OPERATION BBQ

200+ SMOKIN' RECIPES
FROM COMPETITION GRAND CHAMPIONS

★ ★ ★ ★ ★ ★ ★ ★ ★ ★ ★ ★ ★

STAN HAYS
CEO AND CO-FOUNDER OF OPERATION BBQ RELIEF®
WITH TIM O'KEEFE

COMPILED BY CINDI MITCHELL

PAGE STREET
PUBLISHING CO.

PAGE STREET
PUBLISHING CO.

First published in 2019 by

Page Street Publishing Co.

27 Congress Street, Suite 105

Salem, MA 01970

www.pagestreetpublishing.com

Distributed by Macmillan, sales in Canada by The Canadian Manda Group.

23   22   21   20   19   1   2   3   4   5

ISBN-13: 978-1-62414-359-5

ISBN-10: 1-62414-359-8

Library of Congress Control Number: 2018955316

Cover and book design by Laura Gallant for Page Street Publishing Co.

Photography by Ken Goodman

Printed and bound in China

A portion of the proceeds from the sale of this book will be donated to Operation BBQ Relief.

THIS BOOK IS DEDICATED TO ALL OPERATION BBQ RELIEF VOLUNTEERS AND OUR PARTNERS. WITHOUT OUR VOLUNTEERS, MEALS WOULD NOT GET SERVED, AND WITHOUT OUR PARTNERS, WE WOULD NOT HAVE THE RESOURCES TO SERVE THOSE MEALS! THANK YOU TO EVERYONE WHO SUPPORTS OPERATION BBQ RELIEF.

TABLE OF CONTENTS

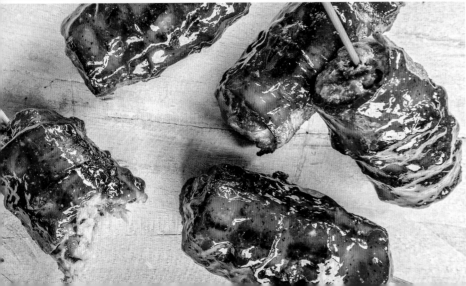

INTRODUCTION

Barbecue is about family, friends and good food. But for a small percentage of people, barbecue is also about competing and seeing who has the best food any given weekend. The one thing we all have in common are the good memories shared around barbecue.

On May 23, 2011, these two groups of BBQ lovers came together after the devastating EF5-rated tornado hit Joplin, Missouri. Competition BBQ teams and BBQ enthusiasts from nine states came together to help the community. In the parking lot at the corner of 7th Street and Rangeline Road, Operation BBQ Relief was founded. The BBQ family was doing what they knew to do, and that was cooking hot barbecue comfort food to help those affected and the first responders. In eleven days, a couple hundred volunteers helped serve approximately 120,000 hot meals. Before we left that parking lot we knew that we were going to make Operation BBQ Relief a nonprofit organization. On February 9, 2012, the IRS granted Operation BBQ Relief its 501(c)(3) public charity.

The BBQ community giving back is nothing new, though. They've been giving back for years—to their communities, churches, kids' schools, sports teams and the list goes on and on. What Operation BBQ Relief did was bring the passion of the BBQ family together to do good on a larger scale.

OBR has had several major milestones since that first experience in Joplin and as many or more struggles. Below are several significant milestones:

November 2012: Hurricane Superstorm Sandy caused major damage in New Jersey and New York. This was the first deployment where we had five separate locations serving over 100,000 BBQ meals in twelve days. The gridlock around the areas created logistical challenges for BBQ teams.

May 2013: Almost two years after the Joplin tornado, Moore, Oklahoma, was hit by a massive EF5-rated tornado. Our teams responded within hours from surrounding states and served over 143,000 hot BBQ meals in twelve days.

August 27, 2016: On this day we served our one-millionth hot BBQ meal in the Hammond/Baton Rouge area. In that area alone we served 313,874 hot BBQ meals. When we left the parking lot in Joplin, we never thought about the day we would serve our millionth meal. Now we are looking toward our two-millionth meal.

2017: This year proved to be the busiest year yet with the largest hurricanes since Katrina and Rita. Hurricane Harvey hit the Texas Gulf Coast on August 25, 2017, causing a record amount of damage and affecting a record number of people. OBR responded and served hot meals for eleven days in downtown Houston, as well as Victoria, Texas. Over those eleven days, we served 371,760 hot BBQ meals to more than 215 different churches, civic groups, nongovernmental and governmental organizations. We served an OBR record of 55,575 meals on September 6, 2017. During our response, CNN, Fox News, the Weather Channel and other media outlets filmed the work our group was doing to help the Texas community. After eleven days of meal service, we broke camp and started to move our equipment from Texas to Florida.

On September 10, 2017, Hurricane Irma hit the Florida coast. Our teams were en route to set up and help serve those communities affected by the hurricane. We ended up setting up outside Fort Myers, Florida. In the nine days following the hurricane, we served 126,400 hot BBQ meals. We worked with different groups like FedEx to get hot meals airlifted to the Florida Keys and a network of volunteers helped serve the communities from southern Florida up to the Orlando area.

We ended 2017 serving 569,450 meals in six states from eight disasters. OBR has now deployed to 51 different disasters in 25 states and served over 1.78 million hot BBQ meals. The majority of those meals were prepared by Grand Champion and World Champion pitmasters. We received additional recognition for our work from the City of Houston, and co-founder and CEO Stan Hays was recognized as one of the Top 10 CNN Heroes for 2017.

The recipes in our book are what these Grand Champion and World Champion pitmasters like to cook for their friends and family in their backyards, and we know you will enjoy them as well. Please share your experiences and pictures with us as you BBQ for your friends and family. We at Operation BBQ Relief are blessed to have such an amazing BBQ family and by buying our book and supporting us, we want to welcome you as the newest member of our BBQ family!

For more information about volunteering or donating to Operation BBQ Relief, go to our website at http://OperationBBQRelief.org.

Additional links to follow us as the BBQ family gives back after disasters:

www.facebook.com/OperationBBQRelief

www.twitter.com/OpBBQRelief

www.instagram.com/OpBBQRelief

www.snapchat.com/OpBBQRelief

www.linkedin.com/company/operation-bbq-relief

CHAPTER 1

PORK

BECAUSE OF ITS VERSATILITY, pork is enjoyed not only for family meals but also for special occasions. It is budget friendly and can be grilled, slow cooked, brined, stuffed or smoked with your preference of wood flavors. In this chapter, you will find many delicious ways not only to cook competition-style meats, but to make an elegant meal for company. On the next page is a listing of the most popular cuts of pork.

PORK LOIN: The large, tender loin is from the pig's back, and it is best roasted. Lean pork loin can dry out if cooked beyond 140°F (60°C), so use an instant-read thermometer to make sure you cook it correctly. You can buy the loin bone-in or boneless.

PORK CHOPS: Pork chops come thin or thick cut; bone-in or boneless; and from the sirloin or from the shoulder, rib or center of the loin. To avoid overcooking, cook lean chops to an internal temperature of 145°F (63°C). For extra insurance against dried-out chops, brine them before cooking.

PORK BUTT: To coax the most from pork butt, slowly smoke, roast or braise it to tenderness. This cut, also called Boston butt, comes bone-in or boneless, weighs 6 to 8 pounds (2.7 to 3.6 kg) and is often shredded after cooking.

PICNIC SHOULDER: Just below the pork butt, where the pig's front leg meets its torso, is the picnic shoulder, also called the pork shoulder. Like the pork butt, the shoulder is fatty and needs long cooking. The picnic shoulder has a considerable cap of fat and skin—perfect for making crackling. Don't confuse picnic shoulders with picnic hams: the latter are smoked.

SPARERIBS: Cut from near the fatty belly of the pig, spareribs include the rib bones, the meat between them and the brisket bone near the pig's chest. They can weigh more than 4 pounds (1.8 kg) per rack. St. Louis cut ribs fit better on a backyard grill because the bones and meat from the brisket section have been removed. They cook more quickly and evenly, too.

BABY BACK RIBS: These ribs come from the back of the pig, along the vertebrae. They're smaller than spareribs, usually less than 2 pounds (910 g) per rack. These ribs have more meat and less connective tissue than spareribs do, which is good, but there is a drawback— baby backs are relatively lean, so they can easily dry out if overcooked.

COUNTRY-STYLE RIBS: These ribs are made from halved or butterflied rib chops from the blade shoulder end of the tenderloin. They contain both dark meat from the shoulder and light meat from the loin. Brining them keeps the white meat moist and pounding them to an even thickness helps the dark meat cook through faster.

PORK TENDERLOIN: Pork tenderloin, the muscle that runs down either side of the backbone, is lean, mild and tender. It's the tenderest part of the pig. Sear tenderloins and then finish them on the cooler part of the grill using indirect heat. Before you start cooking, trim off the shiny membrane (silver skin).

FRESH HAM: Fresh ham is simply the pig's upper hind leg. Whole fresh hams can weigh up to 25 pounds (11.3 kg), so they're usually broken down into the sirloin (or "butt") end closer to the torso and the tapered shank end. Tip: Brine fresh ham before cooking it to keep it moist.

CURED HAM: Cured hams are wet-cured in brine, while country hams are dry-cured in salt and then aged. If the label says anything more than "ham" or "ham with natural juices," don't buy it. Also avoid boneless hams, which can be spongy.

PORK BELLY: The fatty, succulent pork belly has become a hugely popular restaurant cut. Chefs braise and sear sections of the belly to create a dish that's crisp on the outside and unctuous within. Bacon is pork belly that's been salted, (usually) sugared and smoked. Pancetta, sometimes called Italian bacon, is similar but not smoked.

PORK SHANK: A cheap, low-cost item that's often found in soups, pork shank is the lower leg region, below the knee. Shanks tend to be rather tough and require a lengthy cooking time to help the meat break down and become tender. While shanks are usually cooked using moist heat, such as braising, they're also wonderful when prepared on the smoker.

7-DAY JAMBONNEAU

LAKESIDE SMOKERS BBQ TEAM

Mike and Kris Boisvert won an astounding seventeen grand championships in just a short five years before moving on from competition barbecue. Mike was one of the first to jump in to volunteer with Operation BBQ Relief during Superstorm Sandy, and he still loves to cook for a crowd. This recipe is for Mike's Christmas jambonneau. It is for sixteen fresh (uncured) pork shanks, covered with a savory rub, slow-smoked until it pulls apart easily and drizzled with a sweet glaze.

YIELD: 16 SERVINGS • COOK TIME: 7 HOURS

BRINE

2½ gal (9.5 L) water

3 cups (724 g) salt

4 cups (880 g) brown sugar

1 tbsp (17 g) Prague powder (pink salt)

1 large Spanish onion, quartered

4 cloves garlic, smashed

4 scallions, chopped

2 tbsp (17 g) whole peppercorns

4 bay leaves

MEAT

16 fresh pork shanks

RUB

2 cups (440 g) brown sugar

2 tbsp (12 g) black pepper

2 tbsp (20 g) garlic powder

2 tsp (5 g) ginger powder

1 tsp ground cinnamon

1 tsp ground nutmeg

GLAZE

2 (8-oz [225-g]) jars Boar's Head Brown Sugar & Spice Ham Glaze or your favorite ham glaze

¼ cup (60 ml) water

To make the brine, combine the water, salt, brown sugar and Prague powder in a large pot over high heat. Bring it to just under a boil to dissolve the salts and sugar. Add the onion, garlic, scallions, peppercorns and bay leaves. Pour everything into a large food-grade bucket and cool overnight in the fridge.

To make the meat, add the pork to the cool brine and put it in the fridge for 7 days. Halfway through the brining process, move the shanks around at least once.

On day 6, fill another food-grade bucket with 2 gallons (7.6 L) of water and put it into the fridge.

After 7 days of brining, take the shanks out of the brine and get rid of the brine. Rinse the bucket out and add the shanks back into it. Add the 2 gallons (7.6 L) of cold water to the shanks and place the bucket back in the fridge for at least 12 hours.

To make the rub, combine all the rub ingredients in a small bowl.

Remove the pork shanks from the fridge; trim some of the excess fat and skin from them. Apply the rub, and leave the rubbed shanks out of the fridge for 2 hours. In those 2 hours, light the smoker.

Stabilize the smoker to around 250°F (121°C) and put the shanks in the smoker. Add a small piece of applewood, and then a few more during the first 2 hours of the cooking process. Total cook time should be right around 6 hours, or until the centers of the shanks are around 180°F (82°C) and a probe slides in easily.

To make the glaze, mix the glaze ingredients in a small pot and cook over medium heat until melted and well combined.

Raise the temperature of the smoker to 400°F (204°C) and brush the glaze on the shanks. Cook for another hour or so.

Take the meat off the bones by slicing as close as possible to the bone with a knife, or use a fork to shred the meat off the bone and serve it as different-sized chunks of meat: big, small and a little pulled. Drizzle a little more of the glaze over the chunks and serve.

OPERATION BBQ RELIEF IN ACTION

My alarm sounds at 5:15 a.m. Not that I need it; I have been wide awake for the past hour. In the darkness, I find my way to the door. A brisk wind welcomes me as I step outside. It's cold, a drastic change from the weather that we've had over the past few days. Everything is damp and dreary. I struggle in the murkiness to finish my final packing before we hit the road. About half an hour later I'm behind the wheel pulling out of Wiseman Park, driving through Lynchburg Square and heading down Route 55. In the early dusk's glow I can see the Lynchburg Welcomes You! sign in my rearview mirror. As we move forward the sign gets smaller and smaller . . . and then it's gone. I get a little sad because I know that that's the last time I will ever see that sign again. It would be the last time in The Hollow, the last time up on The Hill, and it will be the last time competing at The Jack. And as I drive forward I become content and even at peace with our decision. I smile to myself thinking about the amazing times I've had in Lynchburg over the past four years—times and memories that I'll have forever. And as the daylight struggles to break through the clouds, we press on, moving forward with limited stops, as fast as we can. Because driving directly into the path of a hurricane was not only a great idea, but it made perfect sense.

To do well at a BBQ competition, you need two things: you need to cook really good BBQ and you need just a little luck. Over the past few years, we—the Lakeside Smokers—have definitely received our fair share of luck. But fortunately at this year's Jack, we were saving our luck for much bigger things. As we drove up Route 81 through Virginia, a storm front from the west was closing in and a hurricane to the east was racing us up the coast. Stopping only to gas up, we drove twenty hours straight home, with barely enough time to watch the two storms collide into what we now know as Superstorm Sandy. From the comforts of my home I watched as Sandy pulverized the East Coast. The New Jersey Shore was one of the hardest hit. Where I live in New England had minimal damage: we lost power for a few hours but were very, very lucky. We made it home safe and had a slight inconvenience. Others were not so lucky.

A day after the storm, the sun was out and we were cleaning up the RV. I thought to myself just how lucky we were . . . but I had no idea. I went to work the next day only to find out that I didn't get the job that I had planned to go to that week. Seriously, how lucky am I? I now had plenty of time to relax and recharge. I had visions of chilling lakeside and maybe brewing up some beer later that week. Then I turned on the news, and everything changed. The reports out of New Jersey and coastal New York were terrible. Facebook was blowing up with pictures of the devastation. Friends were sharing pictures of their homes: homes that were flooded, hit with trees or completely gone. Heartbreaking indeed.

(continued)

OPERATION BBQ RELIEF IN ACTION (CONTINUED)

A few days went by, a few phone calls were made, and I was on my way to Jersey. Operation BBQ Relief was mobilizing, and the BBQ community came together to help. Friends, family and neighbors helped the efforts by donating money and supplies. When Eric and Cindi Mitchell picked me up, their truck was packed with more supplies. We could barely fit it all in. We hit the road, not really knowing what to expect but just wanting to help. The seven-hour trip to Forked River, New Jersey, turned into ten because we had to search for gas . . . I don't think any of us knew just how bad it was.

I spent two days on the New Jersey Shore, doing whatever I could do to help. Given the magnitude of the devastation, it seemed insignificant . . . and not enough. I thought: some of these people just lost their homes, and I'm giving them a pulled pork sandwich? But, hopefully, it helps. On some level, on a human level, I hope it helps. On the way home, my thoughts were still with the people I had just left. The people I met, the faces of those who lost so much, I won't soon forget. I also thought about just how lucky I really am. I felt fortunate that I even had the chance to offer any assistance, in any way. So many things had to fall into place to allow me this opportunity. I used to think that I was lucky because I've done well at BBQ competitions. But somewhere between Tennessee and New Jersey, I realized just how small that sounds, that I should consider myself lucky for so much more.

—MIKE BOISVERT, *Lakeside Smokers BBQ Team*

BIG UGLY'S MOUTHWATERING BBQ RIBS

BIG UGLY'S BBQ TEAM

Every backyard cook needs to know the proper way to prepare a great rack of ribs. Learn this workflow from a championship cook, and you'll turn out winning ribs each and every time.

YIELD: 8–10 SERVINGS • COOK TIME: 5½–6 HOURS

4 racks of spare ribs

2 tbsp (30 ml) extra-virgin olive oil

2 cups (400 g) favorite rub (Big Ugly team prefers BBQ Bob's Hav'n a BBQ, Alpha Rub)

Apple or cherry smoke wood

1 cup (230 g) low-salt butter

2 cups (473 ml) honey

2 cups (400 g) brown sugar

2 cups (480 ml) barbecue sauce (BBQ Bob's Hav'n a BBQ sauce is a good choice here)

Set the grill/cooker/smoker up for the indirect method and let the temperature stabilize at 250°F (121°C).

Trim the ribs St. Louis style. Try to keep ten bones on the rack. Using a sharp knife, remove any loose fat from the surface of the ribs, along with anything that does not look pleasing.

Flip the rack over and remove the piece of meat and the long, thin membrane from the back of the ribs. Using a knife, pry the membrane up from one bone. Then, using a paper towel, grip the section of membrane you pried up between your thumb and finger, and pull the entire membrane away from the ribs. The paper towel helps provide a better grip and makes it easier to remove the membrane. Removing the membrane allows flavors from the rub to get into the underside of the rack.

Apply a light coating of olive oil to both sides of the ribs. Starting with the underside, apply a light-to-medium coat of the rub. Flipping the ribs over, apply a medium coat to the topside and let it sit for 15 minutes.

Once the cooker is heated up, add your favorite smoking wood, such as apple or cherry. When the ribs have rested for about 15 minutes, place them on the smoker, generally where the temperature is most constant. You need to know your cooker to know where the temperature is consistent.

Let the cooker do its thing for 3 hours. IF YOU'RE LOOKIN', YOU AIN'T COOKIN'! Walk away! Check to make sure the temperature is dialed in, but don't open the cooking chamber unless you absolutely have to.

(continued)

BIG UGLY'S MOUTHWATERING BBQ RIBS (CONTINUED)

Three hours into the cook, you will have to open the door and rotate the ribs. Front to back, side to side, whatever works. This is also a good time to apply a light sprinkle of rub. Visually, you should be able to gauge the level of doneness by looking at the racks. The bones along the edge should be starting to show, and they should have some solid color to them.

About 2 hours after rotating, it's time to wrap the ribs. Tear four sheets of aluminum foil large enough to wrap the ribs. Cut up ¼ cup (56 g) of butter into pieces for each rack. Place a few pieces of butter on the foil followed by a healthy squirt of honey, a handful of brown sugar and a healthy shake of rub. Place the rack of ribs on the foil and reverse the process: shake some rub, add some brown sugar, squirt some honey and then add some more butter to the top of the ribs.

This is also a good time to check the doneness of the ribs. Grab a toothpick and stick it into the meat between two bones. Stick the middle and each end. The toothpick should easily go in and come out with a little resistance, indicating that the rack only needs an hour or so of additional cooking.

Wrap the ribs tightly in the aluminum foil. Place the racks back on the cooker and continue to cook for about 30 minutes to 1 hour.

After an hour, remove the foiled ribs from the smoker. Unwrap the ribs and remove them from the foil. Remember, the liquid inside the foil will be HOT! Brush your favorite sauce onto the ribs and return them to the cooker long enough to set the sauce, about 10 to 15 minutes.

Remove the sauced ribs from the cooker, slice into individual rib sections and plate with some extra sauce on the side.

OPERATION BBQ RELIEF IN ACTION

I got involved in OBR because I believe in the OBR mission—having active involvement and helping others in times of need. The values held by OBR are the same values that we all should have: honesty, compassion, friendship, hard work and respect. Right now, there is a real need for positive role models who help without thought of themselves, who act without hesitation, who are there in a time of need. OBR provides this every day, on every deployment.

—**CHRIS HALL,** *Big Ugly's BBQ*

ANNA'S APPLE PORK CHOP

ANNA HAYS, COUNTY LINE SMOKERS

Eleven-year-old Anna Hays of County Line Smokers started cooking when she was only six years old. She already has two grand championships under her belt, from 2012 and 2017.

The saltiness of the rub, combined with the tart of the apples and the sweetness of the juice gives you a succulent pork loin chop with beautiful cross marks and a great presentation.

YIELD: 1 SERVING • COOK TIME: 7 MINUTES

1 (10-oz [280-g]) thick-cut, center-cut pork chop

Apple juice

1 Granny Smith apple

Pork Mafia's Memphis Mud Rub or favorite rub, to taste

Place the pork chop in a resealable plastic bag and cover with apple juice. Close the bag tightly, and place in the refrigerator for at least 1 hour. Core and cut a Granny Smith apple into slices.

Start your charcoal for the grill. Anna likes hardwood lump and uses Cowboy's Southern Style lump charcoal.

Remove the pork chop from the plastic bag and dust liberally with the Memphis Mud rub. Let it set until the rub starts getting wet on the meat.

Put a clean grate on your grill and spray with nonstick cooking spray. When your grill gets good and hot, usually about 5 minutes, put your pork chop on the grate.

After 2 minutes, turn the chop to get nice cross grill marks. Cook for another 1½ minutes, and then flip over. After 1½ minutes, check the temperature of the chop. It should be getting close to 130°F (55°C) internal. Turn for the cross marks and pull it off at 140°F (60°C). Put it on a plate and cover with foil for around 5 minutes. No sauce necessary.

While the chop is resting, put your Granny Smith apple slices on the grill with a little Memphis Mud rub. Grill them until they are tender, 4 to 6 minutes per side, and serve them with your perfectly grilled apple-marinated pork chop.

*See photo on page 8 (bottom left).

BONE-SUCKING BABY BACK RIBS

SMOKIN' HOGGZ

This baby back rib recipe is what got Bill Gillespie started in the fun and crazy world of competition BBQ. After years of honing his barbecue skills, he's proud of this award-winning rib recipe! Wow your guests when you serve these ribs along with a side of Smokin' Hoggz BBQ Sauce (page 68).

YIELD: 6–8 SERVINGS • COOK TIME: 3½ HOURS

2 racks loin back ribs (baby back), with the membrane from the back side of the ribs removed

½ cup (125 g) yellow mustard

Smokin' Hoggz All-Purpose Dry Rub (page 326), to taste

Applewood chips or chunks (if using chips, soak in water for about an hour)

½ cup (120 ml) honey

½ cup (100 g) brown sugar

Butter

1 cup (235 ml) Smokin' Hoggz BBQ Sauce (page 68) or favorite BBQ sauce

Apply the yellow mustard to both sides of the ribs, just enough to lightly coat them (the purpose of the mustard is to give the rub something to stick to). Sprinkle the meat with the rub and let it sit for about 1 hour, to allow the meat to come to room temperature. A good overall dusting on both sides of the ribs is all you will need.

While the ribs are resting, preheat your smoker for low and slow cooking, 250°F (121°C). If using a water pan, fill it about three-fourths full with hot water. Add your smoke wood about 5 minutes before putting the ribs on the smoker.

Place your ribs on the smoker meat-side up. Let them cook for about 2½ hours. After 2½ hours, lay out two sheets of aluminum foil large enough to wrap the ribs. Drizzle some honey and brown sugar on each sheet, and then add about 1 tablespoon (14 g) of butter. Place the ribs on the honey and brown sugar meat-side down. Pour some of the BBQ sauce on the back side of the ribs. Wrap the ribs tightly in the foil and place them back onto the smoker for another hour, or until done. You will know they are done when you can see the meat shrink from the bone about ½ to ¾ inch (1.3 to 2 cm). Take the ribs out of the foil, glaze them with the juices that collected in the foil and let them rest for about 20 minutes. Cut them up and serve.

*See photo on page 8 (bottom right).

> **NOTE:** Some cooks like to spray ribs with a fruit-juice mixture during the cooking process. While it's more common for cooks who use offset smokers, there is no reason you can't give it a try on your ribs. Typically, spraying the ribs helps add some nice color, a bit of flavor and some moisture. You could try a fifty-fifty mix of apple juice and cider vinegar.

FLAVORFUL BACON-WRAPPED SAUSAGE FATTIES

BOOTYQUE BBQ TEAM

There are many variations to the sausage fatty, and this bacon-wrapped, sweet and meaty appetizer doesn't disappoint. The smell and taste are amazing!

YIELD: 8–10 SERVINGS • COOK TIME: 2 HOURS

1 (8-oz [227-g]) package cream cheese with chive and onion

1 lb (454 g) breakfast sausage

1 bunch scallions, chopped

Sweet Swine O' Mine BBQ Rub or favorite rub, to taste

Captain Rodney's Boucan Glaze or favorite glaze, to taste

1 lb (454 g) bacon

Captain Rodney's Peach Glaze or favorite glaze, to taste

Remove the cream cheese from the refrigerator and allow it to soften.

Flatten the sausage into a thin, rectangular patty about ½ inch (1.3 cm) thick on a lightly greased surface. Spread the softened cream cheese over the entire sausage patty. Cover with the chopped scallions, apply the Sweet Swine O' Mine BBQ Rub and Captain Rodney's Boucan Glaze, and roll into a log, securing the ends. Liberally cover the log with more BBQ rub. Basket weave the bacon and roll it around the sausage log, applying the seasoning rub again.

Cook the meat at 275°F (135°C) over indirect heat to an internal temperature of 165°F (74°C), about 2 hours. Remove it from the heat and glaze with Captain Rodney's Peach Glaze. Let the fatty stand for 1 hour before slicing.

BLACKENED PORK CHOPS WITH GASTRIQUE

SWEET SWINE O' MINE BBQ TEAM

Are you looking for an interesting dinner idea? Pat this spicy rub on some brined, dry-aged pork chops. Then serve them with cheesy grits drizzled with gastrique sauce, and give the family something delicious to come home to!

YIELD: 4 SERVINGS • COOK TIME: 2 HOURS

BRINE

1 gal (3.8 L) distilled water

1 cup (241 g) salt

2 cups (383 g) sugar

4 cloves garlic, chopped

1 onion, chopped

1 large bunch fresh thyme

2 stalks celery, chopped

1 large bunch fresh rosemary

2 bay leaves

½ cup (120 ml) Worcestershire sauce

½ cup (120 ml) soy sauce

MEAT

4 dry-aged Compart pork chops

Spray oil

¼ cup (55 g) blackened seasoning

Dash of cooking oil, for searing

2 tbsp (30 ml) olive oil

1 (8-oz [225-g]) jar sweet cherry peppers, chopped and liquid reserved

Shallot or small onion, chopped

4 tbsp (57 g) butter, divided

4 tbsp (60 ml) honey

GRITS

1 (1-lb [454-g]) box Jim Dandy Grits, prepared according to package directions

2 cups (241 g) shredded white cheddar cheese

Seasoning, to taste

To make the brine, mix the ingredients in a glass container large enough to hold all 4 pork chops. Add the pork chops to the bowl, and brine in the refrigerator for at least 4 hours. Make sure the pork chops are fully submerged in the brining liquid.

To make the meat, remove the pork chops from the brine, and rinse them under cold water. Pat them dry with paper towels, and coat them with a light layer of spray oil. Liberally coat the chops with a prepared blackened seasoning of your choice.

Place a seasoned cast-iron pan on your stovetop over high heat. Let the pan heat up, and then add some cooking oil to the pan. Place the chops in the pan and sear for 1 to 2 minutes. Flip, and sear the remaining side. Using tongs, sear the edges of the pork chops. After browning all sides, remove the chops from the heat and form them into a single layer in the bottom of a baking dish.

Immediately add the olive oil, peppers and shallot to a hot pan and sauté until just translucent, about 6 to 8 minutes. Add half of the butter and then add half of the pepper juice, the honey and the remaining butter. Stir until the mixture is incorporated, then pour over the chops.

Place the chops in a smoker preheated to 250°F (121°C) and cook using indirect heat for about 90 minutes. Using a meat thermometer, obtain the temperature of the pork chops. Continue to cook until the pork chops reach an internal temperature of 145°F (63°C).

To make the grits, follow the instructions on the package. Add the cheese and seasoning to taste.

Serve the chops alongside the cheesy grits, drizzled with the sauce.

APPLEWOOD-SMOKED PORK CHOPS WITH BRANDIED PEACH SAUCE

PHIL THE GRILL BBQ

The sweetness of peaches combines with the boldness of brandy to form a flavorful sauce that matches well with the brined pork chops in this dish. A short 2 hours is all it takes to brine and then smoke your chops to guaranteed tenderness.

YIELD: 4–5 SERVINGS • COOK TIME: 75 MINUTES

BRINE

4 cups (960 ml) water

⅓ cup (80 g) kosher salt

⅓ cup (79 ml) molasses

⅓ cup (79 ml) cider vinegar

MEAT

4–5 thick-cut, bone-in pork chops

1–2 pieces of applewood

BRANDY SAUCE

4 tbsp (57 g) butter

1 tbsp (14 g) minced fresh ginger

1 (16-oz [455-g]) bag frozen peach slices

1½ tbsp (21 g) brown sugar

¼ cup (60 ml) brandy

½ cup (120 ml) Phil The Grill OMG Barbecue Pitmasters Edition Sauce or favorite BBQ sauce

⅛ tsp ground cinnamon

Salt and pepper, to taste

To make the brine, bring the water to a boil and add the salt, molasses and vinegar. Reduce the heat and stir until the salt is dissolved. Remove from the heat and let it cool.

To make the meat, arrange the chops in a lidded plastic container or resealable plastic bag. Cover with the brine, making sure all of the chops are submerged. Seal and let the chops sit in the brine in the refrigerator for no more than 2 hours.

While the chops are brining, set up the grill for an indirect cook that will burn for at least 2 hours at 225 to 250°F (107 to 121°C). Use a drip pan under the cooking grate to catch the fat. Once the grill is up to temperature, add the smoke wood. Applewood works best for pork chops. If using a gas grill, place 2 to 4 cups (454 to 907 g) of soaked wood chunks in the smoker box. If you are using a charcoal grill, toss a fist-sized lump right into the coals. Remove the chops from the brine and arrange them on the grill. Close the lid and cook using indirect heat for 30 minutes. Flip the chops and continue to cook until the chops reach an internal temperature of 145°F (63°C), another 30 to 45 minutes. Remove the chops to a plate and keep them warm.

To make the sauce, in a skillet over medium heat, melt the butter and sauté the ginger until soft. Add the peach slices and brown sugar. Stir until everything is well combined and the peaches have begun to soften, about 6 to 8 minutes. Add the brandy and very carefully ignite. Cook until the flame dies. Add the barbecue sauce, cinnamon and salt and pepper to taste. Ladle the sauce over your pork chops and serve.

CHARCOAL-GRILLED PORK CHOPS *WITH* PEAR-MAPLE SAUCE

STICKS-N-CHICKS BBQ TEAM

A great choice for summer grilling, these glazed, thick and juicy pork chops are delicious and easy to prepare, and they make a great presentation!

YIELD: 4 SERVINGS • COOK TIME: 12 MINUTES

4 boneless pork chop loins
(¾" [2 cm] thick)

1 tbsp (15 ml) olive oil

½ tsp salt

½ tsp ground black pepper

¼ cup (57 g) butter

3 tbsp (44 ml) pure maple syrup

3 tbsp (60 g) peach, apricot or plum preserves

½ tsp dried basil

3 medium pears, cored and thinly sliced

Coat both sides of the pork chops with olive oil and sprinkle with salt and pepper. Fire up the smoker or grill to a temperature of 250 to 325°F (121 to 163°C). Place your chops on the grill, close the lid and cook using direct heat for 4 to 6 minutes.

Flip your chops and continue to cook with the lid down for an additional 4 to 6 minutes, or until the juices run clear.

While the chops are cooking, melt the butter in a small metal bowl placed on the grill. Stir in the maple syrup, preserves and basil. Add the pears and heat them on the grill for about 3 minutes, just until the pears are warmed through and tender.

Serve your chops with the pears and sauce.

OPERATION BBQ RELIEF IN ACTION

I went to school in southeast Kansas at Pitt State University in Pittsburg, about 30 minutes from Joplin. On the night of the tornado, my wife and I were listening to a police scanner, hoping it wasn't as bad as it sounded on the scanner. We had a lot of memories and friends in and around Joplin. When I woke up in the morning, the news showed the devastation. I went online and found Operation BBQ Relief for Joplin on Facebook. I knew Stan and Jeff but only from competing against them. I remember talking to my wife and her looking at me like, "Why are you still standing here?" I reached out to Stan Hays and was soon on my way.

—WILL CLEAVER, *OBR Co-Founder/COO/CFO, Sticks-n-Chicks BBQ Team*

COMPETITION-STYLE PORK BUTT

DIZZY PIG BBQ TEAM

The perfect combination of Dizzy Pig rubs, hickory smoke and gentle heat gives this pork butt a deep mahogany bark while the interior stays moist and juicy.

YIELD: 15–20 SERVINGS • COOK TIME: 10–12 HOURS

MEAT

1 (7–10-lb [3–4.5-kg]) Boston butt (sometimes called pork shoulder blade roast)

INJECTION

2 cups (473 ml) pork stock (preferably homemade with fresh pork bones)

2 tbsp (30 g) salt

4 tbsp (48 g) raw cane sugar

RUB

2 tbsp (36 g) coarse kosher salt

6 tbsp (29 g) Dizzy Pig Crossroads (also excellent: Dizzy Pig Dizzy Dust, Dizzy Pig Raging River or Dizzy Pig Swamp Venom) or favorite salt-free seasoning blend

2–6 chunks of your favorite dry smoke wood (hickory is a natural for pork)

½ cup (120 ml) pork stock

To make the meat, look for the side of the pork butt that contains a fat cap. Leave the fat cap on but trim the excess fat, silver skin and membranes from the rest of the pork butt. Optimally, you want the rub to build a crust on the meat itself, so make sure to trim everything and expose the meat.

To make the injection, combine all the ingredients in a bowl and stir until thoroughly combined. Place the pork butt into a disposable aluminum pan and prepare to inject. Ideally, you want to inject the mixture into all sections of the pork butt.

It is best to punch a hole in the surface of the meat and insert the injector needle at an angle. Push the needle as far as it will go into the meat. As you withdraw the needle, squeeze the injector to release some of the liquid. Just before you pull the needle all the way out, re-insert it at a different angle, so you can inject liquid into a different section of the pork butt. The fewer holes you punch into the meat, the better. Repeat injecting at different angles until all of the injection mixture is used. Re-inject any excess liquid that collects in the pan.

To make the rub, using a paper towel, pat the surface of the pork butt dry. Apply a light dusting of coarse kosher salt all over the butt, and then apply a heavy coating of Dizzy Pig Crossroads (or your favorite Dizzy Pig blend). Using your hands, press in the rub until the entire butt is covered. Cover and rest for at least 30 minutes and up to 3 hours.

Preheat your grill/cooker/smoker with charcoal and hickory chunks, to 240°F (116°C) with an indirect setup. (Place a drip pan between the meat and fire.) Wait for the smoke to turn blue, thin and make sure it smells good. Strong smoke can overwhelm the flavor of your pork and make it very dark in color.

(continued)

COMPETITION-STYLE PORK BUTT
(CONTINUED)

Place the pork butt in your cooker fat-cap down (assuming your heat is coming from below). Cook for 8 to 9 hours, or until the exterior has a rich brown crust, and the temperature in the center of the butt is approximately 165 to 170°F (74 to 77°C).

Remove the meat from your cooker and double wrap it in heavy-duty aluminum foil. Then add your pork stock. For a little extra layer of flavor, finely grind a couple teaspoons of Dizzy Pig Crossroads seasoning and add it to the pork stock.

Return to your cooker and cook until the meat reaches 195°F (91°C) internal temperature in the center, about 2 to 4 hours. Check for tenderness. The meat should wiggle a little like gelatin, and be very tender to your temperature probe. If it's still not tender, return the foil-wrapped butt to your cooker and cook for 15 more minutes, repeating the tenderness check. It is not uncommon to need to cook to an internal temperature of 200 or 205°F (93 or 96°C).

When fully tender, remove the pork butt from your smoker and cover with towels, a blanket or place in the cooler to rest for at least 1 hour and up to 4 hours. Pull, shred, chop or chunk to your preference. Add salt and a fine ground rub to taste.

CRISPED SKIN PICNIC PORK SHOULDER

SMOKIN' HOGGZ

There are two parts to the pork shoulder: the butt and the picnic. The picnic is located on the bottom of the shoulder and usually has the hide still attached. Instead of getting those soft and stringy shredded pieces of meat you'd find with a pork butt, you will have meaty chunks of pork that you can pull apart with your fingers. After the pork shoulder is fully cooked, hit it with some high heat on your charcoal grill to get that skin nice and crispy!

YIELD: 15–20 SERVINGS • COOK TIME: 10–12 HOURS

INJECTION

½ cup (120 ml) apple juice

¼ cup (60 ml) water

¼ cup (49 g) granulated sugar

2 tbsp (36 g) kosher salt

2 tbsp (30 ml) Worcestershire sauce

1 tbsp (15 ml) cider vinegar

SMOKIN' HOGGZ ALL-PURPOSE DRY RUB

½ cup (95 g) granulated sugar

½ cup (110 g) brown sugar

¼ cup (35 g) ancho chile powder

¼ cup (72 g) kosher salt

2 tbsp (15 g) paprika

1 tbsp (6 g) ground black pepper

2 tsp (5 g) garlic powder

2 tsp (5 g) onion powder

1 tsp white pepper

½ tsp allspice

1 (8-lb [3.5-kg]) picnic shoulder

Olive oil

Applewood

To make the injection, mix all the injection ingredients until the sugar and salt have dissolved. Store in the refrigerator until ready to use.

To make the rub, mix all the ingredients together and store in an airtight container.

Prepare your grill or smoker for a 250°F (121°C) indirect cook. Add about 1 gallon (3.8 L) of hot water to the water pan. You can add smoke wood just before you put the meat on.

Trim off any loose fat on the pork. Using a meat injector, inject the picnic shoulder with the injection. Use all of the injection.

Coat the entire pork shoulder with olive oil. Season the shoulder liberally with the dry rub.

When the smoker is up to temperature, add 4 to 6 chunks of apple smoke wood and place the shoulder on the middle rack with the larger surface of skin facing up. Cook the pork to an internal temperature of 190°F (88°C), about 10 hours. Remove it from the cooker and loosely tent with a sheet of heavy-duty foil.

While the shoulder is resting, fire up your charcoal grill for direct grilling. When the grill is ready, about 10 minutes, put the shoulder on the cooking grate directly over the hot coals, and flip it a quarter turn every 2 to 3 minutes, until the skin becomes nice and crispy.

Once the skin is crispy, remove the meat from the grill and loosely tent with foil for about 30 minutes. Using a pair of heat-resistant gloves, shred the pork shoulder. Don't forget to save some of that nice crispy skin to snack on!

CORNBREAD-STUFFED PORK LOIN
WITH RASPBERRY CHIPOTLE SAUCE

SMOKIN' HOGGZ

Pork loin is a tender piece of meat located just underneath the baby back ribs. Some would even call the loin the prime rib of pork. This is a great piece of meat to stuff and smoke. It's very lean and cooks pretty quickly. Here's a fabulous way to cook this wonderful piece of hog heaven: filled with cornbread stuffing and glazed with a little raspberry chipotle sauce.

YIELD: 8 SERVINGS • COOK TIME: 1½–2½ HOURS

MEAT

2–3 pieces of applewood

2 cups (400 g) prepared cornbread stuffing

1 (4-lb [2-kg]) pork loin

2–3 tbsp (30–45 ml) olive oil

1 recipe Smokin' Hoggz All-Purpose Dry Rub (page 326) or favorite rub

SAUCE

1 (7-oz [200-g]) can chipotle peppers in adobo sauce

1 (10-oz [280-g]) jar seedless raspberry jam

To make the meat, preheat your cooker for low and slow cooking, 250°F (121°C), and fill the water pan about halfway with hot water. Add your smoke wood about 5 minutes before putting the meat on.

Follow the instructions on the box to prepare the cornbread stuffing.

Trim the white "silver skin" from the pork loin. Butterfly the pork loin by slicing it across the middle like a hot dog bun, stopping about ½ inch (1.3 cm) from cutting all the way through. Pile on the stuffing and close up the loin, using butcher's string to keep it closed. Fasten a segment of butcher's string every 1½ inches (4 cm). Lightly coat the entire loin with olive oil and sprinkle the rub liberally on all sides of the loin.

Place the pork loin in the smoker and smoke until the internal temperature of the pork reaches 140°F (60°C), about 1½ to 2½ hours depending on the thickness of the meat. Start to check it after 1½ hours.

To make the sauce, take about 3 to 4 of the chipotles from the can and finely dice them. Place the jam in a medium bowl, and stir in the diced chipotles and about 3 tablespoons (45 ml) of the adobo sauce. Mix well and add more adobo sauce until the heat and taste reach your personal preference.

During the last 30 minutes of cooking, apply the sauce and continue cooking to help the sauce set. Remove the meat from your cooker and let it rest for about 15 minutes. Slice the pork and serve with more sauce.

BREAKFAST SAUSAGE–SPICED GRILLED PORK CHOPS

CHRIS LILLY, BIG BOB GIBSON BAR-B-Q

Sometimes you just crave breakfast all day long. Next time you do, take the same seasonings used to make breakfast sausage so delicious and apply them to some pork chops. This seasoning rub, coupled with the grilled flavor of Kingsford Charcoal Briquets with applewood, makes these chops an anytime meal.

YIELD: 4 SERVINGS • COOK TIME: 10–12 MINUTES

RUB

3¼ tsp (16 g) salt

2¼ tsp (10 g) dark brown sugar

1½ tsp (3 g) black pepper

1 tsp dried sage

¼ tsp garlic powder

¼ tsp cayenne pepper

⅛ tsp ground nutmeg

MEAT

4 (6–8-oz [170–227-g]) bone-in pork chops or boneless loin chops (¾" [2 cm] thick)

To make the rub, in a small bowl, combine all the rub ingredients. Season the chops liberally with the rub.

Configure your charcoal grill for direct cooking and preheat to 450°F (232°C).

To make the meat, place the pork chops on the grill and cook over direct heat for 5 to 6 minutes. Flip the pork chops, and continue to cook for 5 to 6 minutes, or to an internal temperature of 145 to 150°F (63 to 66°C). Remove the chops from the grill and let them rest for 5 minutes before serving.

CRUNCHY DEEP-FRIED RIBS

SWEET SWINE O' MINE BBQ TEAM

Mark Lambert came up with this recipe back in 2002 after he had just finished cooking competition hot wings at Memphis in May. Everyone else left the cooking area to go visit with other teams, and he began to clean up. As Mark was returning items to the fridge, he noticed a big pan of rib trimmings from the day before. Tired of barbecue, he decided to try something a little different. This recipe is a great way to use the individual end ribs you cut off a rack when trimming ribs for a competition. While the preferred rib for this recipe is Compart loin back ribs, you can just as easily use baby back or spare ribs.

YIELD: 3–4 SERVINGS • COOK TIME: 10–12 MINUTES

MEAT

Ribs of your choice

2 cups (240 g) chicken fry mix or all-purpose flour

SAUCE

2 (5-oz [148-ml]) bottles tiger sauce

½ cup (115 g) butter

3 tbsp (44 ml) Louisiana hot sauce (Daigles is preferred)

1 tbsp (15 ml) rice wine vinegar

10 cups (2.4 L) cooking oil

NOTE: The cooking oil should come up to temperature in about 10 minutes. If the oil temperature does not rise to 330°F (166°C), then you will have to add more charcoal around the Dutch oven. If the oil temperature rises too high, then you will have to remove some charcoal from the smoker and wait for the temperature of the oil to drop down before frying the ribs.

Preheat your smoker to about 400°F (204°C).

To make the meat, cut the raw ribs into individual bones. Soak the ribs in ice water for 5 minutes. Remove the ribs and toss them in the chicken fry mix or flour (only use wheat flour for this recipe).

To make the sauce, mix the ingredients in a medium bowl and set aside.

Pour the cooking oil into a deep, 5-quart (4.7-L) Dutch oven. Cover the Dutch oven and place it directly on the hot charcoal. After 10 minutes, carefully remove the cover from the Dutch oven.

Using a deep-frying thermometer, monitor the temperature of the cooking oil. Ribs are tough, and when frying, they need a little more cook time until they brown, so you'll want the oil at a slightly lower temperature than conventional deep-frying. When the oil heats up to 330°F (166°C), carefully place the raw, floured ribs into the hot oil using metal tongs.

Deep-fry the ribs for 10 to 12 minutes. The surface of the ribs will turn brown, and the ribs will float when they've finished cooking. You'll also start to see some marrow seep out of the ends of the bones. When the ribs are done, cover the Dutch oven and remove it from the smoker.

Using metal tongs, remove the ribs from the Dutch oven and place them on a paper towel to draw away some of the oil. Toss the cooked ribs in sauce and enjoy, but be careful: these ribs are addictive!

FILIPINO CEBU LECHON-STYLE ROLLED AND STUFFED PORK BELLY

DIVA Q, AKA DANIELLE BENNETT

With just one taste of what citrusy lemongrass does to pork belly, your friends and family will be in awe of your barbecue skills! Serve this juicy stuffed delicacy and you'll be cooking like a rock star.

YIELD: 12 SERVINGS • COOK TIME: 7–8 HOURS

1 (8-lb [3.62-kg]) fresh pork belly, skin on

5 cloves garlic, crushed

5 crushed bay leaves

¼ cup (72 g) kosher salt

3 tbsp (18 g) black pepper

¼ cup (2 g) dried chives

10 lemongrass stalks, bruised

1 bunch garlic chives

1 bunch green scallions

2 cups (473 ml) China Lily Soya Sauce or favorite soy sauce

2–3 pieces of your favorite smoke wood

Lay the pork belly on a cutting board, skin-side down.

In a small bowl, mix the crushed garlic, bay leaves, salt, pepper and chives. Rub this mixture all over the meat side of the pork belly. Place the bruised lemongrass, garlic chives and scallions lengthwise down the center of the pork belly. Roll the pork belly and tie together with butcher twine, making a tight cylinder. Brush the skin side with soya sauce.

Prepare your grill for 250°F (121°C), indirect cooking. Add 2 to 3 pieces of smoke wood.

Place the rolled pork belly on the grill. Baste with soya sauce every 30 minutes. Smoke for 7 to 8 hours, until the skin is crispy and the internal temperature of the pork is 155 to 160°F (68 to 71°C). Let it rest for 15 minutes and then slice thinly.

> **NOTE:** Bruising the lemongrass helps release its aromatic flavorings. To get the most flavor out of this citrusy stalk, trim off the spiky top and the base. Remove and discard the first few outer layers, and then bruise the lemongrass stalk by lightly crushing it with a pestle or a meat mallet.

GRILLED PORK TENDERLOIN
~WITH~ JALAPEÑO-APRICOT GLAZE

COUNTY LINE SMOKERS

Spicy, sweet, very moist and easy to prepare—you're going to love these pork tenderloins. They turn out wonderfully tasty with an awesome array of flavors from the rub and glaze.

YIELD: 3 SERVINGS • COOK TIME: 10–12 MINUTES

GLAZE

3 tbsp (60 g) apricot preserves

3 tbsp (60 g) jalapeño jelly

3 tbsp (44 ml) rice wine vinegar

1–2 tbsp (15–30 ml) agave syrup

1 jalapeño, diced small, optional

1 shallot, diced small, optional

MEAT

1 lb (454 g) pork tenderloin

2 tbsp (30 g) your favorite pork rub

To make the glaze, heat all of the glaze ingredients together in a small saucepan over medium heat, being careful not to burn it. Stirring constantly, bring to a boil and remove from the heat. Keep it warm for basting and for a dipping sauce.

Using a knife, trim the silver skin, along with any loose fat, from the pork tenderloin. Apply a coating of your favorite pork rub to all sides of the meat.

Set your smoker or grill to 300°F (149°C), direct cooking.

Place the tenderloin on the cooking grate. Place the lid on the grill, and cook for 90 seconds. Remove the lid, rotate the pork loin a quarter turn and cook for an additional 90 seconds. Repeat this cooking process until the tenderloin reaches an internal temperature of 125 to 130°F (52 to 54°C) in the thickest area before you start to apply the glaze. There is a large amount of sugar in the glaze, so make sure to move the pork loin to the coolest area of the grill.

Apply several layers of the glaze to the tenderloin. Once the thickest part of the tenderloin reaches 138 to 140°F (59 to 60°C), pull it off the grill. Tent the loin with foil and let it rest for 5 to 8 minutes. Reserve the remaining glaze and keep it warm.

Slice the pork tenderloin on the bias and serve with the remaining glaze as a dipping sauce. This is great with grilled pineapple, apple coleslaw or your favorite side dishes.

HERBED REVERSE-SEARED PORK TENDERLOIN ~with~ CHIMICHURRI SAUCE

BEHIND BBQ

Pork tenderloin, a favorite meat to prepare, is versatile, healthy and delicious. It's also a good value, often purchased with two or three tenderloins per pack. Try to buy natural tenderloin that has not been "enhanced" with any solution. Reverse-searing the meat, as done in this recipe, cooks thoroughly and evenly, without drying out the meat, and creates a delicious crust. Your patience with this method will be rewarded with a juicy, tender finished product.

YIELD: 6–9 SERVINGS • COOK TIME: 25 MINUTES

RUB

1 tbsp (18 g) kosher salt

½ tbsp (3 g) rubbed sage

1 tbsp (3 g) dried rosemary, crushed using your fingers

1 tbsp (3 g) dried thyme

1 tsp ground black pepper

¼ cup (60 ml) regular olive oil (not extra-virgin)

MEAT

2–3 all-natural pork tenderloins, about 1 lb (454 g) each (Each tenderloin should serve 2–3 people.)

CHIMICHURRI SAUCE

1 bunch fresh Italian flat parsley, leaves and small stems only (about 1 cup [60 g])

1 bunch fresh cilantro, leaves and small stems only (about 1 cup [50 g])

½ cup (120 ml) extra-virgin olive oil

1 tbsp (15 ml) champagne vinegar or white wine vinegar

1 medium shallot, peeled and quartered

1 clove garlic, peeled

1 Fresno red pepper, stem and seeds removed, or ¼ tsp red pepper flakes

½ tsp kosher salt

¼ tsp black pepper

(continued)

HERBED REVERSE-SEARED PORK TENDERLOIN ⚭ CHIMICHURRI SAUCE (CONTINUED)

To make the rub, combine all the ingredients in a bowl. Substitute fresh herbs if you like, just triple the amounts and grind them together. Let the rub sit while you trim the meat. Sitting in the oil will open up the herb flavors.

To make the meat, trim any silver skin and membrane from the pork tenderloins. Apply the herb rub all over the tenderloins. Let the tenderloins sit while you prepare the grill.

Set up a two-zone fire in your charcoal grill, with hot coals on one side of the grill and an empty space on the other. If using a gas grill, only light one side of the grill. Oil the grates.

Place the tenderloins on the cool zone of the grill, cover the grill and cook using indirect heat. About every 5 minutes, remove the lid, rotate the pork loins a quarter turn and continue cooking with the lid on. Each time you rotate the tenderloins, spritz with water to help create a bit of a smoke ring.

Cook for 20 to 25 minutes, or until the internal temperature reaches 140°F (60°C).

To make the chimichurri sauce, blend all the ingredients in a food processor until puréed.

When the meat has reached 140°F (60°C), place the tenderloins directly over the hot coals (or over the lit burners of your gas grill) to brown the exterior of the meat. After 60 seconds, rotate the tenderloins a quarter turn, and cook for 60 additional seconds. Repeat two more times so that all four sides develop a flavorful surface crust.

Remove the tenderloins from the grill and let them rest for 5 to 10 minutes. Slice them against the grain and serve with the chimichurri sauce.

NOTES: After 15 minutes of cooking, use an internal probe thermometer or check the temperature with an instant thermometer. If the meat isn't ready, continue to cook and check again every 5 minutes.

While the pork is cooking on the cool side of the grill, you can grill some veggies over the hot coals, such as Savory Grilled Brussels Sprouts (page 258).

PORK RIBS, DIZZY STYLE

DIZZY PIG BBQ TEAM

This recipe for smoky, sweet and spicy pork ribs is made with the perfect balance of spices found in Dizzy Dust All-Purpose Rub.

YIELD: 2 SERVINGS • COOK TIME: 5–8 HOURS

1 rack spare ribs

1 tbsp (15 g) yellow mustard, optional

½ cup (120 g) Dizzy Dust All-Purpose Rub or favorite rub

Pecan and hickory smoke wood chunks

½ cup (120 ml) apple juice

½ cup (120 ml) apple cider vinegar

Remove the sheet of silvery membrane on the back of the rack. Working a knife under the membrane, lift up and then grasp and pull that loose tag with a paper towel. It will quickly and efficiently remove the entire sheet.

Remove the breastbone from the rest of the rack. There's some nice meat here, but it doesn't really present well, so cook it on the side and put the meat into baked beans. To make the side ribs into St. Louis style, continue to trim off the tail end at the last bone, remove any large blobs or extraneous fat as well as the brisket flap of meat that appears on the back of the ribs. Again, this piece is fine for adding to chili or beans, but detracts from "presentation-quality" ribs.

Smear the mustard, if using, onto the ribs to provide a sticky surface for the rub to adhere to. What would a Dizzy Pig recipe be without a generous coating of Dizzy Pig products? A lot less flavorful, that's what! Generously coat the ribs with the rub.

The Dizzy Pig BBQ Team smokes their ribs in a Big Green Egg (BGE) ceramic cooker. However, the ideas used here can be duplicated in your smoker, regardless of brand (and some multiple burner gas grills can do an okay job, with the help of a smoking box and a long, slow cook). After a lump charcoal fire has been established, add some pecan and hickory smoke wood chips. Place three firebricks on top of the cooker's grill to create a barrier between the food and direct flame (for indirect cooking). Place a foil-lined drip pan beneath the cooking rack that holds the ribs. When the temperature stabilizes, the cooking temperature should be in the 225 to 230°F (107 to 110°C) range.

About an hour into the cooking process, the Dizzy Dust rub starts to form a crust on the outside of the meat. Once this has happened, begin to occasionally spritz the surface of the ribs with a combination of apple juice and apple cider vinegar about every half hour for the remainder of the cook, which will total approximately 4 hours but up to 7 depending on exact temperatures and your particular cut of ribs. The ribs should be turned with every other spritz. An additional dusting with the Dizzy Dust rub during this period will contribute a deeper level of crusting, if desired.

NOT-SO-BASIC CROWN ROAST OF PORK

THE BASIC BBQ TEAM

The centerpiece of this dish is a crown roast of pork. A crown roast of pork is a bone-in pork loin tied in a circle with the bones pointing upward, like the points on a crown. Bones should be French trimmed, or exposed, creating a handle for what will eventually be sliced into chops for individual plating. When cooked "hot and fast" in a smoker, the extra flavor element of smoke takes this dish traditionally cooked in an oven for holiday celebrations to a championship level.

YIELD: 12 SERVINGS • COOK TIME: 3 HOURS

BASIC PESTO

¼ cup (55 g) light brown sugar

¼ cup (72 g) kosher salt

2 tbsp (12 g) coarse ground black pepper

1 whole bulb of garlic, diced into small bits or chips (do not pulverize)

1 small package (or just over ¼ cup [7 g]) rosemary, stripped and finely chopped (place leftover stems to the side)

1 small package (or just over ¼ cup [10 g]) fresh thyme, stripped and finely chopped (place leftover stems to the side)

3–4 lengths (or 2 tbsp [2 g]) fresh sage, stripped and finely chopped (place leftover stems to the side)

½ cup (120 ml) extra-virgin olive oil

VEGETABLES AND MEAT

2 lb (907 g) small red potatoes, skin on

1 lb (454 g) small white onions

1 lb (454 g) carrots

Sea salt

Extra-virgin olive oil

1 cup (226 g) Basic Pesto

1 (7-10-lb [3-4.5-kg]) 9-10-bone crown roast of pork

1–2 cups (237–473 ml) fruit juice (apple, white grape or cranberry)

1–2 cups (237–473 ml) water

2–3 pieces cherry wood

To make the pesto, add half of each of the pesto ingredients (except the olive oil) to a food processor. Using the food processor's blade attachment, process the ingredients until they are finely chopped. Scrape the sides of the food processor and add the remaining half of the pesto ingredients. Continue to process the ingredients until it forms a paste. Scrape the sides of the food processor as needed. Add the olive oil and blend until the mixture emulsifies.

To make the vegetables and meat, preheat the smoker to 300 to 325°F (149 to 163°C).

Wash the red potatoes and cut into halves or quarters (½ to ¾ inch [1.3 to 2 cm]).

Peel the white onions and cut each in half. Peel the carrots, cut into 3-inch (7.5-cm) sections and split once or twice. Mix the veggies together, add a liberal amount of sea salt and toss.

Add a couple shakes of olive oil and toss. Add 2 to 3 tablespoons (28 to 42 g) of the pesto and toss. Cover and place in the refrigerator. Place the tied crown roast of pork on a clean surface. Wrap the exposed bones with aluminum foil.

Smear a heavy coat, about 1 cup (226 g) of pesto, all over the pork, making sure to coat the bottom and your fingers to gently push into all the crevices. Once the pork is covered thoroughly, add any of the remaining pesto to the vegetables.

In the bottom of a roasting pan, add the leftover stalks and stems from the fresh herbs, along with 1 to 2 cups (237 to 473 ml) of fruit juice. Add the same amount of water. Your goal is to cover the bottom of the pan with roughly ½ inch (1.3 cm) of liquid.

Place a rack in the pan and place the pork roast bones-up in the center of the pan. Surround the pork tightly with the vegetables. Place the pan in your smoker and add 2 to 3 chunks of cherry wood to the fire. After 1½ hours, remove the foil from the bones and pull the veggies back from around the roast. After 1 more hour, start checking for 140°F (60°C) internal temperature in the center of the loin meat. At 140°F (60°C), remove the roast to a flat surface and tent it with foil. Expect the temperature to rise to about 150°F (66°C).

Cover the pan of vegetables tightly with foil and leave them in the smoker for 20 to 30 minutes.

PERFECT SCORE PULLED PORK

FIRE DOWN BELOW

Since starting in 2013, Fire Down Below has competed in over twenty competitions and has made several upgrades to their smokers and trailers. Ed and Ginny have had category calls in the majority of their competitions. The highlight of their short time on the circuit was a first place call in pork, with a perfect score at the 2014 Jack Daniel's World Championship Invitational. Their winning pulled pork recipe, using their injection, rub and sauce, will have you cooking like these champions in no time!

YIELD: 12–15 SERVINGS • COOK TIME: 10–12 HOURS

WINNING PORK INJECTION

1 cup (237 ml) white grape juice

⅓ cup (79 ml) peach nectar

¼ cup (60 ml) apple cider vinegar

1 tbsp (18 g) kosher salt

1 tbsp (15 ml) Worcestershire sauce

½ tbsp (4 g) onion powder

1 tsp garlic salt

1 tsp MSG, optional

FIRE DOWN BELOW PORK RUB

¼ cup (51 g) turbinado sugar

¼ cup (55 g) light brown sugar

¼ cup (29 g) paprika

2 tbsp (12 g) chili seasoning

2 tbsp (17 g) black pepper

1 tbsp (18 g) kosher salt

1 tbsp (15 g) garlic salt

1 tbsp (7 g) dry mustard

1 tbsp (15 g) celery salt

1 tbsp (15 g) onion salt

1 tsp cumin

1 tsp garlic powder

1 tsp onion powder

¼ tsp cayenne pepper

FIRE DOWN BELOW PORK MARINADE

¾ cup (177 ml) Stubb's Pork Marinade

2 tbsp (29 g) salted butter

2 tbsp (27 g) dark brown sugar

2 tbsp (30 ml) agave nectar

FIRE DOWN BELOW BARBECUE SAUCE

1½ cups (368 g) ketchup

¼ cup (60 ml) molasses

¼ cup (55 g) dark brown sugar

3 tbsp (44 ml) maple syrup

2 tbsp (30 g) prepared yellow mustard

2 tbsp (30 ml) apple cider vinegar

1 tbsp (15 ml) Worcestershire sauce

1 tbsp (15 ml) soy sauce

1 tbsp (15 ml) Heinz 57 Sauce

1 tbsp (15 ml) liquid smoke

1 tsp onion powder

1 tsp garlic powder

½ tsp kosher salt

½ tsp black pepper

½ tsp cayenne pepper

MEAT

1 (8–10-lb [3.5–4.5-kg]) bone-in pork butt

3-4 chunks applewood

To make the injection, combine all the pork injection ingredients in a glass bowl and stir until thoroughly combined. Cover and store in a refrigerator until you are ready to inject the pork butt.

To make the rub, combine all the pork rub ingredients together in a bowl or jar with a lid. Stir the ingredients together, place the lid on the container and set aside.

To make the marinade, combine all the pork marinade ingredients together in a glass bowl. Mix until combined. Cover the bowl, and store in a refrigerator.

To make the sauce, combine all the barbecue sauce ingredients in a small saucepan. Stir to combine all the ingredients. Over medium heat, bring the sauce to a simmer. Remove from the heat and allow the sauce to cool. Then store in a refrigerator.

To make the meat, trim the bone-in pork butt of any loose fat, but keep the fat cap intact.

Using the freshly made pork injection and a marinade injector, slowly inject it into the butt in a checkerboard pattern. Inject about 2 tablespoons (30 ml) of fluid into each spot. Apply the rub generously to the butt, making sure to cover all sides. Wrap the butt in plastic wrap and refrigerate 2 to 8 hours.

About 45 minutes before placing the butt in the smoker, remove it from the refrigerator, unwrap it and apply another generous amount of rub to all areas.

Set your smoker for 250°F (121°C) indirect heat and add 3 to 4 applewood chunks to the fire right before placing the meat inside the smoker. Place the meat, fat-side up, and cook until the internal temperature of the butt reaches 160 to 170°F (71 to 77°C), about 6 to 7 hours.

Once the butt has reached the target temperature, remove from the smoker and place fat-side down on two sheets of heavy-duty aluminum foil, large enough to wrap it. Pour the pork marinade over the butt, and tightly wrap it in foil. Place it back in the smoker and cook until the center of the butt reaches an internal temperature of 190 to 195°F (88 to 90°C), about 3 hours.

Remove the butt from the smoker; open the foil to allow it to cool and stop the cooking process. Let the butt vent for about 10 minutes and then wrap tightly again. Place it in a dry cooler, wrap it in some old towels and let it rest for 1 to 2 hours.

To serve, remove the butt from the cooler, take it out of the foil and place it in a baking or foil pan. Using two forks, pull the meat into small chunks and pour about ¾ cup (177 ml) of warmed barbecue sauce on the meat, along with ¼ cup (60 ml) of apple cider vinegar. Mix together and season with about a tablespoon (8 g) of the leftover rub.

SIMPLE-to-PREPARE PORK TENDERLOIN

BUSH KITCHEN BBQ

Sometimes recipes can quickly get out of control with lots of steps and numerous ingredients. This simple go-to recipe is quick and easy, yet so tasty it's devoured by kids and adults alike.

YIELD: 2–3 SERVINGS • COOK TIME: 30 MINUTES

HERB RUB

1 tsp dried thyme leaves

1 tsp dried rosemary leaves

1 tsp parsley flakes

1 tsp granulated garlic

½ tsp cracked pepper

2 tsp (12 g) kosher salt

MEAT

1 lb (455 g) pork tenderloin

1 tbsp (15 ml) olive or vegetable oil

Sweet chili sauce or jam

To make the rub, combine all the ingredients in a small bowl.

To make the pork tenderloin, remove any fat or silver skin. Rub the oil over the pork and then lightly sprinkle all sides with the herb rub.

Configure your grill for two-zone cooking at medium-high heat (400 to 500°F [204 to 260°C]). Place the tenderloin on the hot zone, and grill for 5 minutes with the lid on. Remove the lid, flip the tenderloin and cook for an additional 5 minutes with the lid on the grill.

Move the tenderloin to the cool zone of the grill, and finish cooking with the lid on. Cook the tenderloin for 15 to 20 minutes to your preferred doneness, or 165°F (74°C). Brush with the chili sauce or jam, leave for an additional 5 minutes and then serve.

Alternatively, cook the tenderloin on a smoker at 250°F (121°C) for about 50 minutes. Monitor the tenderloin until cooked to your preferred doneness, or 165°F (74°C). Brush with the sweet chili sauce and smoke for an additional 10 minutes.

Serve sliced with your favorite salad, vegetables or in a wrap.

OPERATION BBQ RELIEF IN ACTION

When I moved to America from Australia, I became involved with competitive BBQ. It soon became my new family away from home. BBQ and the comradeship forged around the fire is strong. When Operation BBQ Relief started, it was a natural next step to become involved with a great group of people that don't know any other way than to help others in their times of need, whether it is moral support for a newcomer or the need to feed people in times of disaster.

—SAFFRON HODGSON, *Bush Kitchen*

SMOKED SAUSAGE–STUFFED PORK TENDERLOIN

MYRON MIXON

The smoked sausage, the sweet/savory rub and the spicy vinegar sauce send this outstanding fusion of flavors into our BBQ hall of fame!

YIELD: 3 SERVINGS • COOK TIME: 45 MINUTES

JACK'S OLD SOUTH BBQ RUB

¾ cup (165 g) brown sugar

¾ cup (80 g) sweet paprika

¾ cup (216 g) kosher salt

9 tbsp (54 g) black pepper

2 tbsp (18 g) garlic powder

2 tbsp (15 g) onion powder

1 tbsp (8 g) cayenne pepper

1 tbsp (2 g) dried basil

JACK'S OLD SOUTH VINEGAR SAUCE

2 cups (473 ml) apple cider vinegar

1 cup (245 g) ketchup

½ cup (120 ml) hot sauce

2 tbsp (30 g) salt

2 tbsp (12 g) coarsely ground black pepper

1 tbsp (3 g) red pepper flakes

½ cup (96 g) sugar

2 cups (470 g) apple jelly

MEAT

1 large pork tenderloin, about 1½ lb (680 g)

1 lb (454 g) smoked sausage (a large link)

To make the rub, combine all the ingredients and mix well.

To make the sauce, combine the vinegar, ketchup and hot sauce in a stockpot over medium heat. Stir together. Pour in all the remaining ingredients except the apple jelly, and stir. Do not boil. When the spices are thoroughly dissolved, take the pot off the heat.

To make the meat, heat your smoker to 300°F (149°C). Trim any excess fat and membrane from the pork tenderloin. Using a sharp knife with a very long, straight blade, insert the knife through the center of the tenderloin. Take care not to cut out to the sides—just insert the knife blade to the center and then remove it. Push a turkey baster through the slit, enlarging the opening, and then remove the baster.

Trim your smoked sausage link to the exact length of the tenderloin. Stuff it into the opening you cut in the pork tenderloin. Apply the rub thoroughly, coating the outside of the tenderloin. Place the tenderloin in a medium aluminum pan, and place the pan in the smoker. Cook the tenderloin for 20 to 30 minutes.

While the meat is cooking, return the pot with the sauce to medium heat. Add the apple jelly. Stir thoroughly to combine. Make sure the sauce thins out as it heats, about 5 minutes. Then lower the heat and keep it warm until you're ready to use it.

Using a meat thermometer, take the temperature of the pork tenderloin. During the last 15 minutes of cooking time, apply half of the sauce to the meat and put the meat back on the smoker, reserving the remainder of the sauce. Remove the pan from the smoker when the tenderloin reaches an internal temperature of 150°F (66°C). Allow the meat to sit loosely covered for 10 minutes. Cut it into slices about ¼ to ½ inch (0.6 to 1.3 cm) thick and serve with the remaining sauce.

PALATE-PLEASING SLICED PORK LOIN

SMOKE ON WHEELS BBQ TEAM

Ready for a true slice of pork perfection? Just one of the three ingredients, Smoke on Wheels Pork Marinade provides a rich, hearty flavor that'll turn this into the tastiest pork loin you've ever had. It's a crowd-pleaser!

YIELD: 14 SERVINGS • COOK TIME: 45 MINUTES

2 (4-lb [2-kg]) pork loins, trimmed and sliced

2 cups (475 ml) Smoke on Wheels Pork Marinade or favorite marinade

8 tbsp (120 g) pork or rib rub of choice

Place the pork loins into a resealable plastic bag. Dump the marinade into the bag and marinate in the refrigerator for 2 to 3 hours.

Remove the pork loins from the bag and pat them dry using paper towels. Sprinkle all sides with the rub, and let rest for 10 minutes. Preheat the grill to 250°F (121°C).

Place the pork loins on the grill and cook using indirect heat for 30 to 35 minutes. Using a meat thermometer, check the temperature of the pork and continue to cook to an internal temperature of 140°F (60°F), about 10 minutes. Remove the pork from the grill and let it rest 10 to 15 minutes.

Cut the pork loins into ½-inch (1.3-cm) slices and serve.

TY'S HAWAIIAN PORK SKEWERS

GUADALUPE BBQ COMPANY

You will love the sweet and savory flavor combos that this Hawaiian pork recipe offers. The deeply flavorful pork is skewered with pineapple chunks and smoked bacon for a festive, utensil-optional dish everyone will love.

YIELD: 5–6 SERVINGS • COOK TIME: 15 MINUTES

1 (20-oz [567-g]) can crushed pineapple with juice

¾ cup (165 g) brown sugar

½ cup (120 ml) soy sauce

⅓ cup (82 g) ketchup

⅓ cup (79 ml) red wine

¼ cup (60 ml) Worcestershire sauce

1 clove garlic, minced

½ tbsp (7 g) fresh peeled and grated ginger

4 drops liquid smoke (hickory)

1 (3-lb [1-kg]) pork loin, cubed into 2″ x 2″ (5 x 5-cm) pieces

1 fresh pineapple, peeled, cored and cubed into 2″ x 2″ (5 x 5-cm) pieces

10–12 bamboo skewers, soaked in water

1 lb (454 g) smoked peppered bacon, sliced

In a bowl, mix the crushed pineapple with juice, brown sugar, soy sauce, ketchup, red wine, Worcestershire, garlic, ginger and liquid smoke. Pour half of this mixture in a pot to simmer until thickened, about 15 minutes. Add the pork and pineapple chunks to the mixture remaining in the bowl, and marinate for 10 to 15 minutes.

Remove the bamboo skewers from the water and start to assemble the pork, pineapple and bacon skewers. Push the skewer through one end of a strip of bacon. It's important to start with this ingredient so that you can interweave the bacon strip as you add 3 pork pieces and 3 pineapple pieces on the skewer. When it's done, the bacon should resemble a snake going in and out of the pork and pineapple. Repeat this process for each skewer.

Grill over medium-high heat for 6 to 8 minutes, with the goal of getting the bacon cooked and not overcooking the pork. Flip, and continue to cook for an additional 6 to 8 minutes, or to an internal temperature of 160 to 165°F (71 to 74°F) in the center of the pork. During the cooking process, baste with the reduced marinade mixture.

The remainder of the marinade mixture can be served as a dipping sauce. Enjoy!

CHAPTER 2

BEEF *AND* LAMB

Beef and lamb are favorite meats for outdoor cooking enthusiasts. You can cook many of these meats relatively quickly over direct heat, and slow cook others for many hours over charcoal. The outer regions of the animal, such as the legs, chest and neck, do a lot of work and tend to be tougher, while the inner regions tend to be more tender. To better understand the meats used in this chapter, it helps to know about the primal cuts. Although terminology may change across regions and countries, butchers often refer to eight primal cuts in the United States.

CHUCK: Essentially the neck and shoulder region, chuck is rich in flavor with a good mix of meat and fat, making it a common source of ground beef. While slightly tough, this economical cut is often used for stewing, braising, pot roasting and slow cooking. Common cuts from the region include chuck roasts, shoulder clod, blade roasts, and flat iron, ranch and boneless chuck eye steaks.

RIB: Flavorsome and very tender, the rib-eye roast is the preferred selection for many diners. The primal rib region is between the chuck and the loin, and the rib eye is the main muscle in this region. Laying within the ribs, the muscle receives little use, and makes for a delicate finished product. Rib eye can also be sliced into steaks, and its marbled fat content helps the meat naturally retain moisture during cooking. Beef back ribs are cut away from the rib-eye muscle. These ribs typically measure 6 to 10 inches (15 to 25 cm) in length. Beef short ribs tend to be straighter, have more meat than beef back ribs and can be 2 to 6 inches (5 to 15 cm) in length. The lower end of beef short ribs usually connects to the plate region.

LOIN: Part of the upper back, the loin provides choice cuts known for excellent texture. The tenderloin is extremely soft and flavorful. Located close to the spine, this muscle does very little work and has a low fat content. Beef tenderloin is sometimes cooked as a roast, but more often cut into steaks. The tenderloin tapers down at one end and is used to produce filet mignon. Sirloin meat is located above the tenderloin. Many steaks, including strip steaks, come from the loin region. Porterhouse and T-bone steaks are loin cuts that include part of the tenderloin. Tri-tip, a triangular beef roast, is cut from the bottom of the sirloin region. Flap steak, a thin cut of meat located at the bottom of the sirloin butt, is cut into chunks and served as steak tips. Because the meat is somewhat tough, steak tips are usually marinated for several hours and tend to be fairly marbled with a rich flavor.

ROUND: Round refers to the hind leg, with its large, round ends. Fairly lean, with little marbling, these tough pieces of meat are among the least flavorful and often require moist cooking methods. Top round, or the upper portion of the leg, is very lean and slightly more tender than the bottom round, or lower leg. Cuts from this region include top round roasts, rump roasts, bottom round roasts, eye round roasts and eye round steaks.

BRISKET: When properly cooked, beef brisket is a moist and flavorful meat that is enjoyed braised or smoked. Brisket is representative of the chest, a heavily worked muscle region. A full packer brisket is comprised of two muscles: the flat and the point. The flat is the leaner of the two muscles, and is usually cut into slices. The point is more marbled, so the finished product is moister and juicier than the flat. The point can also be served as slices, but it's often turned into a much-loved barbecue delicacy known as burnt ends.

PLATE: The belly region, below the ribs, is known as the plate. Skirt steaks and hanger steaks are cut from the plate. These cuts tend to be inexpensive, but are tough and fatty. While marinades are often used to help tenderize skirt steaks, hanger steaks are surprisingly more tender and flavorful. Pastrami can also be procured from the plate region.

FLANK: Slightly more tender than skirt steak, flank steak comes from the lower chest region, beneath the loin. Tougher than steaks cut from the loin or rib regions, flank steaks are often marinated or cooked using a braising liquid. Meat from the flank region is often ground.

SHANK: The lower leg beneath the knee is the shank. These densely bundled muscles can be braised for hours. While sometimes used in beef bourguignon, shank is more commonly used in beef stock, soups and stews. The toughest of all cuts, shank is very inexpensive.

BEEF TENDERLOIN OVER MUSHROOM RISOTTO ⟋ LOBSTER CREAM SAUCE

NATURAL BORN GRILLERS

John D. Wheeler was the 2008 Memphis in May Grand Champion in Whole Hog and he won First Place Ribs in 2010 and then again in 2013. The co-owner of the Memphis Barbecue Company and winner of 65 Grand Championships, he shares his award-winning recipe for a perfect "company" dish. This beef tenderloin is roasted to perfection.

YIELD: 8–10 SERVINGS • COOK TIME: 1½ HOURS

MEAT

4–5 lb (1.8–2 kg) beef tenderloin, trimmed

Garlic powder, to taste

Salt and pepper, to taste

Hickory and pecan wood chunks

RISOTTO

2 tbsp (29 g) butter

2 tbsp (30 ml) extra-virgin olive oil

1 cup (210 g) Arborio rice

4 cups (946 ml) chicken broth, divided

1–1½ cups (237–355 ml) good-quality dry white wine

½ cup (38 g) finely chopped mushrooms

¼ cup (45 g) shredded Parmesan

LOBSTER CREAM SAUCE

½ cup (115 g) butter

1 cup (237 ml) heavy whipping cream

1 cup (180 g) shredded Parmesan

¼ cup (28 g) shredded mozzarella

Lobster sautéed in garlic butter, or smoked and chopped into small pieces

Freshly ground black pepper

To make the meat, lightly sprinkle the garlic powder all over the tenderloin and rub it in. Repeat with the salt and then the pepper. Start with the garlic so you can see how much you are putting on, and so you don't overdo spots of garlic. Once the salt is on, it's difficult to tell the difference between the two.

Set up your smoker for 250°F (121°C), and use hickory and pecan wood chunks for flavor. Place the tenderloin on the rack and smoke for approximately 1½ hours, or until it reaches an internal temperature of 135 to 140°F (57 to 60°C). Remove from the smoker and place in an aluminum pan. Then let it rest, covered, for 15 to 20 minutes.

To make the risotto, in a skillet over low heat, melt the butter with the olive oil, whisking to emulsify. Add your rice and stir. Heat the rice until it starts to look translucent, but don't let it turn brown, about 3 to 5 minutes. Add 1 cup (237 ml) of broth and a generous splash of wine. Stir constantly over low heat while the rice cooks and soaks up the liquid. When the liquid is almost gone, add another cup (237 ml) of broth and a splash of wine. Repeat until all of the broth is absorbed, about 20 to 25 minutes total. The risotto should be tender but mildly al dente. Stir in the mushrooms and cheese to finish off.

To make the sauce, heat the butter in a skillet over low heat until melted. Add the heavy whipping cream and stir with a whisk to mix thoroughly. Add the Parmesan and mozzarella. Continue to stir until the cheese is melted. Add the lobster. Serve it hot, adding black pepper to finish.

Slice the tenderloin to your desired thickness. Serve on a bed of risotto with lobster cream sauce over the top.

BEEF WELLINGTON ≋ WITH ≋ CHEESY SCALLOPED POTATOES

YABBA DABBA QUE!

Beef Wellington is a wonderful dish that can be both impressive and simple to prepare. There has never been a time that seconds have not been requested, so you may want to double this recipe. Serve with a perfect side dish of cheesy scalloped potatoes and you have a complete meal that's quick to prepare.

YIELD: 5–6 SERVINGS • COOK TIME: 1½ HOURS

CHEESY SCALLOPED POTATOES

3 large white potatoes

3 large sweet potatoes

1 cup (237 ml) milk

1 cup (237 ml) heavy cream

2 tbsp (23 g) dark brown sugar

1 tsp garlic powder

½ tsp kosher salt

Pinches of white and black pepper

Pinch of ground nutmeg

4 tbsp (57 g) unsalted butter, softened, plus more for greasing

2 cups (241 g) grated sharp cheddar

BEEF WELLINGTON

1 (2½-lb [1-kg]) center-cut beef tenderloin, trimmed

2 tbsp (30 ml) olive oil

1 tbsp (18 g) kosher salt

½ tbsp (3 g) ground black pepper

3 tbsp (42 g) unsalted butter, softened

1 minced shallot

½ cup (38 g) minced mushrooms

1 tbsp (2 g) dried thyme

1 tbsp (15 ml) red wine

1 sheet puff pastry, thawed

1 large egg yolk, beaten

To make the scalloped potatoes, set your cooker for 350°F (180°C) indirect heat.

Wash, peel and slice the potatoes into ¼-inch (0.6-cm) slices. In a large bowl, add all the remaining ingredients except the cheese and stir until blended. Grease the bottom and sides of a 9 x 12-inch (23 x 30-cm) casserole dish with butter. Place one layer of potatoes across the bottom, and then add about a fourth of the mixture. Sprinkle with one-fourth of the grated cheese. Repeat these layers until all the ingredients are in the casserole, finishing with a layer of cheese. Place the casserole on a rack and cook for about 50 minutes, until tender.

To make the beef Wellington, trim any silver skin from the tenderloin and let it come up to room temperature. Coat the tenderloin with olive oil, salt and pepper.

Set up your cooker for a direct grill at 450°F (230°C). Once the grill is up to temperature, sear the tenderloin on all sides until browned, about 10 minutes total, and then remove and let it cool on a wire rack.

While the tenderloin is resting, place the butter, shallot, mushrooms and thyme in a frying pan and cook on the grill at a reduced temperature of 400°F (200°C) until the shallot and mushrooms have softened, about 5 minutes. Add the wine and continue to cook for another 5 minutes, until the wine has reduced. Once cooked, remove and let it cool while bringing the temperature of your cooker back up to 450°F (230°C) with an indirect setup.

On a flat surface, lay out the puff pastry sheet and place the cooked tenderloin in the center. Place the cooled shallot and mushroom mixture on top of the tenderloin, wrap it up with the pastry and seal the edges with the beaten egg. Coat the outside with the rest of the beaten egg.

Place the wrapped tenderloin in a roasting pan and bake with indirect heat at 450°F (230°C) for about 15 minutes, or until the internal temperature reaches 125°F (52°C) for rare. Place the cooked Wellington on a cooling rack under foil for about 10 minutes, and then slice it into 1½- to 2-inch (4- to 5-cm) portions to serve.

BRAD'S BRAD-ASS BRISKET

THE SHED BBQ TEAM

A perfectly cooked brisket is a true test of a great backyard cook. In this recipe, Brad Orrison shares tips for the tastiest brisket in the South. One bite, and you'll understand why it's called Brad-Ass Brisket!

Give yourself plenty of time. Put the brisket on early so you will have time to let the brisket rest before serving.

Invest in a good pair of waterproof gloves in case you need to move the brisket during the smoking process.

Have the beer cooler close to the smoker so you can keep a good eye on your temperatures.

Serve with your favorite ShedSpred BBQ sauce.

YIELD: 24–28 SERVINGS • COOK TIME: ABOUT 12 HOURS

BRISKET RUB

1½ cups (362 g) garlic salt

1½ cups (174 g) paprika

¾ cup (72 g) cumin

¾ cup (72 g) fresh black pepper

½ cup (64 g) chili powder

¼ cup (22 g) oregano

1½ cups (310 g) turbinado sugar

12–16 lb (5–7 kg) brisket

To make the rub, combine all the ingredients in a bowl. Rub in and fully cover the brisket with the brisket rub.

Configure your cooker for indirect cooking. Let the cooking temperature stabilize around 260°F (127°C). If you're using a grill versus a smoker, be sure to use indirect heat and rotate the brisket halfway through the cooking process.

Cook the brisket for 10 to 12 hours, or until it reaches an internal temperature of 190 to 195°F (88 to 91°C) to ensure tenderness. Use a probe thermometer.

Let the brisket rest at least 1 hour before serving. Some pitmasters use a clean cooler with a lid to hold it for at least an hour to let the brisket fall or get tender.

When serving, cut across the grain with the knife at an angle to slice your brisket. It will give the best cut for presentation and for eating.

NOTE: Choose a pretty brisket, 12 to 16 pounds (5 to 7 kg), with a good amount of fat. Hold it up, meat-side down, with one hand in the middle. If it lets gravity take over and starts to bend or fold over your hand, it's going to be a beauty: good and tender!

PECAN *AND* APPLE SMOKED CORNED BEEF BRISKET

BBQ GURU

The time it takes to cure this brisket flat is well worth the wait. Don't think so? One savory sampling of this recipe and you will never purchase pastrami from the deli again! Pink curing salt, or Prague Powder #1, is available online or in some specialty shops.

YIELD: 14–16 SERVINGS • COOK TIME: 8–10 HOURS

BRINE

1 gal (3.8 L) water

2 cups (576 g) kosher salt

5 tsp (28 g) pink curing salt (Prague Powder #1)

3 tbsp (20 g) pickling spices

½ cup (110 g) brown sugar

1 tbsp (9 g) whole brown mustard seeds

1 tbsp (5 g) coriander seeds

1 tbsp (4 g) red pepper flakes

2 tbsp (17 g) whole black peppercorns

1 tsp powdered cardamom

6 large bay leaves, crumbled

2 tsp (5 g) ground ginger

½ stick cinnamon

7 whole cloves

8 whole allspice berries

8 whole juniper berries

MEAT

8–10-lb (3.5–4.5-kg) brisket flat

Coarse black pepper and BBQ Bob's Alpha BBQ Rub or favorite rub, for dusting

Your favorite smoke wood

To make the brine, place the water and all the brine ingredients into a large stockpot and bring to a boil, stirring often to dissolve the salts and sugar. Cool the brine down to 45°F (7°C) or less before using.

To make the meat, place the brisket into a large, resealable plastic bag or shallow container with a lid and pour the brine over the brisket to submerge. Store the brining brisket in the refrigerator for 8 to 10 days, checking periodically to make sure the brisket is totally submerged. After 8 to 10 days, remove the brisket from the brine and rinse with cold water.

Once the beef brisket has been properly cured and rinsed, it is ready for the smoker. Use an indirect setup and set the smoker temperature to 275°F (135°C).

Dust the brisket on all sides with coarse black pepper and BBQ Bob's Alpha BBQ Rub. Let it sit for 30 minutes.

Once your smoker is up to temperature, add your favorite smoke wood. Pecan and apple works well here. About 15 minutes before you place the brisket in the smoker, add one small chunk of apple and one small chunk of pecan smoke wood to the hot coals. This will allow the smoke to mellow out and give you a sweeter flavor.

Place the brisket in the smoker and allow it to cook for about 4 hours on the rack. After 4 hours, remove the brisket from the smoker, wrap with heavy-duty aluminum foil and place back into the smoker. Continue cooking until the internal temperature reaches approximately 200°F (93°C) or it is fork tender, 4 to 6 more hours.

Let the brisket rest in a dry cooler for approximately 1 hour before slicing.

BEST-TASTING GRILLED GREEK LAMB CHOPS

RIBS WITHIN BBQ TEAM

Doug Keiles makes these savory and salty chops often, because they are easy to prepare and they pack great flavor. While Doug prefers a Frenched chop, any lamb chop can be used with great results.

YIELD: 4 SERVINGS • COOK TIME: 12 MINUTES

2 tsp (12 g) kosher salt

Juice and zest of 1 lemon

½ cup (120 ml) olive oil

1 tsp black pepper

1 tbsp (3 g) dry oregano

8 lamb chops, about 1" (2.5-cm) thick, 2 per person

Rice or pasta, for serving

Mix the salt, lemon juice and zest, olive oil, pepper and oregano in a bowl. Add the chops, coat them well and cover the bowl. Marinade in the refrigerator 8 to 10 hours, or overnight. You can also do this in a sealed 1-gallon (3.8-L) plastic bag. Mix or flip the bag occasionally.

One hour prior to cooking, remove the chops from the refrigerator and lay them on a flat plate. Turn your grill on high for 5 to 10 minutes to clean and preheat the grates. Oil the grates by putting oil on a paper towel and applying it to the grates with tongs. Leave one burner on hot, one on medium and one on low.

Place the chops on the hot grates and grill for 2 minutes per side. Move them to medium heat and grill 2 more minutes per side. Finally, move to low heat for 2 minutes per side.

Remove them from the grill and let them rest, loosely covered, for 5 minutes. Serve with rice or pasta.

> **NOTE:** This recipe can also be made with boneless chicken thighs or breasts. Cook times change to 3 minutes per side on medium and 1 minute per side on low.

TRI-TIP ~with~ SMOKED GOUDA ON GRILLED TOAST POINTS

PHIL THE GRILL

This lean roast blends a wet rub and a dry rub for incredible flavor. Thinly sliced and lathered in melted cheese, you will want to cook this beefy-tasting roast every time you fire up your cooker!

YIELD: 4–6 SERVINGS • COOK TIME: 40–45 MINUTES

WET RUB

¼ cup (60 ml) olive oil

1 tbsp (30 ml) Worcestershire sauce

2 tbsp (15 ml) soy sauce

2 tbsp (5 g) Creole seasoning

3 lb (1 kg) tri-tip beef roast

DRY RUB

Phil The Grill Rub Me All Over or favorite seasoning blend, to taste

Black pepper, to taste

Kosher salt, to taste

Montreal steak seasoning, to taste

Smoke wood chips, soaked in water and drained

1 loaf French bread

Olive oil

4 slices smoked Gouda cheese

Phil the Grill OMG BBQ Sauce or favorite BBQ sauce

To make the wet rub, combine all the ingredients in a bowl. Apply the wet rub to both sides of the tri-tip.

To make the dry rub, combine all the ingredients in a bowl. Apply a layer of the dry rub seasonings to both sides of the meat. Let it sit for 10 minutes.

Configure your grill for two-zone cooking and preheat to 400°F (204°C). Sear the tri-tip roast, fat-side up, for 10 minutes each side. Add soaked wood chips on top of the hot charcoal. Move the roast to an indirect cooking zone, cover for 20 minutes and roast to an internal temperature of 130°F (54°C). Remove it from the heat, tent loosely with a sheet of aluminum foil and let rest for 15 minutes.

Slice your French bread into ¾-inch (2-cm) slices, brush with olive oil and grill for 30 to 40 seconds per side. Place the bread on indirect heat, layer on the smoked Gouda slices and cook for 1 to 2 minutes, or until the cheese melts. Remove from the heat, thinly slice the beef and layer it on top of the cheese. Drizzle with the BBQ sauce, plate and serve.

HIGH-HEAT SMOKY BRISKET

SMOKIN' HOGGZ

This is a great method for cooking briskets, not only because it takes less time, but also because the results are fantastic! The finished brisket is tender and very flavorful. If you learn this high-heat cooking method for brisket, we think you're going to come back to it again and again!

YIELD: 20–30 SERVINGS • COOK TIME: ABOUT 4½ HOURS

INJECTION

1 cup (237 ml) beef broth

1 cup (237 ml) water

1 tbsp (15 ml) beef broth concentrate

2 tbsp (30 ml) Worcestershire sauce

¼ cup (60 g) phosphates

2 cloves garlic, roughly chopped

1 onion, chopped

RUB

¼ cup (72 g) kosher salt

¼ cup (49 g) sugar

1 tbsp (6 g) coarse black pepper

1 tbsp (10 g) garlic powder

1 tbsp (7 g) onion powder

1 tbsp (8 g) chili powder

2 tsp (4 g) ground cayenne

MARINADE

1½ cups (355 ml) dark beer

¼ cup (60 ml) apple cider vinegar

¼ cup (60 ml) Worcestershire sauce

1 tbsp (15 ml) sodium-free beef broth concentrate

1 tbsp (10 g) garlic powder

1 tbsp (7 g) onion powder

1 tbsp (15 g) brisket rub

1 tsp celery seed

2 tsp (10 g) MSG

1 tsp cayenne pepper

MEAT

1 (10–15-lb [5–7-kg]) brisket

Your favorite smoke wood chunks

BBQ SAUCE

1 cup (245 g) ketchup

½ cup (118 ml) apple cider vinegar

¼ cup (60 ml) molasses

1 tbsp (15 ml) Worcestershire sauce

1½ cups (330 g) packed light brown sugar

2 tbsp (16 g) chili powder

1 tbsp (18 g) kosher salt

2 tsp (4 g) coarse black pepper

1 tsp garlic powder

1 tsp onion powder

To make the injection, the day before using, mix all the injection ingredients in a saucepan and heat over medium heat. Cool and store in the refrigerator.

To make the rub, combine all the ingredients in a bowl.

To make the marinade, in a saucepan over medium heat, mix all the ingredients and simmer for about 15 minutes. Cool and store in the refrigerator. Mix and heat right before use.

To make the meat, trim all of the loose fat and silver skin from the flat side of the brisket. Remove most of the fat from the point. Inject the brisket with injections in a checkerboard pattern, every 2 inches (5 cm). Apply the rub liberally all over the brisket and let it sit in the fridge for 4 hours to overnight.

Set up your smoker for hot and fast cooking, 350°F (177°C). You will also want to line your water pan with some heavy-duty aluminum foil, as this will greatly help with cleanup when you are done. Add your choice of wood chunks and place the brisket on the cooking rack. Cook for 2½ hours or until the brisket reaches an internal temperature of 165°F (74°C).

When the desired internal temperature is reached, remove it from the cooker and prepare for wrapping. Lay out a sheet of heavy-duty foil large enough to completely wrap the brisket.

Place the brisket on the foil, add the heated brisket marinade, wrap and cook for an additional 1½ to 2 hours, until you reach an internal temperature of 200°F (93°C). Remove the brisket from the smoker and vent the foil for about 10 minutes to help stop the cooking process. Wrap it back up, set it aside in a dry, empty cooler and let it rest for about an hour.

To make the BBQ sauce, mix all the ingredients in a medium saucepan over low heat and simmer for about 15 minutes.

After an hour of rest time, unwrap the brisket and save the juices contained in the foil. Take the brisket, and separate the flat from the point. To do this, place a long slicing knife between the point and flat. Slice at an angle, going toward the end of the flat. It should be like slicing through warm butter. Cube up the point into 1-inch (2.5-cm) pieces, place them into a pan, add some BBQ sauce and put it back on the cooker for an additional 30 minutes. Slice the flat into ¼-inch (0.6-cm) thick slices and put them back into the foil juice for about 10 minutes. This will help add a little flavor to this already delicious brisket.

JACK DANIEL'S WHISKEY-INFUSED STEAK TIPS

SMOKIN' ACES

What's better than beef marinating in Jack Daniel's, teriyaki and maple syrup? NOTHING! The sugars in the marinade caramelize and add a great taste to steak tips. The whiskey infuses the beef to create a nice, beefy bite.

YIELD: 4 SERVINGS • COOK TIME: 8 MINUTES

MEAT

2 lb (907 g) steak tips, trimmed of visible fat and silver skin

MARINADE

⅓ cup (79 ml) olive oil

1 tbsp (8 g) freshly ground ginger

½ cup (120 ml) Jack Daniel's Tennessee Whiskey

3 cloves garlic, minced

1½ cups (355 ml) teriyaki sauce

⅓ cup (79 ml) maple syrup

To make the meat, place the trimmed meat into a resealable plastic bag.

To make the marinade, combine the ingredients in a bowl and blend. Pour the marinade over the steak tips, and seal the bag well. Place it in the refrigerator and marinate for at least 2 hours. Do not marinate for more than 24 hours.

Heat your grill to a high heat, around 450°F (232°C). Place the tips on the hot grill and cook to medium rare, about 4 minutes per side, or to 140°F (60°C) internal temperature. Enjoy!

JUICY ✦ BONELESS PRIME RIB ON A DRUM SMOKER

BIG POPPA SMOKERS BBQ TEAM

Beautifully marbled with fat, this roast is not only juicy and tender—it's a feast for the eyes! For this recipe, you will need a meat thermometer, drum smoker (or any charcoal, pellet or wood smoker) and you may want a roast rack.

YIELD: 8–10 SERVINGS • COOK TIME: 110 MINUTES

1 (6½-lb [3-kg]) Wagyu boneless prime rib (Snake River Farms)

Cuckoo Racha Sriracha Chili Dust (Big Poppa Smokers) or favorite seasoning blend, to taste

Double Secret Steak Rub (Big Poppa Smokers) or favorite rub, to taste

Peppered Cow Rub (Simply Marvelous) or favorite rub, to taste

Preheat your drum smoker or grill to 250°F (121°C), no deflector needed.

Trim the prime rib of any excess fat. Season the trimmed meat with Big Poppa Smokers Cuckoo Racha Chili Dust, season with a generous layer of Big Poppa Smokers Double Secret Steak Rub and finish with a light coating of Simply Marvelous Peppered Cow Rub.

Put the prime rib on your drum smoker (with or without a rack). Flip the meat after 1½ hours or the meat has reached 105°F (41°C) internal temperature. Remove from the smoker when it reaches 127°F (53°C) internal temperature, about 20 to 30 minutes. Loosely tent with foil, and rest for 15 to 20 minutes before carving.

PRO TIP: Do not slice the entire prime rib roast all at once. Instead, slice as you serve your guests. Presentation carving like a hotel buffet is best so you can control portions for each of your guests while also maintaining the temperature of your roast.

MARINATED GRILLED SKIRT STEAK WITH HERBED CHIMICHURRI SAUCE

THREE MEN AND A BABYBACK BBQ TEAM

Hot and caramelized on the outside, tender and juicy on the inside, this steak has incredible flavor and tenderness. Wine adds a subtle, sweet background flavor to the marinade and the perfectly grilled beef gets topped with a slightly spicy Argentinean chimichurri sauce.

YIELD: 2–4 SERVINGS • COOK TIME: 8 MINUTES

MARINADE

1 small onion, diced

3 cloves garlic, minced

½ cup (120 ml) olive oil

¼ cup (60 ml) white wine vinegar

2 tbsp (30 ml) Worcestershire sauce

2 tsp (8 g) sugar

1 tsp salt

1 tsp black pepper

¼ cup (60 ml) Worcestershire sauce

¼ cup (60 ml) red wine

2 (10-oz [280-g]) skirt steaks, trimmed of any excess fat

Salt and pepper, to taste

Fresh herbs, for garnish

CHIMICHURRI SAUCE

½ cup (120 ml) red wine or sherry vinegar

3–4 cloves garlic, thinly sliced or minced

1 shallot, finely chopped

1 jalapeño, finely chopped

2 cups (96 g) minced fresh cilantro

1 cup (60 g) minced fresh flat-leaf parsley

⅓ cup (15 g) finely chopped fresh oregano or thyme

¾ cup (177 ml) extra-virgin olive oil

Salt and pepper, to taste

To make the marinade, combine all the ingredients in a bowl. Reserve 1 cup (235 ml) of the marinade and save the rest for another use. Mix the reserved marinade, Worcestershire sauce and wine together in a bowl. Then add the skirt steaks and let them sit for 3 hours or overnight in the refrigerator.

To make the chimichurri sauce, combine the vinegar, garlic, shallot, jalapeño, cilantro, parsley and oregano in a small bowl. Using a whisk, add the olive oil. Season with salt and pepper and set aside.

Remove the steaks from the marinade and season with salt and pepper. Discard the marinade. Grill the steaks over a very hot flame for about 3 to 4 minutes on each side, until the meat is nicely charred (no more than medium-rare, or 130 to 135°F [54 to 57°C]). Transfer the steaks to a cutting board and allow them to rest for 5 to 10 minutes.

Thinly slice the steak, drizzle chimichurri sauce over top and garnish with fresh herbs.

*See photo on page 54 (top right corner).

PECAN-SMOKED BEEF FILLET

SWEET SMOKE Q BBQ TEAM

What is better than this easy, melt-in-your-mouth buttery beef cooked to perfection on the grill? Go on and give up thinking about it because you won't be able to think of anything better!

YIELD: 4 SERVINGS • COOK TIME: 12–14 MINUTES

MEAT

4 (6–8-oz [170–227-g]) beef fillets

½ cup (120 ml) Sweet Smoke Q Beef Juice concentrate

1 cup (237 ml) water

Pecan smoke wood chunks

Salt and freshly ground black pepper

8 slices applewood smoked bacon, cooked and crumbled

GARLIC CHIVE BUTTER

½ cup (115 g) unsalted butter, softened

2 cloves garlic, minced

2 tsp (2 g) fresh chives

½ tsp salt

½ tsp fresh ground black pepper

To make the meat, an hour before cooking, remove the fillets from the refrigerator. In a resealable plastic bag, mix together the Sweet Smoke Q Beef Juice and the water. Place the fillets in the bag containing the marinade for about an hour.

To make the butter, combine the ingredients in a small bowl, mix well and roll into a log. Place it in the fridge to harden.

Prepare a charcoal grill for two-zone cooking, with a fire on one side at medium-high heat. Add some pecan wood chunks directly onto the hot charcoal. Remove the fillets from the marinade and season both sides with salt and pepper. Place the fillets on the cool zone of the charcoal grill, covered, for 10 minutes to absorb the smoke. Move the fillets over the direct heat and cook until you get a good sear, about 1 to 2 minutes each side. Finish cooking when the internal temperature reaches 125°F (52°C), for medium-rare. Remove from the grill and add a teaspoon of the compound butter and the bacon crumbles. Let it rest for 5 minutes before cutting into the meat.

REVERSE-SEAR CAP *of* RIBEYE

WILBUR'S REVENGE

This ribeye cap is perfect every time. With a sizzling, dark, flavorful crust, it is perfectly cooked on the inside—tender and juicy with big, bold flavor. While the reverse sear method ultimately takes longer to cook than other methods, this dish is ready to eat immediately because you've rested the ribeye prior to the sear—so you can eat it nice 'n' hot!

YIELD: 3 SERVINGS • COOK TIME: 51 MINUTES

1 (18-oz [510-g]) cap of ribeye

Fresh ground sea salt

2 tbsp (28 g) your favorite brisket rub

Take the cap of ribeye out of your refrigerator. Season it with salt with a light-medium coverage. Let it sit at room temperature for 2 hours.

Preheat the smoker to 225°F (107°C).

Season the ribeye with medium coverage of your favorite brisket rub. Place it in the smoker. When the cap of ribeye hits 102°F (39°C) internal temperature, approximately 45 minutes, place it on a 500°F (260°C) grill. Cook for 1½ minutes, rotate a quarter turn and cook an additional 1½ minutes to achieve nice grill marks. Flip the beef and cook for another 1½ minutes followed by a quarter turn again. Then cook until your desired doneness. For a perfect medium-rare, pull the ribeye after 1½ minutes and let it rest for 5 minutes. Slice it on a bias ¼ inch (0.6 cm) thick and serve.

ROBERT'S BOLD *AND* SPICY MEATLOAF

ROBERT SIERRA, S&S PIT CREW

This bold and spicy meatloaf is cooked on a homemade offset smoker named "The Black Pearl." The cook time may vary for your smoker, but give this recipe a try and you'll quickly learn that a smoked meatloaf is kind of like a barbecue treasure: simple, savory and delish!

YIELD: 4–6 SERVINGS • COOK TIME: 3 HOURS

2 lb (907 g) ground chuck

3 large eggs

½ cup (120 ml) Heinz Texas Style Bold & Spicy BBQ Sauce, divided

⅓ cup (45 g) finely chopped onion

1 tsp salt

½ tsp black pepper

½ tsp granulated garlic

½ tsp cumin

2 sleeves saltine crackers

Place the ground chuck in a quarter aluminum pan. Add the eggs, ¼ cup (60 ml) of the Heinz BBQ Sauce, onion, salt, pepper, garlic and cumin and mix thoroughly. Crush the saltine crackers in a ziplock bag. Add them to the meat mixture and mix thoroughly. Top the meatloaf with the remaining ¼ cup (60 ml) of Heinz BBQ Sauce.

Preheat the smoker to 250°F (121°C). Place the pan on the rack and cook for 3 hours, or to an internal temperature of 160°F (71°C). Remove the pan and let it rest for 5 to 10 minutes; then slice and enjoy!

SMOKEY JOE'S CAFÉ BBQ SHORT RIBS

FAMOUS DAVE ANDERSON

This juicy dish features beef short ribs slow-smoked in a tasty broth, grilled to perfection and mixed with a tangy and sweet sauce.

YIELD: 6–8 SERVINGS • COOK TIME: 3½ HOURS

8 lb (3.6 kg) beef short ribs

Famous Dave's Steak Seasoning or your favorite seasoning blend, to taste

½ tsp coarse ground black pepper

1 large onion, quartered and separated

1 (10-oz [296-ml]) can beef consommé

2 cups (473 ml) Famous Dave's Barbecue Sauce or your favorite BBQ sauce

2 tbsp (31 g) sweet pickle relish

Preheat your smoker to 300°F (149°C), indirect heat.

Sprinkle the ribs generously on all sides with the steak seasoning and pepper. Place the ribs in a heavy roasting pan. Top with the onion. Pour the consommé around the ribs, being careful not to knock the seasoning off the ribs.

Place the ribs on the preheated smoker, covered, for 2½ hours. Remove the pan from the smoker. Place the ribs on a platter. Skim the fat from the juices in the pan. Remove the beef from the bones, discarding the bones. Place the beef back in the pan containing the juices.

In a bowl, combine the barbecue sauce and pickle relish and pour over the beef. Cover and bake for 45 minutes. Remove the cover and bake for 15 minutes longer.

MARK ⟨AND⟩ MARK'S TANGY SUMMER SAUSAGE

SWEET SWINE O' MINE BBQ TEAM

Sweet Swine O' Mine, established in 1996, is a two-time World Grand Champion BBQ team out of Memphis, Tennessee. One taste of these wonderfully seasoned sausages and you'll understand why they've won numerous awards. This recipe is unique but certainly something an aspiring novice could do. The recipe makes a 25-pound (11-kg) batch and freezes well.

YIELD: ABOUT 100 (6″ [15-CM]) SAUSAGES • COOK TIME: ABOUT 8 HOURS

12½ lb (6 kg) lean beef or venison

12½ lb (6 kg) semi-lean pork (you can go with more beef/venison if you prefer it leaner)

1 oz (30 g) Cure #1, also known as Prague Powder #1 (a mixture of sea salt and sodium nitrate, which must be accurately weighed, not measured)

12½ tbsp (189 g) salt

5 tbsp (35 g) onion powder

5 tbsp (42 g) garlic powder

5 tbsp (32 g) black pepper, coarsely ground

2½ tbsp (28 g) mustard seed

5 tbsp (60 g) sugar

5 tsp (11 g) ground nutmeg

5 tsp (3 g) dried basil

5 tsp (8 g) coriander seed, cracked

1½ cups (192 g) powdered milk OR 2 oz (60 ml) 414 Binder

2½ cups (600 ml) buttermilk

2 oz (57 g) buttermilk powder

3 lb (1.5 kg) high-temperature cheese, optional (see note in directions)

2½ lb (1 kg) chopped jalapeños, optional

About 70′ (21.5 m) sausage casings

Grind all the meats through a ⅜-inch (1-cm) plate on your meat grinder. Add the rest of the ingredients, except the cheese and jalapeños, and mix well. Rest the mixture for an hour and regrind through the ³⁄₁₆-inch (0.5-cm) die.

If you want to add cheese and jalapeños, now is the time to do so. For a 25-pound (11-kg) batch, use 2½ to 3 pounds (1 to 1½ kg) of high-temperature cheese. Note: High-temperature cheese is specially made so that it will not melt under normal cooking temperatures up to 400°F (204°C). If adding jalapeños, you can use either raw or roasted. Refrigerate overnight for the cure and spices to meld into the meat mixture.

The next day, stuff the meat into the casings to your desired length. Place the stuffed casings in your smoker at 130°F (54°C) for 2 hours with no smoke, to dry the casing so the casing and sausage can take on smoke later in the cooking process.

Turn your smoker up to 150°F (66°C) and smoke them for 4 hours with a light, moderate or heavy smoke (depending on your preference). You want a slow rise in heat. If you smoke too hot, you will not get the right results. Bump the heat to 170°F (77°C) and cook for another hour. At this point, it's optional if you continue to use smoke during the cooking process.

To finish cooking, increase the smoker temperature to 190°F (88°C) and continue to cook until the internal meat temperature is at least 150°F (66°C).

Once you reach your internal temperature, it is time for an ice water bath to rapidly bring down the meat temperature. This also helps to prevent wrinkly casings forming on the summer sausage. After the ice water bath, hang them at room temperature for a couple of hours and then refrigerate overnight.

Pack the sausages in the freezer . . . but only after some taste testing.

SMOKY TAMARI-LIME TRI-TIP

SMOKE ON WHEELS BBQ TEAM

Andy's tri-tip recipe has a rich, thick and dark marinade. This recipe tastes gourmet, will impress your guests and will have them begging for seconds and thirds!

YIELD: 6–8 SERVINGS • COOK TIME: 16 MINUTES

MARINADE

½ cup (120 ml) grapeseed oil

⅓ cup (79 ml) tamari

4 scallions, washed and cut in half

4 large cloves garlic

1 small red onion

¼ cup (60 ml) lime juice

¼ tsp red pepper flakes

¼ tsp chipotle pepper

½ tsp ground cumin

3 tbsp (44 g) dark brown sugar

MEAT

1 (3-lb [1-kg]) tri-tip roast

Steak seasoning of your choice

To make the marinade, blend the ingredients in a blender or food processor until puréed.

To make the meat, place the tri-tip on a cutting board and remove the silver skin and excess fat.

Place the roast in a shallow container and pour the marinade over it. Refrigerate, covered, for 2 to 3 hours. Drain the marinade from the meat. Season the meat with the steak seasoning and let the meat come to room temperature.

Grill the roast directly over high heat for 7 to 8 minutes per side.

Once the internal temperature is 125°F (52°C), remove from the grill and cover, allowing the beef to rest for at least 10 minutes. Thinly slice against the grain and on a bias to serve.

CHAPTER 3

POULTRY

YOU WILL NEVER BURN, underseason or undercook your chicken or turkey again once you use the recipes and cooking times given for these grilled and smoked poultry dishes. Follow the time tables, use a good thermometer and always allow the meat to rest for at least ten minutes before slicing into it, and you will have a juicy winner every time.

Do you know which cooking methods are best suited to each cut for the most appetizing results?

The location of the cut of chicken determines the texture and flavor; this can make the difference between whether the meat is suitable for grilling, braising, using as an ingredient in chicken salad or casseroles or serving with sauces.

Here's a primer on the different cuts of chicken and their best uses.

WHOLE CHICKEN: This one's just what it sounds like—the whole bird. Well, usually minus the head. Whole chickens can be purchased fresh or frozen. Roasted chicken is an absolute classic, and there are many variations, from rotisserie-style to bacon-wrapped. A whole chicken can also be broken down into the other cuts listed, in which case, the cooking methods are virtually unlimited, including: grilling, braising, frying, baking and broiling.

EIGHT-PIECE CUT: The whole bird is cut into two breast halves with ribs and back portion, two wings, two thighs with the back portion and two drumsticks. They can also be sold as "whole cut chicken." One cooking method that works for just about any part of the eight-piece cut of chicken is braising. This slow-cooking method not only maximizes the flavor of chicken, but keeps it nice and moist.

HALF CHICKEN: The whole chicken is split from front to back through the backbone and keel, resulting in two basically mirror-image halves. Like a whole chicken, this is a great cut for roasting, but be careful to not let it dry out. Unlike a whole chicken, its more manageable size makes it well suited for grilling.

BREAST QUARTERS: A cut that includes a portion of the back, the breast and the wing. Your favorite method of cooking a chicken breast will work with the breast quarter. Roast it, grill it, bake it, but don't overdo it.

SPLIT BREAST: A breast quarter with the wing removed, which may come with or without a portion of the back.

BONELESS, SKINLESS CHICKEN BREAST: A split breast that has been deboned and skinned. It can be grilled, pan-fried or baked. Since it is white meat and doesn't have the fat from the skin to contain juices, watch any cooking method to prevent the chicken from drying out.

WHOLE CHICKEN WING: This all-white meat portion of the chicken is a versatile cut, but keep in mind that since it is all white meat, it contains lower fat, so it is more prone to drying out. Be sure not to overcook.

WING DRUMETTES: The portion of the wing between the shoulder and the elbow is a common cut that can be grilled, braised, baked or broiled.

WING MIDSECTION: Also referred to as the "wing flat" or "mid-joint," this is the section between the elbow and the tip. Probably its most famous use is Buffalo wings. This cut is very versatile though: it can also be broiled, baked or grilled.

WHOLE CHICKEN LEG: A combination of both drumstick and thigh in one unit, it is different from the leg quarter. It doesn't include a portion of the back. The whole chicken leg is available bone-in and with skin, or boneless and skinless. With the thigh and the leg, these are great braised or grilled. Given their balance of fat and flavor, they are also particularly delicious when fried. The boneless, skinless version is best cooked with moisture, as it can dry out without the added fat and protection of the skin. Marinate and grill, or braise it for tasty results.

THIGHS: The portion of the leg cut above the joint of the knee. Thighs are available bone-in with skin, or boneless and skinless. Being a more "worked" muscle, the thighs are well suited for braising, which softens the chicken and maximizes the thighs' rich flavor. Grilling and smoking are popular methods of cooking chicken thighs.

DRUMSTICKS: The lower portion of the leg quarter between the joint of the knee and the hock, drumsticks can be prepared in a variety of ways. They are well suited

CROWD-PLEASING SPICY ASIAN BBQ WINGS

SWEET SWINE O' MINE BBQ TEAM

Brined and then grilled until crispy, these spicy Asian chicken wings are delicious bites of sweetened joy!

YIELD: 8 SERVINGS • COOK TIME: 32 MINUTES

ALL-PURPOSE BRINE

1 gal (3.8 L) distilled water

1 cup (241 g) salt

2 cups (383 g) cane sugar

4 cloves garlic, chopped

1 onion, chopped

1 large bunch fresh thyme

2 stalks celery, chopped

1 large bunch rosemary

2 bay leaves

½ cup (120 ml) Worcestershire sauce

½ cup (120 ml) soy sauce

3 lb (1.4 kg) chicken wings

Boar's Night Out (BNO) White Lightning seasoning

Spray cooking oil

SWEET AND SPICY CHILI SAUCE

2 cups (473 ml) Frank's RedHot Sweet Chili Sauce

2 tbsp (29 g) minced ginger

2 whole chopped scallions or 1 diced shallot, plus more for garnish

½ cup (24 g) chopped cilantro, divided (reserve ¼ cup [12 g] to top the wings)

1 tbsp (15 ml) toasted sesame oil

1 tsp toasted sesame seeds

1 tbsp (15 ml) Ponzu

2 tbsp (30 ml) Sriracha

1 tsp minced garlic

Black pepper, to taste

To make the brine, place the brine ingredients in a large bowl and mix together until the sugar dissolves. Add the chicken wings to the bowl and brine in the refrigerator for at least 4 hours. Make sure the wings are fully submerged in the brining solution.

Remove the wings from the brine and pat them dry. Season with Boar's Night Out (BNO) White Lightning or your favorite all-purpose, low-sugar seasoning. Spray with cooking oil.

Configure your grill for indirect cooking, and let the grill heat up to 350°F (177°C). Arrange the wings on the cool side of the grill and cook using indirect heat with the lid on for 30 minutes. Lift the lid and remove the wings from the grill. Using metal tongs, carefully spread out the hot coals into a single layer. Char the wings over direct fire, turning frequently to brown them, for about 2 minutes. This will finish the wings so that the skin is nice and crispy.

To make the sauce, combine all the sauce ingredients in a bowl. Toss the wings in the sauce to coat them. Add the reserved ¼ cup (12 g) of cilantro and some additional chopped scallion, if desired, and serve.

BASIC'S CRANBERRY-BRINED SMOKED TURKEY

THE BASIC BBQ TEAM

This delicious hickory-smoked turkey recipe brings a Cape Cod twist to your Thanksgiving table. Smoked turkey is a holiday delight and sure to be the centerpiece of a meal your guests will enjoy!

YIELD: 10–12 SERVINGS • COOK TIME: ABOUT 5 HOURS

TURKEY

20 lb (9 kg) whole turkey

BASIC'S CRANBERRY POULTRY BRINE

½ gal (2 L) cranberry juice

¾ cup (216 g) kosher salt

1 tbsp (6 g) Bell's Seasoning

1 tbsp (8 g) black pepper

½–¾ gal (2–3 L) water

VEGETABLES AND SEASONINGS

1 large yellow onion, quartered

3 stalks celery, split down the center

3 peeled carrots, split down the center

1 (1-oz [28-g]) box Bell's Seasoning

Butcher BBQ Honey Rub or favorite rub, to taste

GRAVY PAN

1 qt (946 ml) chicken stock

2 cloves garlic

1 cup (237 ml) white grape juice

1 green bell pepper, seeded and sliced

2 onions, quartered

3 carrots, chopped into 2" (5-cm) pieces

Celery seeds

Turkey neck

3 bay leaves

1 tsp Bell Seasoning

Dried thyme

½ cup (115 g) butter

To make the turkey, start with any size bird you prefer. This recipe uses amounts that are adequate for birds between 15 and 25 pounds (6.8 and 11.3 kg). Feel free to adjust ingredient quantities up or down in order to meet your needs.

To make the brine, in a large bowl, mix together all the ingredients for the brine.

Prepare the turkey for the rigors of smoking by brining overnight. Get a 5-gallon (19-L) bucket or small cooler large enough to hold the bird. Line the container with an unscented plastic garbage bag. Place the bird in the bag and place the bag in the container. Pour the brine over the bird. Close the bag, shake the container and cover the closed bag with ice. Leave it overnight or for a minimum of 12 hours. We have left the bird in the brine for as long as 24 hours.

Two hours before placing your bird in the smoker, remove from the brine and rinse thoroughly, both inside and out. Expect the skin to take on an unusual cranberry/pink color from the brine. Do not worry: it will look normal when cooked.

After washing, dry the bird thoroughly and place in the refrigerator for 30 minutes to dry some more.

(continued)

BASIC'S CRANBERRY-BRINED SMOKED TURKEY (CONTINUED)

For the vegetables and seasonings, place the yellow onion, celery and carrots inside the cavity of the bird. Next, lightly sprinkle Bell's Seasoning on both the inside and outside of the bird. Then, apply a medium coating of Butcher BBQ Honey Rub to the exterior of the bird.

Next, tie or truss the bird. There are many ways to do this. There is no right or wrong way. Do some research, choose a technique and tie that bird. Use a traditional brown butcher's twine.

To make the gravy pan, place all of the pan ingredients in a pan. I like to use a 4-inch (10-cm) deep aluminum pan. Use what works for you, but I suggest you do not use a pan/rack that allows the bird to sit in the bottom of the pan. Place the turkey in the smoker on a rack that keeps the bird above the gravy pan.

At this point your cooking temperature and cooking times really depend on your smoker. The Basic BBQ Team likes to cook this recipe on a pellet smoker and use 100-percent hickory pellets. Let the bird absorb a lot of smoke by keeping the cooker at a very low 200°F (93°C) for the first hour.

After 1 hour, increase smoker temperature to 300°F (149°C). A rough estimate of total cooking time is about 15 minutes per pound (455 g).

After the first 3 hours, baste the bird every 30 minutes. About three-quarters of the way through the cook (roughly 3 to 4 hours depending on the size of the bird) you should check the skin. Once the skin is a golden brown, tent it with foil.

Continue cooking the turkey for about 1 to 2 more hours depending on the size of the bird. The bird is done when the center of the breast meat reaches 165°F (74°C). The legs and thighs will be up around 190°F (88°C). Once the bird reaches these temperatures, remove it from the cooker and let it rest in a cold oven or on a countertop. Strain the lovely concoction that is in the gravy pan and place the strained liquid into a smaller pot.

At this point you should turn your au jus into gravy. There are many ways to make gravy, so let's just state that this is the best gravy base ever tasted. You can season it how you like to make it your own. Let the bird rest for not more than 1 hour before carving and serving.

TIM'S HONEY-GLAZED HOT WINGS

FEEDING FRIENDZ

Marinated in hot sauce, and lathered with butter spray, these honey-glazed wings have a nice, crispy skin and a touch of heat. This recipe was the Feeding Friendz BBQ Team's winning entry in the "People's Choice Wing" competition at Chillin' Country BBQ State Competition, held in York, Maine.

YIELD: 8 SERVINGS • COOK TIME: 14 MINUTES

3 lb (1 kg) chicken wings, cut into sections, tips discarded

1 cup (236 ml) Frank's RedHot sauce or your favorite hot sauce

1 tbsp (5 g) cayenne

Butter spray

1–2 cups (236–473 ml) clover honey, divided

Marinate the wings in Frank's RedHot. If you use a vacuum tumbler, marinate for 20 minutes; otherwise marinate the wings overnight in a resealable plastic bag.

After marinating, lightly and evenly sprinkle both sides of the wings with cayenne.

Prepare a charcoal grill for direct medium heat, about 350°F (177°C). Place the wings on the grill and spray liberally with butter spray. Place the lid on the grill and cook for about 5 minutes.

Remove the lid, flip the wings over and spray the other side of the wings with butter spray. Cover the grill and cook for 3 to 4 minutes, until crispy.

Drizzle half of the honey over the wings and grill for about 5 minutes more, or until the wings are done and the internal temperature reaches about 180°F (82°C).

Remove the wings from the grill and drizzle the remaining honey over the side not already coated with it.

CHICKEN SATAY SKEWERS *with* SWEET *and* SPICY PEANUT SAUCE

CARLO CASANOVA, KG COOKERS

Flavorful Thai-style chicken skewers are marinated and then grilled to tender, juicy perfection and enjoyed with a sweet and spicy peanut sauce. Serve with white rice for a complete meal.

YIELD: 4 SERVINGS • COOK TIME: 15 MINUTES

CHICKEN

4 boneless, skinless chicken breasts, cut into 1" (2.5-cm) cubes

¼ cup (60 ml) soy sauce

1 tbsp (9 g) cornstarch

2 cloves garlic, finely chopped

1" (2.5-cm) piece fresh ginger, peeled and finely chopped

12 bamboo skewers

PEANUT SAUCE

2 tbsp (30 ml) peanut or vegetable oil

½ onion, finely chopped

1 clove garlic, finely chopped

¼ cup (64 g) chunky peanut butter

¼ cup (60 ml) water

½ tsp chili powder

To make the chicken, place the chicken cubes in a dish or bowl. Mix the soy sauce, cornstarch, garlic and ginger together and pour it over the chicken. Cover and let it sit in the refrigerator for a couple of hours. Soak the bamboo skewers in cold water for at least 30 minutes.

Preheat your grill for a hot, 400°F (204°C) direct cook.

Thread the chicken pieces onto the pre-soaked bamboo skewers. Oil the grates and transfer the skewers onto the hot pit. Cook to an internal temperature of at least 165°F (74°C), about 8 minutes, turning every 2 minutes.

To make the peanut sauce, heat the oil in a saucepan, add the onion and garlic, and cook over medium heat, stirring frequently, for 3 to 4 minutes until softened. Add the peanut butter, water and chili powder, and simmer for 2 to 3 minutes, until thin and softened.

Serve the skewers immediately with the warmed peanut sauce and enjoy!

CHICKEN SPIEDINI

SMOKE ON WHEELS BBQ TEAM

Spiedini is an Italian-inspired dish that features marinated, breadcrumb-coated chicken breast rolled and skewered and then grilled to tasty perfection. The zesty flavors in the Smoke on Wheels marinade really make this dish pop.

YIELD: 2 SERVINGS • COOK TIME: 10 MINUTES

4 boneless, skinless chicken breast halves

1 cup (235 ml) Smoke on Wheels BBQ Marinade or favorite marinade

⅔ cup (80 g) Italian seasoned breadcrumbs

⅓ cup (60 g) grated Parmesan cheese

1 tbsp (3 g) chopped fresh parsley

2 cloves garlic, minced

Put the breast halves between sheets of plastic wrap or in a resealable plastic bag. Using a mallet, gently pound the chicken until they are ¼ inch (6 mm) thick. Place the chicken in another resealable plastic bag and pour the marinade into the bag. Marinate in the refrigerator for 4 hours.

On waxed paper, combine your breadcrumbs, Parmesan, parsley and garlic. Dip the chicken into the remaining marinade and coat with the crumb mixture. Tightly roll the pounded chicken and fasten together using toothpicks. Cut your chicken into 1-inch (2.5-cm) thick pieces and thread them onto a metal skewer. Remove the toothpicks. Repeat this process with the remaining chicken.

Place the skewers on an oiled grill over medium-hot coals. Cover the chicken and grill for about 5 minutes per side, or until it reaches 165°F (74°C). To serve as appetizer bites, skewer each chicken roll with a toothpick for easy snacking.

AWARD-WINNING HIGH-HEAT CHICKEN LOLLIPOPS

SMOKIN' HOGGZ

Meat on a stick: a dish with its own built-in utensil. These chicken lollipops are sure to be a hit at your next cookout, particularly with the kids. One look and your friends and family will think you are the next television food star!

YIELD: 12 CHICKEN LOLLIPOPS • COOK TIME: 75 MINUTES

INJECTION

1½ cups (355 ml) chicken broth

1½ tsp (7 g) Accent (MSG)

2 tsp (5 g) dehydrated butter powder

SMOKIN HOGGZ DRY RUB

½ cup (95 g) granulated sugar

½ cup (110 g) brown sugar

¼ cup (35 g) ancho chile powder

¼ cup (72 g) kosher salt

2 tbsp (15 g) paprika

1 tbsp (6 g) ground black pepper

2 tsp (5 g) garlic powder

2 tsp (5 g) onion powder

1 tsp white pepper

½ tsp allspice

CHICKEN

2–3 chunks sugar maple or applewood

12 chicken drumsticks, skin on

SAUCE

1½ cups (355 ml) Sweet Baby Ray's Honey Chipotle BBQ sauce

¼ cup (60 ml) honey

½ cup (120 ml) white grape juice

To make the injection, combine the chicken broth, Accent and butter powder, making sure the Accent dissolves completely. Store refrigerated until ready to use.

To make the rub, mix all the rub ingredients together and store in an airtight container.

To make the chicken, prepare your smoker or grill for hot and fast cooking, 300 to 350°F (149 to 177°C). Add 2 to 3 chunks of sugar maple or applewood about 10 minutes before putting the chicken on.

With a paring knife, cut the tendons at the narrow end of each drummette. Scrape the meat down as far as possible without removing the meat completely, to form a round lollipop shape. With a pair of pliers, remove all the ligaments and smaller bones and discard. Make sure all the meat is down to one end of the bone and be sure the skin is covering all the meat; trim excess skin if necessary.

With a meat injector, inject about 1 to 2 tablespoons (15 to 30 ml) of injection and mix all throughout each piece of meat.

Season the drums with Smokin' Hoggz Dry Rub and place the chicken in your smoker or grill. Cook using direct heat for about 1 hour, or until the chicken reaches an internal temperature of 165°F (74°C).

To make the sauce, in a medium saucepan, heat the barbecue sauce, honey and grape juice.

Remove the chicken drums from your smoker. Using tongs or gloved hands, submerge each drum into the warm sauce. Shake off any excess sauce and place the drums back on the smoker or grill, directly on the grate. Cook until the sauce is caramelized, about 15 minutes.

Remove the chicken drums from your smoker. Let them rest for 10 minutes and serve.

ORANGE-HONEY SRIRACHA WINGS

BARK BROTHERS BBQ

Try this spicy, sweet and savory chicken wing recipe, and you will see why Bark Brothers BBQ has had numerous calls at contests all over Ohio!

YIELD: 8–10 SERVINGS • COOK TIME: 1 HOUR

DRY RUB

½ cup (110 g) brown sugar

½ cup (58 g) paprika

1 tbsp (6 g) ground black pepper

1 tbsp (18 g) kosher salt

1 tbsp (8 g) chili powder

1 tbsp (10 g) garlic powder

1 tbsp (7 g) onion powder

1 tbsp (5 g) cayenne pepper

CHICKEN WINGS

5 lb (2.25 kg) chicken wings (sectioned into drums/wingettes; remove wing tips)

Olive oil

Your favorite smoke wood

SAUCE

1 (18-oz [510-g]) jar orange marmalade

⅓ cup (79 ml) Sriracha

⅓ cup (79 ml) honey

⅓ cup (73 g) light brown sugar

To make the rub, combine all the rub ingredients in a bowl.

To make the wings, rinse the wings and pat them dry. Coat the wings lightly with olive oil and apply the dry rub to all sides of the wings.

Set up your smoker or grill for indirect cooking at 300°F (149°C). Add your favorite smoke wood for flavor (Bark Brothers BBQ prefers cherry wood on chicken).

Oil the cooking grate and place the wings on your grill or smoker. Cook with the lid on for 30 to 40 minutes, or until the chicken reaches an internal temperature of 165°F (74°C).

Make the sauce while the wings are cooking. Combine the sauce ingredients in a heavy saucepan and heat over medium heat. Bring to a boil, stirring constantly to dissolve all the sugar. Once the sugar is fully dissolved, remove the sauce from the heat.

When the wings have reached an internal temperature of 165°F (74°C), remove them from the grill. Toss the wings in a large bowl with the orange honey sauce.

Return the wings to the grill for 10 minutes to set the glaze. Remove the wings and toss them in the glaze for a second time. Place the wings back on the cooker for an additional 5 to 10 minutes. Remove your wings from the cooker and devour!

ORANGE-KISSED SWEET & SPICY ASIAN WINGS

A MAZIE Q

These chicken wings, grilled to perfection and sauced with a spicy, tropical citrus tang, will be gone from the serving platter before you know it.

YIELD: 16 SERVINGS • COOK TIME: 30 MINUTES

CHICKEN WINGS

5 lb (2 kg) chicken wings

1 cup (240 g) your favorite rub

SAUCE

1½ cups (355 ml) orange juice

¼ cup (60 ml) rice wine vinegar

¼ cup (55 g) brown sugar

½ cup (123 g) ketchup

¾ tsp ground ginger

½ cup (120 ml) sweet chili sauce

1 tsp sesame oil

Juice of 1 lime

1 tbsp (15 ml) honey

1 bunch fresh cilantro, chopped

Limes, cut into wedges

To make the chicken wings, lightly season the wings with your favorite rub. Keep in mind that the wings you make using this recipe will be pretty sweet, so try to stay away from overly sweet rubs or ones that contain a lot of cinnamon. Many commercial rubs contain sugar and cinnamon. The level of cinnamon in many commercial rubs can be overwhelming and dominate the flavor profile. If you use a rub with a lot of sugar, the sugar will likely burn during the cooking process.

To make the sauce, pour the orange juice into a saucepan. Bring it to a boil on your stove and reduce by half. Add the remaining sauce ingredients, whisk and then reduce the heat. Simmer for 15 to 25 minutes, until the flavors are blended and well balanced. Set the sauce aside to cool.

Use a smoker or configure your grill for two-zone cooking. Allow your cooker to heat up to a temperature of 225 to 250°F (107 to 121°C). Place the wings in the smoker or on the cool zone of the grill, and cook using indirect heat for 20 to 30 minutes.

Finish the wings off by grilling them over direct heat to obtain a nice, flavorful and slightly charred skin, about 2 minutes per side.

Place the wings in a bowl and toss them with the wing sauce. Garnish with cilantro and lime, and get ready to watch everyone do a happy dance!

LO'-N-SLO' JUICY ROASTED TURKEY

LO'-N-SLO' BBQ TEAM

Fruits and vegetables placed in the cavity to impart moisture and flavor, and fresh herb butter placed under the skin, give this brined turkey a big punch of flavor.

YIELD: 12 SERVINGS • COOK TIME: ABOUT 3 HOURS

BRINE

8 cups (2 L) apple cider

1½ cups (432 g) kosher salt

1½ cups (330 g) dark brown sugar

1½ cups (355 ml) agave

1 cup (236 ml) apple cider vinegar

½ cup (120 ml) orange juice

¼ cup (60 ml) lemon juice

¼ tsp ground cloves

¼ tsp poultry seasoning

1 tbsp (8 g) whole black peppercorns

6 bay leaves

TURKEY

1 (12–14-lb [5–6-kg]) turkey

NOTE: You should prepare the brine approximately 4 to 5 hours before you are ready to brine the turkey.

HERB BUTTER

½ cup (115 g) unsalted butter, softened

3 cloves minced garlic

1 tbsp (3 g) minced fresh rosemary

1 tbsp (3 g) minced fresh thyme

1 tbsp (3 g) minced fresh oregano

1 tbsp (3 g) minced fresh parsley

1 tbsp (3 g) minced fresh sage

STUFFING

1 orange, cut into 8 wedges

1 lemon, cut into 8 wedges

1 lime, cut into 8 wedges

1 apple, cut into 8 wedges

1 medium onion, cut into 8 wedges with skin on

4 cloves garlic, slightly crushed with skin on

4 sprigs fresh rosemary

Small bunches of parsley, oregano, thyme and sage leaves

To make the brine, combine all the ingredients in an 8-quart (7.5-L) pot. Bring the liquid to a boil over high heat, stirring occasionally. Remove from the heat and add 8 cups (2 L) of cold water to the pot, stirring well. Allow the liquid to cool to room temperature, and then refrigerate until cold.

To make the turkey, place the turkey breast-side down in a tub or pot large enough to hold the turkey and the brine. Add the brine and refrigerate for 8 to 12 hours. Make sure the turkey is submerged beneath the brining liquid.

Remove the turkey from the brine. Rinse and dry the turkey, and then discard the brine. Place the dried turkey on a tray and place the tray in the refrigerator, uncovered, for 3 hours. This will help to dry the surface for a crispier skin.

To make the herb butter, place the softened butter in a bowl and mix together with all the ingredients.

Remove your turkey from the refrigerator. Carefully slide your hands under the skin of the turkey to loosen it from the breast meat. Using your fingers, spread the herbed butter mixture directly on the breast meat, being careful not to tear the skin.

Stuff the body and neck cavities with wedges of the orange, lemon, lime, apple, onion, garlic and herbs. Place the turkey in a roasting pan. Fill a resealable plastic bag with ice, and place the bag on the breast meat of the turkey. Allow the turkey to rest on the counter for 1 hour. This process chills the white meat to even out the cooking time of the white meat and the dark meat.

Preheat your smoker to 350°F (180°C). Place the roasting pan on the rack and cook for 1½ hours. After 1½ hours, remove the lid. If there is not a lot of liquid in the bottom of the roasting pan, add 2 cups (470 ml) of liquid (water, turkey broth, white wine, etc.).

Continue cooking until an instant-read thermometer registers 165°F (74°C) in the breast. This will take approximately 1¼ to 1½ hours, depending on the size of the turkey. Remove the roasting pan and let the turkey rest 15 to 20 minutes.

Remove the stuffing, carve and serve.

SHREDDED CHICKEN–STUFFED POBLANOS

BBQ GURU

BBQ Bob's Alpha Rub, used here to grill boneless chicken breasts before shredding, is a very flavorful seasoning that balances sweet, heat, savory and salt. Alpha Rub gives you that wonderful and traditional barbecue flavor. These stuffed and grilled poblano peppers stay firm with great flavor.

YIELD: 4 SERVINGS • COOK TIME: 30 MINUTES

3 chicken breasts (skinless/boneless)

1 tbsp (15 ml) olive oil, plus more for coating, divided

1 tbsp (8 g) BBQ Bob's Alpha Rub or favorite rub

1 small Spanish onion, diced small

2 medium tomatoes, diced

½ tsp sea salt

¼ tsp black pepper

¼ tsp cumin

8 oz (227 g) black beans, cooked

½ cup (120 ml) chicken broth

4 poblano peppers, halved and seeded

8 oz (227 g) Mexican cheese, shredded, divided

1 lime

2 avocados, sliced

Set your grill to 350°F (177°C) with a direct setup.

Lightly coat the chicken breasts with olive oil, and then dust with BBQ Bob's Alpha Rub.

Grill over direct heat for 5 to 7 minutes. Flip the breasts and continue to cook until the chicken reaches an internal temperature of 170°F (77°C). Remove the chicken breasts from your grill and set aside.

In a disposable half pan, place 1 tablespoon (15 ml) of olive oil, the onion, tomatoes, salt, pepper, cumin and black beans. Stir occasionally until the onion is cooked thoroughly and the flavors have blended, approximately 10 to 15 minutes.

Shred the chicken breast meat and add it to the black bean mixture in the half pan. Add the chicken broth and stir the ingredients well.

Fill the poblano pepper halves with the chicken and black bean mixture, and then top with half of the shredded Mexican cheese. Grill the stuffed peppers for about 20 minutes, then add the remaining shredded Mexican cheese to the tops and continue to cook until the cheese melts. Serve with a squeeze of fresh lime juice and sliced avocado.

SIMPLE SMOKED SWAMP CHICKEN

SWAMP BOYS BBQ TEAM

Barbecued chicken is so good in so many recipes. Besides being great by itself, smoked chicken is better than chicken prepared any other way, for homemade tacos, burritos, quesadillas, chicken salad, pulled chicken sandwiches, chicken pot pie or anything else that involves chicken. This is the simple way the Swamp Boys barbecue chicken.

YIELD: 4 SERVINGS • COOK TIME: 1 HOUR

1 (3–4-lb [1–2-kg]) whole chicken

½ cup (120 g) Swamp Boys Original Rub or your favorite rub, to taste

1–2 pieces of smoke wood

1 (12-oz [336-g]) bottle Parkay squeeze butter

Remove the chicken from their packaging and thoroughly rinse. Orientate the chicken so the wings face toward you, with the breast-side down.

Using kitchen shears, cut down both sides of the backbone and remove it. Lay the chicken open, skin-side down. Pull out the breast/keel bone, and use it and the backbone to make some stock for another culinary project. Slice where the keel bone was, separating the chicken into two halves. Cut away any chunks of fat.

At this point you can inject, brine, marinate or do whatever you want to the chicken. We like to keep it super simple and just use Swamp Boys Original Rub to season it. Season the chicken under the skin, using your fingers to help spread it around anywhere you can get. Season the bottom and inside of the bird. Season the skin side of the bird last. Use a nice and even layer of rub to make it pretty.

Preheat your smoker to 300 to 325°F (149 to 163°C), and place the chicken on the grate, skin-side up. Use just a small amount of wood for smoke. It's very easy to overdo it with chicken. Check the chicken for a nice golden color at about the 45-minute mark. If the color is where you want it, put the halves into a disposable pan, still skin-side up, and squeeze the butter all over them. Cover and seal with foil and cook 15 minutes more. Check for doneness with a thermometer. You want at least 175°F (79°C) in the thighs.

Now you have some very tasty and moist chicken to eat as is, or pull it off the bones and use in your favorite recipe.

SLOW-GRILLED CHICKEN

DIZZY PIG BBQ TEAM

Combining Dizzy Pig seasoning, a small controlled fire and a little patience just might create the best chicken you've ever tasted. For any doubters, we dare you to try!

YIELD: 4 SERVINGS • COOK TIME: 1½ HOURS

4–5 lb (1.8–2.3 kg) fresh chicken pieces: wings, drumsticks, thighs

1 cup (80 g) Dizzy Pig Dizzy Dust (though all Dizzy Pig flavors are good on chicken) or favorite seasoning blend

Start your grill. The preference for this recipe is cooking over charcoal. If you have a gas grill, you want the fire as low as you can get it. A small fire is best, so don't use too much charcoal. Stabilize the temperature at 275°F (135°C) and wait for clean smoke.

Sprinkle a fairly generous layer of Dizzy Dust (or your rub of choice) on the chicken. Let it sit until the rub adheres, and then coat the other side. Place the chicken, skin-side up, on a raised grate. For the best results, chicken should be at least 12 inches (30 cm) above the charcoal or fire. If you are using a gas grill, consider cooking on the warming shelf above the cooking grate. Keep the lid closed and maintain the heat at 275 to 300°F (135 to 149°C). Rotate the grate or rearrange the chicken pieces every 15 minutes for even browning.

After 45 to 60 minutes (a bit less for wings), a nice, brown crust should have formed on the bottom of the chicken. If the chicken is getting really dark or looks burnt after 20 to 30 minutes, then you are cooking too hot. You should reduce the cooking temperature by either turning down your gas grill or closing the vents partway on your charcoal grill. Alternatively, on some grills, you can try to raise the cooking grate further away from the fire.

Once the chicken is golden, flip the chicken skin-side down. Continue to cook the chicken for 30 to 45 minutes. Remember to rotate the cooking grate or rearrange the chicken pieces every 15 minutes for even browning. The chicken is done when the skin is browned and the meat reaches an internal temperature of 185 to 195°F (85 to 91°C).

Remove it from the grill and let it rest for 5 to 10 minutes. Then enjoy!

SMOKED CORNISH GAME HEN ~WITH~ CHIPOTLE-CITRUS MOJO SAUCE

KEN HESS, BIG BOB GIBSON BAR-B-Q

This smoked Cornish game hen is bursting with fantastic orange, cilantro and lime flavors. These moist and delicate little chickadees will certainly have your guests telling their friends about a memorable meal.

YIELD: 8 SERVINGS • COOK TIME: 30 MINUTES

DRY RUB

¼ cup (29 g) paprika

3 tbsp (54 g) kosher salt

2 tbsp (12 g) fresh ground black pepper

2 tbsp (17 g) garlic powder

2 tbsp (14 g) onion powder

1 tbsp (8 g) chili powder

1 tbsp (8 g) chipotle powder

2 tsp (4 g) ground cumin

MOJO SAUCE

6 cloves garlic, peeled

1 cup (236 ml) fresh orange juice

Zest and juice of 1 lime

½ cup (24 g) roughly chopped fresh cilantro

1 tbsp (15 ml) honey

1 tbsp (18 g) kosher salt

1 tsp chipotle powder

1 tsp fresh ground black pepper

½ cup (120 ml) extra-virgin olive oil

CORNISH GAME HENS

2-3 chunks your favorite smoke wood

4 whole Cornish game hens

To make the rub, combine all the rub ingredients in a mixing bowl and blend well. This rub can be stored in an airtight container for up to 3 weeks.

To make the sauce, place all of the sauce ingredients except the olive oil into a blender. Purée on high until smooth. With the blender running, slowly incorporate the olive oil. You can make the mojo sauce an hour ahead of time. If the sauce separates, just mix it until it comes back together.

To make the game hens, set your grill up for indirect grilling using charcoal and 2 to 3 wood chunks. Bring the temperature of the grill to 350°F (177°C).

Spatchcock the Cornish game hens by removing the Pope's Nose, or fleshy surface that protrudes from the back end of the chicken, and then slice along one side of the backbone. Press on the inside of the legs until the bird flattens out. Remove the sternum bone from its cartilage. Flip the bird over and tuck the wings under the breast meat. Repeat for each hen.

Season the hens liberally with the dry rub. Smoke them skin side up for 15 minutes. After 15 minutes, open the smoker and check the color on the surface of the hens. The hens should have a noticeably darker color. If the desired color is not achieved, then let the hens smoke for 5 more minutes.

Once you have achieved the desired skin color, flip the hen skin side down. Baste with the mojo sauce and continue cooking for 10 to 15 minutes or until the thighs reach an internal temperature of 175°F (79°C). Once cooked through, remove the hens and baste the skin side with the mojo sauce. Cover loosely with foil and let the hens rest for 10 minutes.

Split the hens in half and serve one half per guest.

*See photo on page 84 (lower right corner).

SOUTHEAST ASIAN CURRY GRILLED CHICKEN WINGS

KEN HESS, BIG BOB GIBSON BAR-B-Q

Fragrant aromatics and the extra zing of lime juice make these grilled wings burst with deep flavors. Marinated with coconut milk, ginger, lime juice, sesame oil and soy sauce, this recipe never fails to deliver!

YIELD: 8 SERVINGS • COOK TIME: 25–30 MINUTES

CHICKEN

3 lb (1 kg) chicken wing pieces

SAUCE

½ cup (113 g) prepared Thai green curry paste

¾ cup (177 ml) lite coconut milk

½ cup (120 ml) soy sauce

½ cup (120 ml) honey

2 tbsp (30 ml) sesame oil

2 tbsp (30 ml) fish sauce

1 tbsp (15 ml) Sriracha

1 tbsp (15 g) sambal oelek chili paste

1 tbsp (3 g) chopped cilantro

2 tbsp (28 g) minced fresh ginger

2 tsp (10 ml) lime juice

1 tsp kosher salt

GLAZE

½ cup (120 ml) honey

¼ cup (60 ml) rice wine vinegar

To make the chicken, place the chicken wings in a gallon-size (3.8-L) resealable plastic storage bag.

To make the sauce, combine all of the sauce ingredients in a mixing bowl. Whisk the mixture until all of the ingredients are blended together well. Pour the marinade over the wings and place them in the refrigerator for at least 1 hour.

To make the glaze, combine the honey and the rice wine vinegar until the honey is thinned down enough to brush on the wings. Cover and set aside.

Set up your grill for two-zone cooking. Once your grill has reached 500°F (260°C), sear both sides of the chicken wings using direct heat. Cook for approximately 3 to 4 minutes per side.

After you have seared both sides of the chicken wings, reduce the heat to 350°F (177°C), and move the wings to the cool zone of the grill. Brush the glaze on the wings and cook for about 10 minutes. Flip the wings over and brush them with glaze. Continue to cook the wings until they reach an internal temperature of 190°F (88°C), about 9 to 12 minutes longer. Enjoy!

HOT OFF *the* DRUM SPICY ASIAN WINGS

LUCKY Q [SAUCE RECIPE GIVEN BY ARTIE INOUYE]

The spicy glaze of these chicken wings is a showstopper made with a tempting combination of hot sauce and teriyaki sauce. Try these chicken wings as an alternative to regular hot wings—we think you're gonna like 'em!

YIELD: 8–10 SERVINGS • COOK TIME: 30 MINUTES

1 (3–4-lb [1.4–1.8-kg]) package whole wings

Olive oil

½ cup (120 g) Big Poppa Smokers Desert Gold seasoning or your favorite seasoning blend

1 (12-oz [355-ml]) bottle Three Brothers (Different Mothers) Barbecue Sauce

Yoko's Spicy Teriyaki Marinade and Grilling Sauce or your favorite marinade

1 (12-oz [355-ml]) bottle Frank's RedHot sauce

Set up your smoker or grill to 350 to 375°F (177 to 191°C), indirect heat. Separate the wings into wingettes and drumettes, discarding the tips. Toss the trimmed wings with olive oil, seasoning with a light to medium coat of Big Poppa Smokers Desert Gold. Let the wings sit 20 to 30 minutes in the refrigerator until the rub dissolves.

Place the wings on your cooker, not directly above the heat source. Cook for 20 minutes using indirect heat with the lid on.

While the wings are cooking, combine equal parts Yoko's Spicy Teriyaki and Frank's RedHot sauces. Stir them together and set aside.

After 20 minutes, check the color of the wings. If the wings show good browning, flip and baste them with the sauce mixture. Baste the wings every 5 to 10 minutes until they reach an internal temperature of 170°F (77°C). Then, flip once more and coat the other side of the wings with sauce.

Wings are best served when they have reached 180°F (82°C) internal temperature.

TEXAN-ASIAN GLAZED AND GRILLED CHICKEN

GUADALUPE BBQ COMPANY

Chicken breasts, marinated in an easy-to-make, Asian-inspired sauce, are grilled and then glazed to delicious perfection. There is honey for sweetness, soy for saltiness and jalapeño for heat. Sure, it's slightly spicy, but the sweetness of the honey tames the heat for a balanced flavor.

YIELD: 4 SERVINGS • COOK TIME: 14 MINUTES

¼ cup (60 ml) soy sauce

4 tsp (20 ml) sesame oil

2 tbsp (40 ml) honey

1 tbsp (15 ml) light Caro syrup

½ tbsp (7 g) fresh peeled and grated ginger

1 tbsp (15 g) minced shallot

2 cloves garlic, minced

2 jalapeño peppers, cored and minced

4 skinless, boneless chicken breasts

Combine all the ingredients except the chicken in a large bowl. Place the chicken breasts in the bowl, and marinate in the refrigerator for 30 minutes to an hour.

Get the grill hot at 300 to 400°F (149 to 204°C), direct heat.

Remove the chicken from the marinade. Transfer the marinade to a metal pot and bring the liquid to a boil. Simmer for 10 to 15 minutes to kill any raw chicken bacteria and set aside for basting.

Place the chicken on the grill. Cook using direct heat for 5 to 7 minutes, with the lid on the grill. Open the lid, and flip and baste the chicken. Continue to cook with the lid down for an additional 5 to 7 minutes or until the chicken breast reaches an internal temperature of 165°F (74°C). The chicken will look golden brown with a heavy sheen and will be ready to serve right away.

TASTY THREE-STEP TERIYAKI SMOKED AND GRILLED WINGS

KIM PERRY, BEHIND BBQ

These marinated wings are braised in butter and then smoked and grilled, creating the perfect combination of smoke and spice that everyone will love. You'll always have company at the smoker when you're making these teriyaki wings; sometimes, they don't even make it to the platter before they're gone!

YIELD: 8 SERVINGS • COOK TIME: 1 HOUR AND 10 MINUTES

---

3 lb (1 kg) chicken wings

WING MARINADE

¼ cup (60 ml) soy sauce

2 tbsp (30 ml) apple cider vinegar

2 tbsp (28 g) brown sugar

1 tbsp (6 g) five-spice powder

¼ cup (60 ml) oil

½ cup (115 g) salted butter

Peach, cherry or applewood for smoking

1 (13.25-oz [375-g]) bottle Bone Suckin' Yaki Teriyaki Sauce or favorite teriyaki sauce

Sesame seeds

Remove the chicken wings from their packaging, rinse and pat dry.

To make the marinade, combine all the marinade ingredients in a resealable plastic bag, squishing the bag to mix well. Place the chicken wings in the bag, toss them to coat and marinate overnight in the refrigerator.

Drain and discard the marinade. Place the wings in an even layer in aluminum half pans. Cut the butter into 16 slices. Scatter the butter slices over the wings.

Place the pans in your smoker, uncovered. Using one chunk of peach, cherry or applewood for flavor, cook the wings at 250°F (121°C) for 1 hour.

Preheat a grill to medium-hot (350°F [177°C]). Using tongs, transfer the wings to the grill to brown and crisp the skin. Turn frequently to avoid burning. When the skin is browned, about 3 to 5 minutes, remove the wings from your grill and place in a clean pan. Add Bone Suckin' Yaki sauce, and toss the wings to coat.

Place the wings back on the grill. Allow 5 minutes for the sauce to set, being careful not to burn.

Sprinkle with sesame seeds and serve.

> **NOTE:** As an entrée, plan on 8 to 12 wing sections per person. If using whole wings, separate them into flat and drum sections, trimming off the tips and saving them for when you make stock.

VERMONT MAPLE CHIPOTLE CHICKEN WINGS

SWEET BREATHE BBQ TEAM

Hailing from Vermont means maple, and Sweet Breathe BBQ team does it well on these sweet and spicy maple-glazed wings.

YIELD: 2–3 SERVINGS • COOK TIME: 50 MINUTES

12 chicken wings, tips removed

½ cup (64 g) your favorite BBQ rub

Maple or fruitwood chips

½ cup (115 g) unsalted butter

4 cloves garlic, minced

1 cup (236 ml) pure maple syrup

4 tsp (20 g) chipotles in adobo, puréed

½ tsp salt

Remove the wings from their packaging, and rinse and pat dry. Season the wings with your favorite BBQ rub, and let the rub set for about 10 minutes.

Prepare a two-zone medium fire at 350 to 450°F (177 to 232°C). Place a handful of maple or fruitwood chips on the fire. Place the wings on the cool zone of the grill. Cook the wings with the lid on, using indirect heat for 30 minutes.

While the wings are grilling, prepare the sauce. In a small saucepan over medium heat, melt the butter. Add the garlic and sauté until fragrant, about a minute. Add the maple syrup, chipotle purée and salt. Bring it to a slight boil and reduce the heat to low. Reduce the liquid until the sauce thickens enough to coat a spoon, about 5 minutes.

Move your wings to the hot zone of the grill. Cook the wings using direct heat for 6 minutes a side. Remove the wings, coat with sauce and return to the cool zone of the grill for 5 to 10 minutes to set the sauce. Using a meat thermometer, confirm the wings reached an internal temperature of at least 165°F (74°C).

CHAPTER 4

BURGERS AND SANDWICHES

SOMETIMES YOU JUST CRAVE A GOOD BURGER. Melted cheese and a juicy patty—what's not to love? In this chapter, you'll find several burger recipes to help you get your fix.

But one look at the following recipes, and burgers won't be the only tasty items you'll be craving that are served between toasted breads and layered with flavorful spreads.

This chapter also contains roasted pork sandwiches, grilled chicken hoagies, breakfast wraps and stuffed portobello mushrooms. Drawing hints of inspiration from German, Greek, Italian, Japanese, Mexican, Portuguese and Spanish influences, there's sure to be something for everyone. The best part is that several of these sandwiches can be cooked in 20 minutes or less, so you won't have to keep your hungry guests waiting for long. And that's great because the first car just pulled into your driveway . . .

GROUND BEEF HAMBURGERS ~the~ WISCONSIN WAY

ELYSE BROWN

Seven-year-old Elyse Brown was the 2016 Kid's Que Grand Champion at the Gold Ribbon BBQ Festival in Green Bay, Wisconsin. Cooking on a Weber Smokey Joe, she presented the judges with a mouthwatering burger that was juicy and spicy. There's a good chance you and your guests will like this burger just as much as the judges did!

YIELD: 4 SERVINGS • COOK TIME: 8 MINUTES

1 lb (455 g) ground beef

2 tbsp (5 g) dry ranch seasoning

1 oz (28 g) diced jalapeños

1 egg

¼ cup (33 g) small diced natural onion and garlic cheddar cheese from Renard's Cheese

1 tsp Big Poppa Smokers Happy Ending Finishing Rub or your favorite rub

¼ cup (60 ml) Farm Boy Original BBQ Sauce or your favorite sauce

2 tbsp (30 ml) water

4 hamburger buns

Your favorite burger toppings

Configure your grill for direct cooking and heat to 400°F (204°C).

Mix the beef, ranch, jalapeños, egg and cheese together and make 4 patties. Season with the Happy Ending rub, and let the patties rest while your grill gets hot and the temperature stabilizes.

In a small bowl, mix 2 parts Farm Boy Sauce with 1 part water.

To grill the burgers to medium doneness, grill for 3 minutes on the first side, flip, and brush on Farm Boy Sauce mixture. Cook for an additional 5 minutes, or to an internal temperature of 135 to 150°F (57 to 66°C). Place the burger into a bun, add your favorite toppings, serve and enjoy!

CHORIZO AND SCRAMBLED EGG BREAKFAST WRAPS

STICKS-N-CHICKS BBQ TEAM

Smoky chorizo sausage and spicy salsa give these wraps a hint of Spanish flair. They're ready in less than ten minutes and are great for breakfast, brunch or as a snack!

YIELD: 6 SERVINGS • COOK TIME: 8 MINUTES

1 (12-oz [340-g]) package fully cooked chorizo, casing removed and chopped

8 large eggs, lightly beaten

1 cup (130 g) shredded Monterey Jack cheese

½ cup (130 g) prepared deli salsa

6 (10" [25-cm]) flour tortillas

Sliced avocado, sour cream and cilantro, optional, for toppings

Set your cooker to 250 to 300°F (121 to 149°C).

In a large skillet or plow disc, cook the chorizo over medium heat for 3 to 4 minutes or until heated through. Add the eggs and cook for 2 to 3 minutes or until the eggs are set. Add the cheese and salsa, stirring until the cheese is melted, and remove from the heat.

Spoon the egg mixture into the center of each tortilla. Fold one side of each tortilla over the egg mixture and roll to enclose.

Serve with avocado, sour cream and cilantro, if desired.

CHICKEN BOMB HOAGIES

CAN U SMELL MY PITS

Grilled chicken, sautéed veggies and melted cheese served on a toasted bun is one of Can U Smell My Pits' go-to team dinners at competitions, and it's perfect for summer gatherings. This recipe makes three very hearty hoagies, or one 24-inch (61-cm) party-sized French bread sandwich.

YIELD: 3 SERVINGS • COOK TIME: 24 MINUTES

1½ lb (680 g) boneless chicken breast

1 tbsp (14 g) your favorite chicken rub

2 tbsp (30 ml) olive oil

1 cup (151 g) chopped onion

1 red bell pepper, seeded and chopped

1 green bell pepper, seeded and chopped

1 cup (66 g) sliced mushrooms, optional

5 slices Hoffman's cheddar cheese (this cheese melts awesome and does not separate like regular cheddar)

3 hoagie rolls or 1 French bread loaf

Salt and pepper, to taste

Configure your grill for direct cooking and let the temperature stabilize at about 400°F (204°C).

Rub the chicken with your favorite chicken rub, and let the rub set in for about 10 or 15 minutes.

Place the chicken breasts on the hot cooking grate, and cook for 6 to 8 minutes per side.

Place a skillet on the grill to heat it up. When the pan is hot, add the olive oil, onion, bell peppers and mushrooms (if using). Sauté the vegetables for about 5 minutes, or until they soften.

When the chicken reaches 170°F (77°C) internal temperature, chop it into small cubes and add it to the skillet. Place the sliced Hoffman's cheese on top of the chicken. Remove the skillet from the heat, cover with foil and set it aside.

Slice the hoagie rolls or French bread and toast on the grill for 2 to 3 minutes. Remove the foil from the skillet, stir the contents, load up those rolls and enjoy.

GREEK BURGER (AKA KOFTA BURGER)

STAN HAYS, COUNTY LINE SMOKERS

Chopped herbs, grilled onion and fresh tzatziki sauce provide a rich flavor to these lamb burgers. Think outside the bun and grill a lamb burger. If you've never tried one before, we think you're in for a real treat!

YIELD: 1 SERVING • COOK TIME: 19 MINUTES

LAMB BURGER

½ lb (227 g) ground lamb (may substitute ground beef, turkey or pork)

½ tsp fresh parsley

½ tsp minced garlic

1 tbsp (9 g) minced onion

Pinch of salt

Pinch of black pepper

⅛ tsp garlic powder

TZATZIKI SAUCE

1 cup (200 g) plain Greek yogurt

½ cucumber, peeled and finely chopped

2 cloves garlic, minced

2 tbsp (8 g) chopped parsley

Juice of ¼ lemon

Pinch of salt

Pinch of pepper

1 tbsp (5 g) finely minced red bell pepper

Vegetable oil, for the grate

2 thin slices red onion

1 bun, pita or naan bread

2 oz (55 g) crumbled feta cheese

To make the burger, mix the ground lamb with parsley, garlic and minced onion. Season with salt, black pepper and garlic powder

To make the sauce, add all of the ingredients in a bowl and stir until thoroughly combined. Refrigerate until ready to serve.

Prepare your grill for direct cooking at medium-high heat (400 to 500°F [204 to 260°C]). Oil the grate and place the lamb patty on the hot grill. Cook for about 6 minutes, flip and continue cooking for another 8 to 10 minutes, or to an internal temperature of 160°F (71°C). Remove the burger from the heat, cover and let it rest.

Grill the thinly sliced red onions and toast the bun/bread for 2 to 3 minutes. Top the onion slices with crumbled feta cheese while still on the grill.

Remove the onion and cheese from the grill. Add to the burger and top with tzatziki sauce. Then serve on the grilled bun or bread.

GRILLED ITALIAN PORK SANDWICHES

PORK BARREL BBQ

The Italian pork sandwich may be overshadowed by its sibling sandwich, the cheese steak, but it's no less of a Philadelphia classic. Get ready to give the cheese steak sandwich a run for its money by grilling pork to perfection, with a smoky flavor to the deliciously crispy, crunchy bark on the surface of the meat. This is one sandwich Rocky Balboa would consider a knockout!

YIELD: 6 SERVINGS • COOK TIME: 53 MINUTES

2 tbsp (19 g) minced garlic, divided

1½ tbsp (3 g) finely chopped fresh rosemary

7 tbsp (104 ml) extra-virgin olive oil, divided

1 tbsp (18 g) kosher salt

2 tsp (6 g) freshly ground black pepper

1 (2½–3-lb [1.1–1.3-kg]) boneless pork loin

1 bunch broccoli rabe

½ tsp red pepper flakes

12 slices smoked provolone cheese

6 sandwich rolls

Stir together 1½ tablespoons (14 g) of garlic, rosemary, 3 tablespoons (44 ml) of olive oil, salt and pepper in a small bowl. Place the pork in a baking dish and rub with the garlic marinade. Cover and chill for at least 2 hours.

Remove the pork from the refrigerator and let it sit at room temperature for 45 minutes. Meanwhile, preheat one side of the grill to medium-high, 350 to 400°F (177 to 204°C), to create a two-zone cooking configuration. Place the pork loin directly over the hot charcoal, and cook with the grill lid on for 4 minutes. Remove the lid, flip the pork loin and cook with the lid on for an additional 4 minutes.

Move the pork loin to the indirect zone. Place the lid on the grill and cook using indirect heat for 30 minutes, or until a meat thermometer inserted into the thickest portion of the pork reads 145°F (63°C). Remove the pork from the grill and let it stand for 5 minutes covered with aluminum foil before slicing.

Remove the florets from the broccoli rabe. Trim and discard ½ inch (1.3 cm) of the stem from the bottom of the broccoli rabe. Cook the leaves and stems in boiling water for 2 minutes; then add the florets and cook for an additional 5 minutes.

Drain the broccoli rabe, reserving ½ cup (120 ml) of the cooking water, and plunge the broccoli rabe into an icewater bath. Heat the remaining 4 tablespoons (60 ml) of olive oil in a large skillet over medium heat and add the remaining ½ tablespoon (5 g) of garlic and the red pepper flakes. Sauté for 1 minute. Add the broccoli rabe and sauté for 5 minutes. Add the reserved ½ cup (120 ml) of cooking water and cook for 2 more minutes.

To serve, arrange 2 slices of smoked provolone on the bottom of the sandwich rolls, and top with the sliced pork loin and broccoli rabe.

GRILLED MEATBALL BURGER *with* PESTO *and* SPICY MARINARA ON A BRIOCHE ROLL

BBQ GURU

Here is a fun way to enjoy the Italian flavors you love. Spicy marinara sauce and fresh pesto add to the layers of flavor—try this meatball burger sandwich once and it won't be long before you find yourself craving it again!

YIELD: 8 SERVINGS • COOK TIME: 30 MINUTES

MEATBALL BURGERS

2 lb (1 kg) meatloaf mix

2 eggs

1 cup (121 g) Italian breadcrumbs

1 cup (180 g) grated Romano cheese

⅝ cup (150 ml) warm water

2 tsp (4 g) Italian seasoning

1 tsp salt

1 tsp black pepper

PESTO

3 cups (72 g) packed fresh basil leaves

2 cloves garlic

¾ cup (135 g) grated Parmesan cheese

1 cup (236 ml) olive oil

¼ cup (34 g) pine nuts

¼ cup (39 g) roasted, unsalted almonds

SPICY MARINARA

1 (10-oz [284-g]) can crushed tomatoes

1 tbsp (15 ml) olive oil

1 tsp kosher salt

Pinch of black pepper

1 tsp chopped fresh oregano

Pinch of sugar

¼ cup (45 g) Romano cheese

1 tsp red pepper flakes

FOR SERVING

1 spaghetti squash

Olive oil

Salt and pepper, to taste

Shredded Parmesan cheese

Fresh mozzarella

Butter

8 brioche buns

(continued)

To make the burgers, mix all of the meatball ingredients together by hand and form into eight 4-ounce (115-g) patties.

To make the pesto, place the pesto ingredients in a food processor. Pulse the food processor three to five times to coarsely chop the ingredients, and then mix for 20 to 30 seconds until the pesto is thoroughly combined.

To make the marinara, simmer all the marinara ingredients in a pot over medium heat for 20 minutes, and then set aside.

Configure your grill for direct cooking. Preheat the grill to 400°F (204°C). Cut the squash in half lengthwise. Remove the seeds, brush with olive oil and season with salt and pepper to taste. Roast the squash on the grill for about 30 minutes or until tender. Shred and set aside. (It's best to prepare this before you cook the burgers.)

Next, place the patties on the grill. Cook for 3 to 5 minutes. Flip and cook an additional 4 to 5 minutes or until the patties reach an internal temperature of 130°F (54°C). Remove the patties from the grill and tent them in aluminum foil.

For serving, place a small handful of shredded Parmesan onto a medium-hot skillet and allow it to melt. Once golden brown, remove it from the heat and set aside. Repeat for every burger.

Slice the mozzarella into ½-inch (1.3-cm) thick slices and set aside.

Butter both sides of the brioche buns and grill for 1 minute, until you have golden brown grill marks. Spread the pesto on the bottom half of the brioche bun. Then place the Parmesan crisp on top of the pesto. Set the burger onto the crisp and then add some shredded spaghetti squash, a few slices of mozzarella and a spoonful of spicy marinara. Cover with the top half of the brioche bun and serve.

LAUREN'S HAWAIIAN BURGERS

RECKLESS AND BRAVE BBQ

These Hawaiian burgers are made from smoky ground beef topped with a pineapple and pepper relish, so you know they don't run short on flavor. These patties are juicy, tender and spicy . . . basically everything you want in a perfect burger and more!!

YIELD: 2 SERVINGS • COOK TIME: 8 MINUTES

PINEAPPLE RELISH

1 (20-oz [567-g]) can pineapple rings, grilled, then chopped

2 tbsp (30 ml) canola oil

½ cup (75 g) minced red onion

¼ cup (20 g) minced green bell pepper

1 jalapeño pepper, minced

2 cloves garlic, minced

¼ cup (60 ml) apple cider vinegar

Zest and juice of 1 lime

1 tbsp (16 g) whole grain mustard

Salt and pepper, to taste

BURGERS

1 lb (454 g) ground beef

Slab's Beef Rub

4 slices provolone cheese

King's Hawaiian hamburger buns

Crispy bacon, chopped

Prepare your grill or smoker for two-zone cooking. You will want to grill the burgers over a hot fire at 500 to 600°F (260 to 316°C), and you will need a cooler zone around 400°F (204°C) for toasting the buns.

To make the relish, grill the pineapple rings over direct heat for about 2 to 3 minutes per side. Remove the pineapple from the grill, chop and set aside. In a cast-iron skillet over direct heat, add the oil and sauté the onion, green pepper, jalapeño and garlic until soft, about 5 minutes. Add the grilled pineapple, cider vinegar, lime zest and juice and whole grain mustard. Season with salt and pepper, and set aside to cool.

To make the burgers, mix the hamburger with the beef rub and half of the cooled pineapple relish. Mold four ¼-pound (115-g) patties.

Place the burgers over the hottest part of the grill, and then leave them alone for at least 2 minutes. For crosshatched grill marks, rotate each burger 90 degrees and continue cooking on that same side for 2 minutes more. Flip the burgers and continue cooking for another 3 to 4 minutes, rotating 90 degrees on the grate after 2 minutes. Top with provolone cheese until melted. Remove the burgers from the grill; then toast the buns on the cooler part of the grill for 1 to 2 minutes.

Place the burgers onto the bottom buns, and top with a spoonful of pineapple relish and some of the chopped crispy bacon. Place the top bun onto the burger and get ready to enjoy!

GRILLED TERIYAKI SALMON TACOS

DIVA Q, AKA DANIELLE BENNETT

In this pineapple-poblano combination, the golden sweetness of pineapple is offset by the smoky spice of the peppers. Serve this salsa with your favorite chips, or over steak, pork or chicken. It also works great in fish tacos. You will always be pleased with the results of this juicy and flavorful fish taco, but topping it with Diva Q's grilled pineapple salsa makes for an out-of-this-world dish!

YIELD: 8 SERVINGS (3 TACOS PER SERVING) • COOK TIME: 27 MINUTES

FISH

2 lb (907 g) salmon fillets

1 cup (236 ml) teriyaki sauce

1 tbsp (10 g) minced garlic

GRILLED PINEAPPLE POBLANO SALSA

Canola oil

1 large ripe pineapple, trimmed

1 large white sweet onion, thickly sliced

1 whole poblano pepper, seeded and halved

1 jalapeño pepper, seeded and finely minced

1 red bell pepper, finely minced

2 tsp (10 ml) canola oil

Juice and zest of 2 limes

¼ cup (40 g) finely minced red onion

1 small bunch cilantro, finely chopped

Salt and pepper, to taste

TOPPINGS

24 soft tortillas

1 cup (340 g) cabbage slaw

To make the fish, place it in a large, resealable plastic bag with the teriyaki sauce and minced garlic. Seal the bag and turn to coat all sides of the salmon. Refrigerate for 2 to 4 hours.

To make the salsa, prepare the grill for medium-high heat (400 to 500°F [204 to 260°C]). Oil the grates with canola oil. Slice the pineapple into ½-inch (1.3-cm) thick slices. Grill the pineapple slices directly, turning often until just tender and lightly charred, about 3 to 4 minutes. Grill the white onion and poblano, turning often until softened and the skin has blistered on the pepper, about 7 to 9 minutes. Remove the pepper's skin. Cube the grilled pineapple, dice the onion and chop the poblano into small pieces. Place in a bowl. Add the remaining ingredients to the bowl and stir to combine.

Oil the grates of the grill again. Place the salmon on the grill skin-side down. Grill for 5 to 7 minutes per side, until the fish flakes easily. Remove the skins from the salmon.

Serve in tortillas filled with salmon and topped with the salsa and slaw.

JIMMY'S EPIC SAUCE BACON CHEESEBURGER

LIL' LOOT BBQ

Jimmy's Epic Sauce recipe will turn your plain ole bacon cheeseburger into a flavorful masterpiece. This sauce requires very little preparation time and consists of simple ingredients that are almost always on hand. Make sure you hit both sides of the bun with this sauce—you'll be glad you did!

YIELD: 4 SERVINGS • COOK TIME: 8 MINUTES

BURGERS

2 lb (907 g) 80/20 ground beef

8 tsp (43 g) Loot N' Booty BBQ What's Your Beef? Rub or your favorite rub, divided

2 tsp (10 ml) extra-virgin olive oil, divided

JIMMY'S EPIC SAUCE

½ cup (110 g) mayonnaise

¼ cup (60 g) ketchup

1 tsp hot sauce, such as Cholula

1 tsp Loot N' Booty BBQ Everything Rub or favorite rub

2 tsp (10 ml) extra-virgin olive oil

FOR SERVING

Pecan wood

4 slices cheddar cheese

4 potato hamburger buns

8 slices cooked bacon

1 Roma tomato, thinly sliced

1 head iceberg lettuce, shredded

Fill your chimney with lump charcoal and light with a Weber lighter cube.

To make the burgers, portion the ground beef into 4 equal patties. Season the top of each patty with 1 teaspoon of the rub. Drizzle ¼ teaspoon of extra-virgin olive oil over each patty, on top of the seasoning. Flip the patties over and repeat the seasoning and olive oil process. Let the patties rest at room temperature until your grill is ready.

To make the sauce, combine all the ingredients in a bowl and mix thoroughly.

When the coals have "grayed over" (this takes between 15 to 20 minutes), dump them into the bottom of the grill with the bottom vent 100-percent open. Spread the hot coals evenly and place a small chunk of pecan wood in the center of the coals. Put the cooking grate in place and the grill lid on. Fully open the top vent.

After approximately 15 minutes, or when the smoke coming from the top vent is light and blue, remove the lid and place the patties evenly around the center of the grill. Place the lid on and close the vent to 75-percent open.

After 1½ to 2 minutes, remove the lid, slide a spatula under each patty and give each a 90-degree turn. After another 1½ to 2 minutes (or until your desired doneness), remove the lid and flip the burgers over. Cover and cook for another 1½ to 2 minutes. Remove the lid, give each patty another 90-degree turn and cover. Cook for 1½ minutes, then place a slice of cheddar cheese on top of each patty. Cover and cook for 1 minute, or until the cheese is nice and melty. Remove the patties and cover with foil.

Open the buns and spread ½ tablespoon (7 g) of sauce on the top and bottom. Place the patty on the bottom bun and lay 2 slices of bacon in an "X" across each patty. Spread another ½ tablespoon (7 g) of sauce on top of the bacon and patty. Place 3 to 4 slices of tomato on top and cover the tomatoes with a small handful of shredded lettuce. Add the top bun and take a big bite!

PARMESAN *AND* HERB-STUFFED PORTOBELLO BURGER

WILBUR'S REVENGE

These meaty, flavorful mushrooms are marinated in Italian dressing and gussied up with fresh vegetables and cheese, then stuffed and grilled to perfection! They're the perfect burger for your vegetarian friends and are great for "Meatless Monday" grilling.

YIELD: 4 SERVINGS • COOK TIME: 8 MINUTES

4 portobello mushrooms

1 (16-oz [473-ml]) bottle Italian salad dressing

1 small bunch fresh parsley

1 small bunch fresh oregano

1 cup (113 g) Parmesan cheese, shaved

½ cup (115 g) butter, at room temperature

4 sandwich buns

1 head romaine lettuce

Olive oil

Salt and pepper

1 large tomato, sliced

Before firing up your grill, prepare the mushrooms. Remove the stems and, if necessary, use a spoon to scrape some of the mushroom out of the cavity. Rinse the mushrooms.

Marinate the mushrooms in the Italian dressing for at least 1 hour and no more than 4 hours.

Finely chop the parsley and oregano, and mix together. Wrap the herbs in paper towels and run them under cold water. Squeeze the water from the paper towel. Repeat a second time. Mix 2 tablespoons (5 g) of herbs with the Parmesan cheese.

Prepare your grill at 325 to 350°F (163 to 177°C) for medium heat.

Place the mushrooms on the grill, with the cap facing up, and cook for 3 to 4 minutes. Flip them cap-side down. Fill the cap with the Parmesan cheese mixture.

Butter the buns and place them on your grill. After 1½ minutes, rotate the caps a quarter turn. Cook another 1½ minutes, or until done. Do not burn the caps. Crisp the buns and remove after about 1 minute.

Place the mushrooms, cheese-side up, onto the buns. Chiffonade the romaine, lightly oil, sprinkle with salt and pepper, and then put it on a grill pan in a mound. Toss the romaine to get a light char, about 2 minutes. Pile the romaine on top of the mushrooms. Add sliced tomato, then the bun and serve.

*See photo on page 116 (top right corner).

OPERATION BBQ RELIEF IN ACTION

At the onset of the 2012 BBQ competition season, I never expected to make the Sam's Club finals, nor did I know anything about Operation BBQ Relief. As the competition season drew to an end, on Friday, October 12, I found myself seeking shelter from a thunderstorm at the Sam's Club finals. Finding refuge under an outdoor pavilion, a fellow competitor, Stan Hays, and I started chatting. He began to tell me about Operation BBQ Relief, the organization he helped found, and all the amazing things they had already accomplished. Being a Famous Dave's Franchisee, I told Stan I would see how I could get our organization involved. At the time, I did not realize how quickly that would happen.

On October 29, Hurricane Sandy came barreling up the East Coast. Once the skies cleared, I found that my home and all six of my restaurants were unaffected. But I saw the devastation all around me and on the news. I knew that I was the lucky one, and I needed to do something. I was sure OBR would mobilize, and I emailed Stan to see what I could do and how I could help. I assembled some food supplies, packed my bags, hooked up my Southern Pride trailer to my truck and Wilbur's Revenge was on the move.

I arrived in Brick, New Jersey, and had one of the greatest experiences of my life. I was part of a team that was helping real people in real need. We cooked meals for 10,000 people over the four days I was there, and I was never prouder to be part of an organization. I made some lifelong friends, despite sleeping on a gym floor and in my truck during a Nor'easter. When I left Brick, I knew I had made a difference and I knew OBR had a bright future.

—DAVID MARKS, *Wilbur's Revenge*

NATE'S PERFECT SCORE BURGER

NATHAN HAYS, COUNTY LINE SMOKERS

This burger did indeed win a perfect score for Nathan Hays, the twelve-year-old member of Country Line Smokers and already a four-time reserve grand champion.

YIELD: 1 SERVING • COOK TIME: 12 MINUTES

Weber's Gourmet Burger Rub

½ lb (227 g) hamburger (80/20 chuck)

2 slices Colby Jack cheese (or your favorite cheese)

1 Italian sausage link

Your favorite BBQ sauce

Bun (I like an egg bun)

Preheat the grill to 400°F (204°C).

Sprinkle ½ tablespoon (4 g) Weber's Gourmet Rub over the hamburger meat, mix it in and form 2 patties. Take one piece of cheese and fold it over twice, forming a square. Take one patty, place the square of cheese in the middle, and then put the other patty on top. Pinch the edges together to ensure the cheese does not leak out. Sprinkle a little more rub on top of the burger.

On a hot grill with clean grill grates, place the burger over the hot spot for about 2 minutes; then turn it a one-half turn for another 2 minutes. Flip the burger and move it to a clean area of the grill grates.

Slice the sausage lengthwise and place it onto the grill. Cook for 2 minutes, and then rotate a half-turn for the crosshatch marks. Continue to cook for 2 to 3 minutes. Brush some BBQ sauce on top.

When the burger reaches 160°F (71°C), pull it off the grill. Put the second piece of cheese on top and let it rest, tented with foil.

Flip the sausage and finish cooking for about 4 minutes or until the sausage reaches an internal temperature of 160°F (71°C).

Grill the bun for 1 to 2 minutes. Remove it from the grill and add a little more BBQ sauce to the bun. Add the burger to the bottom half of the bun, put the sausage on top of the burger and then add the top half of the bun. Time to eat!

PIGGY JUICY LUCY

COUNTY LINE SMOKERS

This charred hot dog stuffed inside a grilled hamburger, along with your favorite cheese, is a handheld masterpiece that is easy to prepare and will certainly WOW your guests! Easily adaptable, you can customize the recipes with ingredients you have on hand. You can whip this up as sliders or full-sized burgers. Similarly, you can enjoy this treat with grilled sausages inside instead of hot dogs. This item is great for tailgating, for parties or just hanging with the family.

On the *Chopped Grill Masters* show, these burgers were served on brioche slider buns, with quick pickled zucchini pickles.

YIELD: 4 SERVINGS • COOK TIME: 20 MINUTES

2 all-beef hot dogs or sausage of your choice

1 lb (454 g) ground chuck, 80/20, divided

1 block of your favorite cheese, sliced ¼" (6-mm) thick

Salt and pepper

FINISHING SAUCE

¼ cup (60 ml) Worcestershire sauce

1 tbsp (15 ml) honey

Sriracha, to taste

Preheat the grill to 400°F (204°C).

Grill the hot dogs or sausage over direct heat to get some char and flavor on them. Cook for approximately 4 to 5 minutes with the lid on. Remove the lid, flip the hot dogs and continue to cook with the lid on for an additional 4 to 5 minutes or until the hot dogs reach an internal temperature of 160°F (71°C). Remove them from the grill and set aside to cool.

Once the hot dogs are cooled, take ¼ pound (113 g) of the ground chuck, split the meat in half and form 2 patties. Place the cheese in the center of one patty. Cut the hot dog into 2-inch (5-cm) segments. Slice one segment in half lengthwise, and put it on top of the cheese. Place the other patty on top, and pinch the edges of both patties together to form a thick, stuffed burger.

Repeat the process to form 3 more stuffed burgers.

To make the sauce, whisk the sauce ingredients together in a bowl.

Liberally sprinkle salt and pepper on both sides of the stuffed burgers. Place the stuffed burgers on the grill and cook directly over the hot coals with the lid on. Cook for 4 to 5 minutes. Flip the burgers and cook for an additional 4 to 5 minutes.

You do not want to turn the stuffed burgers too often, and you should only flip them once. Cook the burger medium, approximately 145°F (63°C) internal temperature. Prior to removing the burgers from the grill, baste with some finishing sauce. Allow the sauce to set for 1 to 2 minutes.

NEW YORK DELI BURGER

STICKS-N-CHICKS BBQ TEAM

What could be better than this juicy burger, spiced with sage sausage and topped with fresh, warm slices of pastrami, spicy mustard and a delicious creamy horseradish sauce? I say NOTHIN'!

YIELD: 4 SERVINGS • COOK TIME: 8 MINUTES

1 lb (454 g) ground beef

½ lb (227 g) sage sausage

1 tbsp (17 g) Montreal steak seasoning

1 egg

Dash of A1 Steak Sauce

8 slices marble rye bread, buttered on one side

Horseradish cream sauce

½ lb (227 g) sliced pastrami, warmed

Spicy mustard

In a bowl, mix the beef, sausage, steak seasoning, egg and steak sauce until just combined, and then form into 4 patties.

Preheat the grill for medium-high heat (400 to 500°F [204 to 260°C]) and place the burgers on the grate. Grill for 3 to 4 minutes and flip. After the burgers are flipped, cook for another 3 to 4 minutes or to an internal temperature of 160°F (71°C).

On the outer edges of the grill, place the rye slices butter-side down to toast. Place a cooked patty on the toasted rye. Top with horseradish sauce, warm pastrami slices, mustard and the remaining bread . . . ain't nothin' better!

ONIONY TURKEY BURGERS

UNCLE KENNY'S BBQ

Quick and easy, these juicy turkey burgers pack an oniony bite! Spice them to your preference with your choice of barbecue rub to make it all your own. I like to cook this recipe on a Smoking Brothers pellet cooker, but you can cook it on your choice of grill. Serve on a toasted hamburger bun or with your favorite side dish.

YIELD: 4 SERVINGS • COOK TIME: 20 MINUTES

BURGERS

1 lb (454 g) ground turkey

1 (1.3-oz [35-g]) envelope onion soup mix

1 cup (121 g) shredded cheddar cheese

1 tsp breadcrumbs

1 tsp garlic salt

1 tsp your favorite barbecue seasoning

FOR SERVING

4 slices cheese, optional

4 buns

Lettuce

Sliced tomatoes

To make the burgers, mix all the ingredients together except the seasoning, and form the mixture into 4 patties. Season both sides of the patties with your favorite barbecue seasoning.

Preheat your grill to 300 to 325°F (149 to 163°C). Place the patties on the grill and cook over direct heat for 8 to 10 minutes. Flip the burgers, and cook for an additional 8 to 10 minutes or to an internal temperature of 165°F (74°C). If you want to make this a cheeseburger, add a slice of cheese to the top of each burger during the last minute of cooking. Serve on buns with lettuce and tomato.

SHOW-STOPPING GRILLED BEEF *AND* CHICKEN SOUVLAKI *WITH* CUCUMBER-DILL TZATZIKI

BEHIND BBQ

This well-cooked and seasoned grilled meat, garnished with a cooling tzatziki sauce and wrapped in a delicious, crispy pita, tastes like a bite of heaven.

YIELD: 8–10 SERVINGS • COOK TIME: 20 MINUTES

TZATZIKI SAUCE

1 qt (980 g) plain regular yogurt

1 seedless cucumber, diced

1 clove garlic, minced

¼ cup (60 ml) extra-virgin olive oil

1 handful fresh dill, chopped

3 scallions, finely sliced

1 tsp kosher salt

½ tsp ground black pepper

BEEF MARINADE

¼ cup (60 ml) balsamic vinegar

½ cup (120 ml) olive oil

1 tbsp (5 g) dried oregano

1 tbsp (9 g) minced garlic

1 tbsp (18 g) kosher salt

1 tsp ground black pepper

CHICKEN MARINADE

¼ cup (60 ml) lemon juice

½ cup (120 ml) olive oil

1 tbsp (5 g) dried oregano

1 tbsp (9 g) minced garlic

1 tbsp (18 g) kosher salt

1 tsp ground black pepper

MEAT AND VEGETABLES

3–4 lb (1–2 kg) top sirloin steak

3–4 lb (1–2 kg) boneless chicken breasts

20 mini red, orange and yellow bell peppers

3 large Vidalia onions

1 cup (236 ml) Italian dressing

TOPPINGS

2 seedless cucumbers, diced into ½" (1.3-cm) pieces

3 tomatoes, diced into ½" (1.3-cm) pieces

1 red onion, diced into ½" (1.3-cm) pieces

1 tbsp (5 g) dried oregano

1 tsp kosher salt

½ tsp ground black pepper

8–10 pita bread wraps (look for thick, fluffy ones)

2 cups (300 g) crumbled feta cheese

(continued)

SHOW-STOPPING GRILLED BEEF *AND* CHICKEN SOUVLAKI *WITH* CUCUMBER-DILL TZATZIKI (CONTINUED)

The night before you plan to serve this dish, begin the tzatziki sauce by draining the yogurt. Line a large, resealable container with a doubled cheesecloth. Place your plain regular yogurt on the cheesecloth, pulling the cheesecloth out to create space underneath the yogurt to drain away the liquid. Snap on the cover of the container, securing the cheesecloth, and place the container in the fridge.

To make the beef marinade, combine all the beef marinade ingredients in a resealable bag.

To make the chicken marinade, combine all the chicken marinade ingredients in a separate resealable bag.

Trim the excess fat off the steak, and then cut into 1-inch (2.5-cm) cubes. Place the cubes into the beef marinade bag. Seal the bag and shake to cover all the meat. Place the bag in a bowl and refrigerate for 2 hours and up to overnight.

Trim the excess fat off the chicken and cut into 1-inch (2.5-cm) cubes. Place the cubes into the chicken marinade bag. Seal the bag and shake to cover all the meat. Place the bag in a bowl and refrigerate for 2 hours and up to overnight.

Trim and cube the bell peppers and onions. Place the vegetables in a resealable bag and add the Italian dressing. Seal the bag, toss to coat and then place the bag in the fridge.

To finish the tzatziki sauce, place the drained yogurt in a medium bowl. Mix in the remaining tzatziki ingredients and chill.

To prepare the toppings, combine all the ingredients in a bowl and let them sit until ready to serve.

Set up a large grill for two-zone cooking and preheat to 400°F (204°C).

Drain the marinated vegetables and discard the marinade. Using a perforated grill pan, grill them over the flames, stirring often, for 5 to 7 minutes, or until the vegetables soften and begin to change color as they caramelize. Transfer them to a foil pan, cover and let rest.

Drain the marinated beef, and discard the marinade. Using a grill pan, cook the beef over the hot coals, leaving space between the pieces and turning often. Cook for 3 to 6 minutes, or to an internal temperature of 130 to 135°F (54 to 57°C). Transfer them to a foil pan, cover and set aside.

Drain the marinated chicken, and discard the marinade. Using a grill pan, cook the chicken over hot coals, leaving space between the pieces and turning often. Cook for approximately 6 to 8 minutes, or to an internal temperature of 160 to 165°F (71 to 74°C). Transfer to a foil pan, cover and set aside.

Grill the pita bread wraps over the coals, turning until puffed and just starting to crisp, about 1 minute.

Serve family-style, allowing your guests to make their own pitas. Spread a small amount of tzatziki on the pita. Then, add cubes of meat, grilled veggies, fresh toppings, feta and more tzatziki on top. *OPA!*

SLOW-ROASTED PORK *WITH* BROWN GRAVY *AND* BACON SAUERKRAUT ON A FRESH GERMAN ROLL

BBQ GURU

Is your mouth watering yet or what? Slow-roasted pork with gravy and sauerkraut, made even better with everyone's favorite five-letter word: BACON! It's all served up on a German sandwich roll and tastes so good you'll be yelling "danke!"

YIELD: 6 SERVINGS • COOK TIME: 4 HOURS

1 (2–4-lb [1–2-kg]) pork shoulder roast

½ tsp kosher salt

¼ tsp ground black pepper

⅛ tsp garlic powder

¼ tsp onion powder

2 cups (300 g) sauerkraut

5 slices bacon, cooked and crumbled

½ cup (62 g) all-purpose flour

6 German-style sandwich rolls

Set up your grill or smoker for indirect cooking, and allow the temperature to stabilize at 275°F (135°C).

Season the pork shoulder roast with salt, pepper, garlic powder and onion powder. Put the seasoned pork in a pan, and then place the pan on the smoker. Cook for approximately 4 hours or until the internal temperature is around 200°F (93°C). Let the pork roast rest for 20 minutes, and then pull the meat apart. The meat should easily pull apart.

Towards the end of the cooking process, place the sauerkraut in a small pan and warm over medium heat for about 5 minutes. Add the crumbled bacon and set aside.

After the pork has finished cooking, pour the drippings into a gravy separator. Let it sit for 10 minutes for the fat to separate.

Pour the au jus from the separator into a saucepan. Heat over medium-high for 3 to 5 minutes. Taste for salt preference, and add flour to thicken the gravy to your likeness.

Place the pork pieces into the saucepan of gravy and stir to coat evenly. Spoon some pork onto a German roll, then top with a scoop of bacon sauerkraut.

PORK BELLY BURNT END SANDWICH

WILBUR'S REVENGE

These morsels of pork amazingness are always worth the wait. Slow roasted and slathered in barbecue sauce, this tender and flavorful pork belly is so magical you'll be thinking of it again and again and again . . .

YIELD: 6–8 SERVINGS • COOK TIME: 3 HOURS

3-4 lb (1.4-1.8 kg) pork belly

1 cup (240 ml) your favorite pork rub

1-2 cups (240-480 ml) your favorite BBQ sauce

6-8 buns, optional

Preheat the smoker to 300°F (149°C).

Slice the pork belly into 2-inch (5-cm) wide strips and season with your favorite pork rub.

Place the pork belly strips in the smoker and cook using indirect heat for 1½ hours. Remove the pork belly strips from your smoker and place them on heavy-duty foil. Pour your favorite BBQ sauce on the pork and tightly wrap the foil.

Raise the temperature of the smoker to 400°F (204°C). Place the foiled meat back on the smoker and cook for 1½ hours. Remove the pork from the smoker and foil, and cut into ¾-inch (2-cm) squares, reserving the liquid.

Place a cast-iron skillet on the smoker and heat. When the pan is hot, place all the contents from the foil (pork cubes and reserved liquid) into the hot pan to caramelize the sauce on the pork, about 10 to 15 minutes.

Place the pork on a bun and drizzle with more barbecue sauce, or you can just eat them straight from the pan.

JALAPEÑO *AND* APPLEWOOD BACON BURGERS *WITH* SMOKED VERMONT CHEDDAR *AND* CRISPY VIDALIA ONIONS

THREE MEN AND A BABYBACK BBQ TEAM

This juicy burger, topped with a creamy and spicy sauce, crispy bacon and crunchy, fried Vidalia onions, will keep your mouth happy with each and every bite!

YIELD: 6 SERVINGS • COOK TIME: 15 MINUTES

CRISPY VIDALIA ONIONS

Frying oil (canola, corn or peanut oil)

1 cup (125 g) all-purpose flour

1 tbsp (10 g) garlic powder

1 tbsp (7 g) onion powder

1 tbsp (7 g) paprika

1½ tsp (3 g) cayenne

Salt and pepper, to taste

1 Vidalia onion, very thinly sliced

SAUCE

1 cup (220 g) mayonnaise

½ cup (120 ml) Peter Luger Steak Sauce or favorite steak sauce

2 tbsp (30 ml) Sriracha

2 tbsp (30 ml) chopped dill pickles

Salt and pepper, to taste

BURGERS

1½ lb (680 g) ground sirloin

2 jalapeño peppers, seeded and chopped

½ lb (227 g) thick-cut bacon (preferably applewood smoked), diced into ½" (1.3-cm) pieces

2 chipotle peppers in adobo sauce, chopped

TO SERVE

2 tbsp (30 ml) olive oil

Salt and pepper, to taste

6 slices Grafton Village Maple Smoked Cheddar

6 brioche rolls, split in half

2 tbsp (29 g) salted butter, melted

6 slices cooked applewood smoked bacon

To make the onions, preheat a deep fryer or kitchen counter fryer to 350°F (177°C). Mix the flour and spices together in a mixing bowl. Lightly dredge the onion in the flour until evenly coated. (Note: The moisture from the onion will allow the flour to adhere, so do not dry the onion.) Fry the floured onion in the fryer until golden brown and crispy, about 5 minutes. Drain on paper towels and season immediately with salt and pepper. Set aside.

To make the sauce, combine all the ingredients in a mixing bowl and set it aside.

To make the burgers, mix all the ingredients together in a bowl. Divide into 6 equal portions and form each portion into a 4-ounce (115-g) patty. Set aside.

Configure your grill for two-zone cooking and preheat to 400°F (204°C).

Lightly brush the burgers with olive oil and season with salt and pepper. Grill the burgers over the hotter portion of the grill (towards the center), and cook for 3 to 4 minutes. Flip the burger and cook for 2 to 3 minutes. Place one slice of cheese on each burger and cover the grill with the lid until the cheese is melted (about 2 minutes). Ideally, you want the finished burger to be medium rare, 135°F (57°C). Remove the burgers from the grill and allow to rest for 1 minute.

(continued)

JALAPEÑO & APPLEWOOD BACON BURGERS WITH SMOKED VERMONT CHEDDAR & CRISPY VIDALIA ONIONS (CONTINUED)

Lightly coat the inside of the brioche rolls with the melted butter. Place the rolls cut-side down on the outer perimeter of the grill. (Placing the bread on the outer perimeter where it's not as hot will prevent burning.) Toast the rolls until lightly browned and set them aside, usually about 1 minute.

Place each burger on a brioche roll bottom. Top with a slice of bacon and a small amount of the crispy onions. Drizzle 1 tablespoon (15 ml) of the burger sauce over the top and place the top of the bun over the composed burger.

OPERATION BBQ RELIEF IN ACTION

As the chief volunteer officer of Operation BBQ Relief, I have had the distinct privilege of working alongside ordinary people doing extraordinary things since 2012. This family of 7,500 volunteers has yet to surprise me on how far we will travel or how much we will sacrifice to provide a hot meal to victims who have lost everything or a rescue worker on their 24th hour of rescues.

My OBR adventure started in 2012 with Superstorm Sandy. It was an amazing sight to see cook teams who compete against each other come together for a common cause. The organization and the vision of its founders just made sense to me. Since 2012, I have been involved with virtually every deployment since Sandy, whether on the ground working hand in hand with our volunteers or from behind the scenes ensuring they have everything they need to do what they do best. I see the distance we have traveled, the meals we have served, the obstacles we clambered over and the smiles and laughs that our volunteers provided to those who have lost everything.

—DANA REED, formerly of Three Men and a Babyback, now of Reed Boyz BBQ

SPICY BUTTERFLIED CHICKEN BREASTS & APPLE SLAW ON A PRETZEL BUN

LUCKY Q

Simple flavors come together for a memorable sandwich when you combine perfectly seasoned spicy chicken breasts with melted cheese and sweet apple slaw on a pretzel bun. Are you ready to make some memories?

YIELD: 2 SERVINGS • COOK TIME: 6–8 MINUTES

COLESLAW

1 (16-oz [454-g]) bag of coleslaw

2 apples of choice, core removed and very thinly sliced (julienned)

1 tbsp (15 ml) apple cider vinegar, or to taste

2 tsp (4 g) ground mustard

¼ large onion, diced

Mayonnaise, to taste

Salt and pepper, to taste

Olive oil

2 tsp (6 g) minced garlic

Big Poppa Smokers Little Louie's Seasoned Garlic Salt or favorite garlic salt

Big Poppa Smokers Cuckoo Racha Chili Dust or favorite chili blend

Juice of 1 lemon or lime

2 large chicken breasts

4 slices Muenster, Havarti or Gouda cheese

Butter

2 pretzel buns

To make the coleslaw, mix the coleslaw ingredients together in a large bowl, cover and let it sit in the refrigerator. The slaw is best when it's made at least a couple hours in advance.

In a disposable plastic bag, mix 4 to 5 tablespoons (60 to 75 ml) of olive oil, garlic, 5 shakes of Big Poppa Smokers Little Louie's seasoning, 5 shakes of Big Poppa Smokers Cuckoo Racha seasoning (more or less to taste) and the citrus juice.

Butterfly the chicken breasts by placing one chicken breast on a cutting board, and then putting one hand on top of the chicken to secure it in place. Holding the knife parallel to the cutting board, carefully cut across the chicken breast, starting from the thickest side of the meat. Do not cut all the way through the meat; leave about a ¼ inch (6 mm) along the length of the chicken breast, so the two pieces remain attached. Repeat for the other chicken breast; then place them in the bag containing the marinade and marinate for at least 30 minutes.

Set up your grill or drum to 350 to 375°F (177 to 191°C) for direct cooking, grill grates preferred. Lay the butterflied chicken breasts flat on the grate, directly over the heat. Grill for about 3 minutes per side, or until the internal temperature reaches 152 to 155°F (67 to 68°C). Remove the chicken breasts from the grill and top each one with 2 slices of cheese. Tent with foil and let them rest at least 5 minutes.

Slice and butter the pretzel buns. Lay the buttered side on the cooking grate for up to 1 minute to toast, watching carefully not to burn. Assemble the chicken on the toasted pretzel bun and top the chicken generously with coleslaw.

SMOKED PULLED CHICKEN SANDWICH

LOCAL SMOKE BBQ TEAM

Brining a whole chicken before you cook it on a smoker helps the meat retain moisture, and we think it'll be evident when you taste this pulled chicken sandwich! With a hint of smokiness, and a whole lot of sweet and spice, it won't last long on your dinner table, so take a moment to savor the taste.

YIELD: 4–6 SERVINGS • COOK TIME: 3 HOURS

1 gal (4 L) water, divided

1 cup (288 g) kosher salt

½ cup (110 g) brown sugar

¼ cup (56 g) your favorite barbecue rub, divided (we like our Uncle Dick's Sweet & Spicy BBQ Rub)

1 (3–4-lb [1–2-kg]) whole chicken

½ cup (120 ml) your favorite barbecue sauce, divided (we like our Original Sweet BBQ Sauce)

2 tbsp (30 ml) buffalo-style hot sauce

4–6 buns

Coleslaw, for serving

Bring ½ gallon (2 L) of the water, salt, brown sugar and 2 tablespoons (28 g) of the BBQ rub to a boil, stirring until completely dissolved. Remove from the heat, cover and allow it to cool completely. Add the remaining ½ gallon (2 L) water and transfer it to your brining container. Add the chicken to the brine, cover and refrigerate for 8 to 12 hours.

Remove the chicken from the brine and rinse well with cold water. Pat it dry, and then place it on a baking sheet and sprinkle with 1 tablespoon (14 g) of your barbecue rub.

Slow smoke the whole chicken at 250°F (121°C) until the breast temperature reaches 165°F (74°C) and the thigh reaches 175°F (79°C), about 2 to 3 hours. Remove the chicken and raise the temperature of your smoker to 375°F (190°C).

Remove the skin from the smoked chicken and place it on the baking sheet. Sprinkle it with 1 teaspoon (5 g) of barbecue rub and bake it at 375°F (190°C) for 5 to 7 minutes, or until crispy.

While the skin is crisping, pull all the chicken meat from the bone and place it in a bowl.

Add the crisped chicken skin, 2 teaspoons (9 g) of barbecue rub, ¼ cup (60 ml) of barbecue sauce and the buffalo sauce to a food processor and pulse until the skin and sauces are well blended.

Add the skin mixture and the remaining ¼ cup (60 ml) of barbecue sauce to the pulled chicken and toss until completely coated. Serve on a bun with your favorite slaw.

OPERATION BBQ RELIEF IN ACTION

OBR has a special place in my heart, as I got involved after my parents' house and neighborhood were destroyed by Superstorm Sandy. The locals needed help, and along came OBR. What started as a few of us setting up in a parking lot trying to feed a few hundred people quickly turned into 50+ volunteers feeding thousands a day in the town where I grew up. This continued for what felt like months, as most of the infrastructure in the area was destroyed. It really hit home when a father/son tandem showed up from Maryland saying they "had heard about OBR and wanted to help in any way they could." They had not been affected by the storm, but they spent four days in the bitter cold, sleeping on the floor and doing whatever they could to help. In the beginning, when the entire area was still a disaster, people like David Marks stepped up and led the group in the right direction. The true dedication of everyone involved left a lasting impression for those who were fed a hot meal during such a difficult time. Here we are five years after the storm, still waiting for things to be "normal" again, but I will never forget the smiles we brought to the people's faces that had just lost everything. The lessons learned during Sandy have translated into making OBR a stronger and all-around better organization that can now deploy more efficiently when faced with natural disasters. I will forever be in debt to OBR and look forward to helping in future deployments.

—STEVE RAAB, *Local Smoke BBQ*

SOUTHWEST ROASTED RED PEPPER CHICKEN SANDWICH

WILBUR'S REVENGE

Marinades help make meat tender and flavorful. Something as simple as Italian salad dressing does wonders as a marinade, especially if you let the meat marinate for several hours in the fridge. Cook up these chicken breasts and notice how the marinade really gives the dish some zing!

YIELD: 4 SERVINGS • COOK TIME: 19 MINUTES

4 chicken breasts, skinless and boneless

1 (16-oz [473-ml]) bottle Italian dressing

1 large red bell pepper

4 wheat buns

1 cup (180 g) shredded Parmesan cheese

1 cup (225 g) mayonnaise

French-fried onions, optional

Place the chicken and Italian dressing in a 1-gallon (4-L), resealable bag. Marinate the chicken in the fridge for at least 30 minutes or up to 24 hours.

Configure your grill for direct cooking and preheat to medium-high, 375°F (191°C).

Grill the red pepper and blister the skin. Grill for 2 to 3 minutes per side, on all four sides, about 10 minutes total. Remove the cooked pepper from the grill and place in a baggie. Wait 10 minutes and peel the skin off the pepper. Chop into a fine dice and set aside.

Grill the marinated chicken for 3 to 4 minutes per side or until the juices run clear. Make sure the internal temperature of the chicken reaches 155°F (68°C). Remove the chicken from the grill and wrap in foil. Let it sit for about 5 minutes. The chicken will continue to cook. Allowing the chicken to rest is critical to it staying moist.

Slice the wheat buns in half. Place them on your grill for up to a minute to give them a light char.

Place the diced pepper in a small bowl. Add the shredded Parmesan cheese and mayonnaise; then stir to evenly combine the ingredients. Spoon the mixture on the bottom of each bun.

Remove the chicken from the foil. Slice the chicken on a bias, holding the knife at a 45-degree angle. Lay the chicken slices atop the mayonnaise/cheese mixture, along with French-fried onions, if using. Then add the top to the bun and serve.

CHAPTER 5

FROM SEA TO SEA

LOOKING FOR A MAIN-DISH FISH OR SHRIMP RECIPE? These seafood dish ideas are tasty and easy enough to make on a weeknight for a quick, delicious supper.

The following are recommendations and guidelines from the FDA.gov website:

Most seafood should be cooked to an internal temperature of 145°F (63°C). If you don't have a food thermometer, there are other ways to determine whether seafood is done.

FISH: The flesh should be opaque and separate easily with a fork.

SHRIMP AND LOBSTER: The flesh becomes pearly and opaque.

SCALLOPS: The flesh turns opaque and firm.

CLAMS, MUSSELS AND OYSTERS: The shells open during cooking—throw out ones that don't open.

Never leave seafood or other perishable food out of the refrigerator for more than 2 hours, or for more than 1 hour when temperatures are above 90°F (32°C). Bacteria that can cause illness grow quickly at warm temperatures (between 40 and 140°F [4 and 60°C]).

Carry picnic seafood in a cooler with a cold pack or ice. When possible, put the cooler in the shade and keep the lid closed as much of the time as you can. When it's party time, keep hot seafood hot and cold seafood cold. Divide hot party dishes containing seafood into smaller serving platters. Keep the platters refrigerated until it's time to reheat them for serving. Keep cold seafood on ice or serve it throughout the gathering from platters kept in the refrigerator.

The recipes in this chapter run the gamet from smoky south-of-the-border flavors to sweet Asian glazes to bright and tropical island notes. Spicy Szechuan, Cajun seasonings and tangy barbecue also make appearances. Seafood cooks up quickly, too, so you'll have more time for enjoying company and less time at the grill.

ADOBO HALIBUT WITH CORN, BLACK BEAN AND TOMATO SALSA

YABBA DABBA QUE!

Halibut is a fairly firm white fish that will accept a marinade well. The adobo marinade used in this recipe is really a wet rub. The spices complement the citrus acid well. With each bite, you will taste the sweetness of the fish along with the garlic, cilantro and citrus juices.

YIELD: 8 SERVINGS • COOK TIME: 12 MINUTES

ADOBO MARINADE

¾ cup (177 ml) lime juice

¾ cup (177 ml) orange juice

2 tbsp (30 ml) extra-virgin olive oil

2 tbsp (20 g) chopped garlic

1 tbsp (3 g) chopped fresh cilantro

1 tsp ground cumin

½ tsp kosher salt

½ tsp black pepper

½ tsp dried oregano

2 lb (907 g) halibut fillets

2 tbsp (30 ml) olive oil

1 tsp kosher salt

½ tsp freshly ground black pepper

CORN, BLACK BEAN AND TOMATO SALSA

2 ears fresh corn, husked

1 tbsp (15 ml) olive oil

3 plum tomatoes, seeded and diced

1 cup (194 g) canned black beans, drained

¼ cup (38 g) chopped red onion

¼ cup (60 ml) lime juice

⅓ cup (16 g) chopped fresh cilantro

1 jalapeño pepper, seeded and finely chopped

1 scallion, chopped

½ tsp kosher salt

½ tsp freshly ground black pepper

To make the marinade, in a medium bowl, whisk all the marinade ingredients together until they are well combined. Place the halibut fillets into a resealable plastic freezer bag with the marinade, and refrigerate for 30 minutes to 1 hour.

Set up your grill for 350°F (177°C) direct heat with a drip pan. Make sure the grate is cleaned and well oiled. Remove the fish from the marinade, pat it dry and lightly coat with olive oil. Sprinkle the fillets with salt and pepper.

Place the fish on the cooking grate and cover the cooker. Grill the fish over direct heat for about 4 minutes; then flip and cook for another 3 minutes, or until the internal temperature reaches about 135°F (57°C). When cooked, remove the fish from the grill and place it on a cool rack under an aluminum foil tent. Let the fish rest for 5 to 10 minutes while you prepare the salsa.

To make the salsa, coat the corn with olive oil, place it on the grate and cook over direct heat for about 5 minutes. Turn the corn every minute, and be careful not to burn it! Remove the corn and set it aside to cool. While the corn cools, place the remaining ingredients—plum tomatoes through seasonings—into a bowl. When the corn is cool enough to handle, cut all of the kernels off the ears, place them in the bowl and mix well. Serve the salsa over the cooked halibut.

OPERATION BBQ RELIEF IN ACTION

Packing up our Big Green Eggs, we began the nearly 20-hour drive up the Atlantic Coast from Lynchburg, Tennessee, back home to Bedford, New Hampshire. Hurricane Sandy was practically in the rearview mirror the whole time. We were returning from the site of the Jack Daniel's World Championship Invitational Barbecue. Forty-five minutes after we crossed from Connecticut into Massachusetts, roads and highways were being closed down except for nonessential vehicles in preparation for Sandy's landfall.

The Jack is at the end of the year, so it's sort of the climax of barbecue season for us. There are some things to do still, but after that competition, it's about relaxing. We never got a chance to relax. We unloaded perishables from the trailer shortly after arriving home on October 27, 2012. Turning on the television the following morning, we saw sea-battering scenes coming in from Massachusetts, Connecticut, New York and New Jersey. We immediately decided to get back on the road.

Working through New England Barbecue Society phone contacts, we learned of an OBR effort being coordinated by Cleveland-based Rob Marion of 2 Worthless Nuts BBQ. That day, we loaded up the truck with needed supplies, stopped to pick up Mike Boisvert and his supplies and began the drive back. By Thursday, we had reached Forked River, New Jersey, a town on Barnegat Bay.

There were 10 miles where it was haunting. There was no power and few gas stations. We had waited 2 hours to top off our gas in a Nyack, New York, rest area and saw gas lines backed up nine-tenths of a mile.

Seeing it firsthand was mind-boggling. We had seen it on TV, but the real thing is very different.

Over the next three days, our OBR group made 3,000 meals per day, some boxed for takeout or served backyard-barbecue style, and more still for bulk deliveries of 400 or 500 at a time, sent out with supplies of water.

By Friday, other mid-Atlantic and Northeast teams streaming in were bringing donations of paper towels and canned goods and being directed to efforts in Hoboken, and later Brooklyn and Coney Island. Yabba Dabba Que! moved on to Neptune Township next, 45 minutes up from Forked River.

Barbecue trucks and trailers usually set up in 20 x 20-foot (6 x 6-m) squares for competitions, and they did the same with OBR, setting up cooking sites in a baseball field and senior centers to be accessible.

There were a lot of local volunteers. A group of kids who had nothing to do came out and helped for a while. We were all doing what we enjoy doing . . . it's something more than physically nourishing—it's a nourishment of the soul. Seeing the people who are affected is the biggest takeaway. An eight-year-old boy who had been eating nothing but peanut butter and jelly said he wished he could give something more substantive, but could only donate a one-dollar bill. We told him to keep it, but he insisted, ate some food and asked to get a spot in line the next day.

—ERIC AND CINDI MITCHELL, *Yabba Dabba Que!*

EASIEST CEDAR-PLANKED SMOKED SALMON

BIG UGLY'S BBQ TEAM

This is about as easy and basic as it gets. The fish will give a smoky, sweet flavor that tastes like you worked on it all day instead of only minutes!

YIELD: 2 SERVINGS • COOK TIME: 20 MINUTES

Smoking plank

1 lb (455 g) salmon fillet

1 tsp yellow mustard

2 tbsp (30 g) your favorite BBQ rub

2 tbsp (28 g) light brown sugar

A quick note about smoking planks, as there are many different flavors you can impart with a smoking plank. Big Ugly's BBQ prefers alderwood, but cedar is also a nice choice for a deep, heavy smoke.

Soak the plank in water for a minimum of 2 hours; the longer the better.

Preheat your gas grill to medium (300 to 350°F [149 to 175°C]), or burn charcoal until it is ashen and spread it in an even layer.

Remove the fish from its packaging about 15 minutes before you plan to cook it. Rinse the fish, and pat it dry with a paper towel. This is also a good time to check the fish for any bones left by the fishmonger during processing. You can leave the skin on, or remove it. If you leave the skin on, it helps prevent the fillet from sticking to the plank.

After you pat the fish dry, apply a light coat of yellow mustard. Not a lot, just enough to make the fish tacky to hold the rub and brown sugar. Don't worry, you won't taste the mustard after the fish is cooked.

Next, apply your favorite BBQ rub to the salmon fillet. Coat the fillet evenly from one end to the other, and make sure you cover both sides. Try to use a rub with a lower salt content, but any rub will work well. Lastly, apply the brown sugar, covering the fillet completely.

Place the soaked plank on the grate of the grill. Cover the grill and let the plank heat up. When the plank starts to smell smoky, place the salmon on the plank and close the cover of the grill.

Allow the salmon to cook for about 20 minutes. Use a food thermometer to check the internal temperature. The salmon is done when the internal temperature reaches 145°F (63°C). Remove the fillet, plank and all, from the grill and serve.

ASIAN-GLAZED GRILLED SALMON

BLAZIN' BUTTS BBQ

The grilling plank used in this dish provides a nice, smoky flavor to the fish. Cooking salmon to a medium rare keeps the fillet moist and buttery tasting, with a bit of heat on the back end from the marinade.

YIELD: 4 SERVINGS • COOK TIME: 20 MINUTES

MARINADE

½ cup (120 ml) peanut oil

4 tbsp (60 ml) soy sauce

4 tbsp (60 ml) balsamic vinegar

¼ cup (55 g) brown sugar

3 scallions, chopped

2 cloves minced garlic

1½ tsp (4 g) freshly ground ginger

1 tsp sesame oil

2 tsp (3 g) red pepper flakes

½ tsp salt

1½ lb (680 g) salmon fillet

Cedar or alder grilling plank

Salt and pepper, or your favorite seafood seasoning

To make the marinade, combine all the ingredients in a large bowl. Submerge the salmon, cover the container and place it in the refrigerator for 1 to 2 hours. During this time, soak the grilling plank in water for 30 minutes

Build a medium-sized charcoal fire (about two-thirds of a standard charcoal chimney) or, if using a gas grill, preheat to a medium heat (300 to 350°F [149 to 175°C]).

Place the salmon on the soaked plank. Season the salmon with salt and pepper or your favorite seafood seasoning.

Place the planked salmon on the grill for medium direct heat, and close the lid. Cook for approximately 15 to 20 minutes, checking at the halfway point. The salmon should be cooked to an internal temperature of 150°F (65°C). Remove the salmon, let it rest for 5 minutes and then serve.

BLACKENED GRILLED CATFISH ⟨WITH⟩ TROPICAL SALSA ⟨AND⟩ LEMON-BASIL AIOLI

THREE MEN AND A BABYBACK BBQ TEAM

The sweetness and spice of the tropical salsa really complements the firm, white fillet in this dish. The lemon aioli brings it over the top for flavors that will bring you back to this recipe again and again.

YIELD: 4 SERVINGS • COOK TIME: 17 MINUTES

TROPICAL SALSA

1 mango, diced small

1 guava, diced small

4 (½" [1.3-cm]) slices fresh pineapple

1 jalapeño pepper, minced

4 cloves garlic, minced

2 tbsp (5 g) chopped cilantro

Juice of 1 lime

1 tbsp (15 ml) honey

Salt and pepper, to taste

BASIC MARINADE

1 small onion, diced

3 cloves garlic, minced

½ cup (120 ml) olive oil

¼ cup (60 ml) white wine vinegar

2 tbsp (30 ml) Worcestershire sauce

2 tsp (8 g) sugar

1 tsp salt

1 tsp black pepper

4 catfish fillets, or any firm white fish, i.e., grouper, mahi mahi, etc.

½ cup (115 g) salted butter, melted

3 tbsp (22 g) blackening spice

LEMON BASIL AIOLI

1 cup (220 g) mayonnaise

12 fresh basil leaves, plus more for garnish

3 cloves garlic

Juice from 1 lemon

Zest from 1 lemon, plus more for garnish

Salt and pepper, to taste

2 tbsp (30 ml) white wine

To make the salsa, mix all the salsa ingredients in a small bowl; set it aside.

To make the marinade, mix all the marinade ingredients together in a bowl. Place the fish fillets in the marinade for 20 minutes.

Remove the fish from the marinade and pat dry. Discard the marinade. Dip each fillet into the melted butter, and then generously sprinkle with the blackening spice on both sides.

Configure your grill for two-zone cooking. Set up the grill for the highest temperature (500 to 600°F [260 to 316°C]) and allow it to get hot. If using a cast-iron pan, place the pan directly over the hot coals or heat, and allow the pan to get hot and smoking.

Place the fillets in a cast-iron pan or onto the grill and cover it. Allow the fish to sear until the seasoning begins to get dark and charred, about 3 to 5 minutes. Flip the fillets and repeat this process on the other side. Place the fillets in a buttered pan and place the pan on the cooler side of the grill. Cook the fillets for another 5 to 7 minutes or until the fish is firm.

To make the lemon aioli, combine all the ingredients in a blender or food processor.

Remove the fish from the grill and spoon about ¼ cup (60 ml) of salsa over each fillet. Drizzle with lemon basil aioli. Garnish with lemon zest and basil leaves and serve.

BOURBON ❦ TERIYAKI-GLAZED SALMON ❦ MANGO-PINEAPPLE SALSA

SWEET SMOKE Q

Sweet teriyaki glaze, topped with mango-pineapple salsa and garnished with sesame seeds flavors this delicious grilled salmon dish that needs only a few minutes on your grill.

YIELD: 4 SERVINGS • COOK TIME: 15–20 MINUTES

MANGO-PINEAPPLE SALSA

4 ripe mangoes

½ fresh pineapple

1 small red onion

2–3 jalapeños

Juice of 1 lime

3 tbsp (9 g) finely chopped cilantro

2 tbsp (30 ml) seasoned rice wine vinegar

¾ tsp salt

TERIYAKI GLAZE

½ cup (120 ml) soy sauce

¼ cup (60 ml) water

2 tbsp (30 ml) sweet rice wine

3 tbsp (41 g) brown sugar

¼ cup (48 g) granulated sugar

2 tsp (6 g) minced garlic

1½ tsp (7 g) minced ginger

½ tbsp (5 g) cornstarch

1 tbsp (15 ml) water

1 cedar plank (6" x 14" [15 x 36 cm])

4 (6-8-oz [170–227-g]) salmon fillets

¼ cup (60 ml) bourbon

Salt and pepper, to taste

Toasted sesame seeds

To make the salsa, peel and dice the mangoes, pineapple and red onion in small cubes. Deseed and finely chop the jalapeños. Mix all of the ingredients in a bowl and refrigerate for at least 2 hours.

To make the glaze, combine all the ingredients (except the cornstarch and water) in a saucepan on medium heat until the sugar is dissolved. Mix the cornstarch with the water. Heat the sauce on medium-high heat and add the cornstarch-water mixture. Simmer until thickened.

Soak the cedar plank in salted water for 2 hours, and then drain. Using a sharp knife, remove the skin from the salmon fillets. Run your hand along the fillets, and remove any remaining bones you find in the flesh of the fish. Rinse the salmon under cold running water and pat it dry with paper towels. Brush the fillets with bourbon and generously season with salt and pepper on both sides.

Set up the grill for direct grilling on medium-high heat (400 to 500°F [204 to 260°C]). When ready to cook, place the plank on the hot grate and leave it until there is a smell of smoke, about 3 to 4 minutes. Turn the plank over and place the fish (on what was skin-side down) on the plank.

Cover the grill and cook until the fish is cooked through, about 15 minutes, or until it reaches an internal temperature of 125 to 130°F (52 to 54°C). While the fish is cooking, check the plank occasionally. If the edges start to catch fire, mist them with water or move the plank to a cooler part of the grill. Transfer the salmon and plank to a platter, and drizzle with the teriyaki glaze. Top it off with the mango-pineapple salsa, sprinkle with sesame seeds and serve right off the plank.

BUTTERY SMOKED MULLET

SWAMP BOYS BBQ

Serve this mullet warm, as is, or remove the meat from the skin and make some killer smoked fish dip. There is nothing better on a saltine cracker than some home-smoked fish dip.

YIELD: 5 SERVINGS • COOK TIME: 45 MINUTES

BRINE
2 gal (8 L) cold water

2 cups (576 g) kosher salt

2 cups (440 g) packed brown sugar

5 whole mullet, heads removed and butterflied

Citrus or other light-flavored smoke wood

Swamp Boys Original Rub

Melted butter, for basting

To make the brine, in a large, food-grade plastic bucket, stir together the water, salt and brown sugar until dissolved. Chill in the refrigerator. Place the fish in the brine and refrigerate for 30 minutes.

Remove the fish, rinse and pat dry. Place the fish on a wire rack and refrigerate for 2 hours.

Fire up your smoker and run it at 225°F (107°C). Add a piece of seasoned citrus wood or some other light-flavored smoking wood.

The fish should now be dry and slightly tacky; that is the pellicle that has developed. Evenly season the flesh side of the fish with the rub. Place the fish in the smoker for 45 minutes to let the rub set up. Baste with the melted butter and check for doneness every 15 minutes. When the meat is opaque and flakes easily with a fork, it's ready to serve. The internal temperature should reach 145°F (63°C).

OPERATION BBQ RELIEF IN ACTION

To the best of my knowledge, a few friends from the Florida BBQ Association (FBA) and I carried out what was the first barbecue-based deployment for disaster relief. It was the summer of 2004 and four major hurricanes hit Florida. Hurricane Charley affected our area of central Florida pretty hard. We heard that south of us, in the rural town of Arcadia, folks were really struggling. We also heard that the local grocery store down there lost power and had no backup generators, and that their fresh refrigerated foods and meats were put into reefer trucks, waiting to be cooked. Word spread among some of us with mobile BBQ pits in the FBA, so we left our own messes and made our way through downed trees and such to Arcadia. Once there, we set up our "compound" and started cooking all of the food and feeding the people. We fed about 3,000 people each day. It was because of this event that the "Smoky Angel" award came to be from one of the then-most-popular resources for barbecue information on the Internet, The BBQ Forum. You can read about the history of the Smoky Angel here: www.hawgeyesbbq.com/about_us/charitable_activities.

While the present-day OBR wasn't born until seven years after this, I can't help but think our loosely organized group of barbecue friends carried the spirit and values of today's OBR. I believe that compassion, friendship and the will to help is inherent in many of us, and barbecue provides the outlet. So this is why the OBR holds a special place in my heart.

*—**RUB BAGBY,** Swamp Boys BBQ*

CAJUN CHA-CHA CATFISH & SHRIMP

FAMOUS DAVE'S BBQ

The flavors in this recipe warm the soul. If you have sensitive taste buds, reduce the cayenne by half or this dish just might have you dancing the cha cha!

YIELD: 4 SERVINGS • COOK TIME: 12 MINUTES

CAJUN DYNAMITE DUST

½ cup (58 g) paprika

6 tbsp (108 g) kosher salt

¼ cup (24 g) coarsely ground black pepper

3 tbsp (5 g) dried basil

3 tbsp (18 g) file powder

2 tbsp (20 g) garlic powder

2 tbsp (15 g) dry mustard

2 tbsp (14 g) onion powder

2 tbsp (11 g) dried oregano

2 tbsp (10 g) cayenne, or to taste

2 tbsp (12 g) ground white pepper

2 tbsp (9 g) dried thyme

4 catfish fillets

12 peeled shrimp (26–30 count)

2 tbsp (29 g) unsalted butter

Black beans and rice, for serving

To make the Cajun seasoning, mix all the ingredients in a bowl and store in an airtight container. Use it as a rub for blackened dishes.

Place 1 cup (100 g) of the Cajun seasoning onto a flat plate. Coat each catfish fillet and the shrimp with the seasoning. Using your hands, rub the seasoning into the fillets and shrimp.

Heat a cast-iron skillet on your grill over high heat (500 to 600°F [260 to 316°C]) until very hot, and then add the butter to the skillet. Heat until the butter is sizzling. Place the fish fillets in the skillet. Panfry the fillets, for 2 to 3 minutes per side, until blackened. Remove the fillets from the skillet and place in the shrimp. Cook the shrimp for 3 minutes per side. Pay attention to the shrimp—they cook quickly. When the shrimp curl and turn pink, they are done. Using a thermometer, confirm the catfish and shrimp reach an internal temperature of 145°F (63°C).

Blackened seafood is great served with black beans and rice!

COLOSSAL BACON-WRAPPED SHRIMP WITH PINEAPPLE-JALAPEÑO GLAZE

NATHAN HAYS, COUNTY LINE SMOKERS

In less than 30 minutes, you can dress this crispy bacon-wrapped shrimp in a sweet and spicy glaze for a dynamically delicious appetizer or main dish. Nathan Hays of County Line Smokers took 2nd place appetizer with this recipe at the 2015 World Steak Championship. He was the only minor who qualified for the contest, and he made history, as the minimum age for head cook is now 18 years old.

YIELD: 1–2 SERVINGS • COOK TIME: 24 MINUTES

1 pineapple

1 jalapeño

1 tbsp (10 g) Meat Mitch Whomp Rub or favorite rub

6–8 (12–18 count) shrimp, unshelled

1 (1-lb [454-g]) package low-sodium bacon

1 (10-oz [285-g]) jar pineapple jelly

1 (12-oz [340-g]) jar jalapeño jelly

1 tbsp (15 ml) honey

Configure your grill for direct cooking, and preheat to 375 to 400°F (191 to 204°C).

Place the pineapple on a cutting board on its side. Using a chef's knife, cut off the top and bottom. Hold the pineapple upright with one hand. Using the other hand, slice down along the height of the pineapple and remove the skin. Rotate the pineapple and repeat until all the skin is removed. Use a paring knife to trim off any remaining brown spots. Place the pineapple back on its side and cut into ¼-inch (6-mm) slices. Using a straight apple corer, remove the center of each pineapple slice, creating rings.

Slice the stem off the top of the jalapeño and cut in half. Remove the seeds and cut into ¼-inch (6-mm) strips.

Sprinkle the rub on the shrimp. Place jalapeño slices down the back of a shrimp, and then wrap it in bacon. Use a toothpick to hold the bacon in place. Sprinkle more rub on the outside of the bacon. Repeat for all the shrimp.

To make the glaze, mix equal parts pineapple jelly and jalapeño jelly in a small saucepan. Add the honey, and then place the pan on the grill for 5 to 10 minutes, until warm, and set aside.

Grill the pineapple rings for 2 to 3 minutes per side. Remove them from the grill and cut them in half.

Grill the bacon-wrapped shrimp over direct heat for 3 to 4 minutes per side. Ideally, you want to get the bacon cooked without overcooking the shrimp. As the shrimp cooks and the bacon gets crisp, baste with the glaze. When cooked, remove from the grill and place on top of the pineapple half-ring slices to serve.

MAPLE CHIPOTLE–GLAZED STEELHEAD TROUT

PRAIRIE SMOKE & SPICE BBQ

Below is a two-time 1st place Chef's Choice entry in the Jack Daniel's World Championships. This has a fabulous sweet and spicy glaze basted onto the fish as it grills on a cedar plank. Maple syrup makes all the difference.

YIELD: 2 SERVINGS • COOK TIME: 40–60 MINUTES

Cedar plank

MAPLE CHIPOTLE GLAZE

½ chipotle pepper (from canned chipotle peppers in adobo sauce)

⅔ cup (158 ml) maple syrup

1 tsp adobo sauce (from canned chipotle peppers)

2 steelhead trout fillets

Salt and pepper

Submerge the cedar plank in water for 2 hours.

To make the glaze, finely chop the pepper. Add the maple syrup to a small pan and heat on the stove over medium-low heat, while stirring, for 3 to 5 minutes. Add the chopped chipotle pepper and adobo sauce, and continue stirring. Remove the pan from the heat. Then allow the glaze to cool; it should be lukewarm when it's applied to the fish.

Configure your smoker or grill for indirect cooking, and heat to 300°F (149°C). Remove the cedar plank from the water. Season both sides of the trout with salt and pepper, and then place on the cedar plank.

Place the plank onto your grill and cook with the lid on. After 30 minutes, apply the glaze to the surface of the fish with a silicon brush (or BBQ sauce brush). Repeat every 5 minutes—two to three coats of the glaze should suffice.

After 40 to 60 minutes total, the fish will be done. Remove it from the grill when the fat appears on the surface of the fish and the thickest part of the flesh is opaque and flaky. When using a meat thermometer, you're looking for an internal temperature of 145°F (63°C).

MARYLAND BARBECUED BLUE FIN CRABS

CHECKERED FLAG 500 BBQ

The butter, Sweet Baby Ray's Barbecue Sauce and Old Bay Seafood Seasoning will infuse this dish with barbecue flavors that will have your crabby friends coming back wanting more.

YIELD: 6 SERVINGS • COOK TIME: 15 MINUTES

1½ cups (390 g) fresh corn and red pepper salsa, optional, divided

12 large fresh Maryland blue fin crabs

½ cup (115 g) salted butter, divided

1 (18-oz [510-g]) bottle Sweet Baby Ray's Original BBQ Sauce or your favorite BBQ sauce, divided

½ cup (113 g) Old Bay Seafood Seasoning, divided

Lemon wedges, for serving

Chopped chives, for garnish

Preheat your grill to 350 to 400°F (176 to 204°C). An offset fire to one side of the kettle works best.

Make six sheets of double-thick aluminum foil for packets, about 9 inches (23 cm) long and as wide as the foil roll. Place ¼ cup (65 g) salsa in the center of each piece of foil.

Prepare your fresh crabs by removing the back, gills and insides. Place 2 crabs, laying flat next to each other, on top of the salsa on the first foil packet. Place 1 tablespoon (14 g) of butter in the cavity of each crab. Then, put 1 to 2 tablespoons (15 to 30 g) of Sweet Baby Ray's on top of the butter. Sprinkle 2 tablespoons (28 g) of Old Bay Seafood Seasoning across each crab.

Wrap the packet like an envelope, so that the seam is on the top of the foil packet. This helps prevent the contents from leaking out of the packet. Put the foil packets on the grill (opposite the charcoal on an offset Weber) and cover the grill with the lid.

After 15 minutes, open one of the foil packets and check for doneness. The crabs are done when they are a nice red color and reach an internal temperature of 145°F (63°C).

Reserve some of that great foil juice for a dipping sauce. Serve with lemon wedges and a sprinkling of chopped chives.

RAGING RIVER MAPLE-BUTTER CRUSTED SALMON

DIZZY PIG BBQ TEAM

This Maple-Butter Crusted Salmon recipe by Dizzy Pig BBQ combines maple, butter and Dizzy Pig's Raging River seasoning blend for a tasty piece of fish.

YIELD: 4–6 SERVINGS • COOK TIME: 20 MINUTES

1 (2-lb [1-kg]) salmon fillet

4 tbsp (56 g) Dizzy Pig Raging River Rub or your favorite rub

¼ cup (57 g) butter, melted

¼ cup (60 ml) pure maple syrup

Remove the skin from the salmon and cut the fillet into three 6-inch (15-cm) strips.

Remove the "bloodline." The bloodline is under the skin running down the center of the fillet lengthwise. It is a narrow channel of dark meat that has an especially fishy flavor.

Apply the Dizzy Pig Raging River Rub on all sides of the fillets. Let the rub "melt" in for 20 to 30 minutes while you prepare your grill for direct cooking and medium-hot fire, approximately 400°F (204°C).

Place the fish on a preheated raised grate and cook with the lid on. Combine the butter and maple syrup in a small bowl. After 5 to 10 minutes, liberally brush the mixture on the fillets and cook for an additional 5 to 10 minutes.

When the surface of the fish is browned, carefully flip the fillet over and glaze the top of the fish. Continue to cook with the lid on the grill for about 10 minutes or to an internal temperature of 145°F (63°C).

Brush on one last coating of glaze before removing the fillets from your grill. Place the fillets on a serving plate. While the fish is best served hot, it is surprisingly good cold on crackers.

SPICY SZECHUAN MARINATED SHRIMP

PATRICK BANKS, BOOTYQUE BBQ TEAM

Grilled shrimp is a tasty classic! When properly cooked, shrimp will be pink and juicy with a little snap at the center. This grilled shrimp dish is great served on sliced onion rolls or over pasta with garlic biscuits.

YIELD: 6–8 SERVINGS • COOK TIME: 6–8 MINUTES

2 lb (907 g) jumbo shrimp

2–3 tbsp (30–44 ml) fresh lemon juice

1 bunch scallions, thinly sliced

¼ cup (12 g) chopped parsley

3 cloves garlic, finely minced

2 tsp (1 g) dried basil

1 tsp salt

1–2 tsp (2–4 g) Szechuan pepper blend OR blackened seasoning

Cooking oil

Place the shrimp in a strainer and rinse thoroughly under cold running water. For each shrimp, slip your thumb or finger under the thin shell, peeling and removing it from the shrimp.

Using your thumb and index finger, pinch the tail of the shrimp and wiggle your hand to remove the tail of the shrimp.

Using a paring knife, slice along the back of the shrimp lengthwise. This will expose a dark vein inside the shrimp. Remove the vein, and set the shrimp aside.

Place all of the cleaned shrimp in a glass bowl. Stir the remaining ingredients together, except for the cooking oil, and mix them into the shrimp. Cover, refrigerate, and marinate for 3 to 4 hours.

Configure your grill for direct cooking. Heat the grill to 375 to 400°F (191 to 204°C). Apply the cooking oil to a paper towel or clean cloth rag. Using tongs, rub the paper towel or rag across the cooking grate to prevent the shrimp from sticking.

Lay the shrimp on the cooking grate in a single layer. Cook the shrimp with the lid on for 3 to 4 minutes. Remove the lid, flip all the shrimp and cook with the lid on for an additional 3 to 4 minutes.

Grilled shrimp tastes great if they aren't cooked too long. Shrimp can easily be overcooked, so watch them carefully. When the shrimp is cooked, the flesh turns pink and slightly opaque. You should cook most seafood to an internal temperature of 145°F (63°C).

Remove all the shrimp from the grill and serve immediately.

TEXAS-STYLE GRILLED AHI POKE

GUADALUPE BBQ COMPANY

Soy sauce, ginger and sesame lend fantastic flavor to this ahi tuna dish. Impress someone special with this easy grilled ahi tuna recipe. Hubba hubba, baby!

YIELD: 4–6 SERVINGS • COOK TIME: 4 MINUTES

MARINADE

2 fresh jalapeño peppers, seeded and minced

2 tsp (6 g) grated fresh ginger

2 tsp (10 ml) sesame oil

1 tsp toasted sesame seeds

1 sheet edible seaweed, finely minced

½ cup (120 g) finely chopped shallot

½ cup (24 g) finely chopped chives

4 tbsp (60 ml) soy sauce

FISH

2 (5–9-oz [142–255-g] and ¾–1″ [2–2.5-cm] thick) sushi-grade Ahi tuna fillets

Course sea salt

Freshly ground pepper

Extra-virgin olive oil

4–6 romaine lettuce leaves, to be used as edible bowls

2 tbsp (20 g) toasted white and black sesame seeds, for garnish

To make the marinade, in a glass bowl, mix together the minced jalapeño pepper, ginger, sesame oil, sesame seeds, seaweed, shallot, chives and soy sauce. Divide the marinade in half. You will marinate the fish in half, and reserve the remaining half for later use.

To make the fish, marinate the tuna fillets for about 10 minutes per side. Then remove the fish and discard the marinade. Salt and pepper the fillets.

Configure your grill for direct cooking, and allow it to heat up to 450 to 600°F (232 to 316°C).

Brush your grill clean and oil the cooking grate in preparation to grill the fillets. Place the fillets on the grill over direct high heat. Cook the tuna with the lid on the grill for 2 minutes. Open the lid, flip the fish and cook for an additional 2 minutes.

You're looking for a good sear on the surface exterior and just rare at the interior. Remove the fish from the grill and let it rest on a cutting board for a few minutes. Cut into 1 x 1-inch (2.5 x 2.5-cm) cubes. The tuna should be a nice bright pink on the inside.

Toss the tuna cubes in the reserved half of the marinade/sauce. Divide equally among the romaine lettuce leaves. Garnish with the sesame seeds and enjoy.

CHAPTER 6

CASSEROLES
AND STEWS

ADD SOME FRESH FLAVORS to your menu with these crowd-pleasing dishes. Easy to make and hearty enough to feed a house full of hungry guests, casseroles, stews and soups are even more delicious when made on the grill. All you need is a Dutch oven and a cast-iron skillet.

These dishes are the perfect place to use up leftover pork, beef or chicken from the recipes in other chapters to create a quick weeknight meal. Or double your favorite brisket recipe (the ones on pages 60 and 68 are great options) to throw into enchiladas, a hearty stew made in a bread bowl or a layered Mexican lasagna. The homemade sausage on page 81 can be added to a breakfast egg and sausage bake, creamy casserole or savory frittata, adding another layer of grilled, smoky flavor to an already delicious meal.

Need a break from meat or have some vegetarians visiting? No problem. This chapter also features soup made from smoky baked potatoes, chowder made with char-grilled corn and, of course, the classic favorite, mac and cheese dressed up with your favorite BBQ rub.

With these recipes, you can let a casserole or stew bubble away on the grill while you enjoy time with your guests, then bring the smoldering hot skillet or Dutch oven directly to the table for a casual but filling meal.

FINN'S FINEST BBQ MAC *AND* CHEESE

FINN'S FINEST BBQ

This mac and cheese has a whole different personality than the one on page 266. You can bring your own barbecue preference to this baked macaroni dish by using whatever rub you prefer. Cooking mac and cheese on the grill adds a whole new layer of flavor to this family favorite.

YIELD: 6 SERVINGS • COOK TIME: 1½ HOURS

32 oz (907 g) Mexican-blend shredded cheese

3 eggs

2 cups (473 ml) milk (2% or whole)

½ cup (115 g) butter or margarine, cut into 10 pats, divided

1 lb (454 g) macaroni, cooked per package directions

Salt and pepper, to taste

3 tbsp (42 g) your favorite BBQ rub

Preheat your grill to 325°F (163°C), indirect heat.

Place the cheese in a large bowl. In a separate bowl, mix the eggs with the milk. In a baking dish, layer 5 pats of butter on the bottom of the dish. Add half of the macaroni, half of the cheese, salt, pepper and BBQ rub. Then add the rest of the macaroni, the remaining half of the bowl of cheese and the remaining 5 pats of butter.

Dust the top with your BBQ rub of choice.

Pour the egg and milk mixture evenly over the layered dish until the pan is half full (NO MORE!). Bake using indirect heat for 1½ hours, or until the milk is gone and the macaroni browns on top. Rotate the pan after 45 minutes to help ensure even cooking.

BAKED POTATO SOUP

MIKE AND CHRIS PETERS, HERE PIGGY PIGGY BBQ

This potato soup picks up a hint of smoke from baking the potatoes first, and then finishing the soup on your gas grill's side burner. It makes about 15 quarts (14 L) and will really please your guests!

YIELD: 20 SERVINGS • COOK TIME: 80 MINUTES

8 large baking potatoes

1 tsp extra-virgin olive oil per potato

1½ tsp (9 g) salt

1 tsp black pepper

1⅓ cups (306 g) margarine or butter

1⅓ cups (167 g) all-purpose flour

3½ qt (3 L) milk

1 large onion, chopped

2½ cups (283 g) shredded cheddar cheese

2 cups (241 g) sour cream

Bacon bits, for serving, optional

Configure your grill for indirect cooking and preheat to 400°F (204°C).

Wash the potatoes. Using a fork, poke each potato three to four times. Flip the potatoes and poke three to four additional times. Poking the potatoes helps prevent them from splitting open as they cook. Rub all the sides of the potatoes with olive oil; then sprinkle with salt and pepper. Cut eight squares of aluminum foil. You want them large enough to individually wrap each potato.

Place one potato on each square of foil and wrap tightly. Place the wrapped potatoes on the grill and cook, using indirect heat, for 45 to 60 minutes. The potatoes are done when they are soft. You should easily be able to pierce through the skin of a cooked potato using very little effort. Remove the cooked potatoes from your grill and allow to cool. Then refrigerate them until ready to use.

Using a knife, cut the skins off the potatoes. Slice the cold potatoes into ¾-inch (2-cm) cubes and set them aside.

In a large stockpot over medium heat, melt the butter, stir in the flour and heat and stir until smooth, 2 to 3 minutes. Gradually add the milk, stirring until thickened, 2 to 3 minutes longer.

Add the potatoes and onion and bring to a boil while stirring. Reduce the heat and simmer for 10 minutes. Add the cheese and the sour cream and stir until melted. Remove from the heat and serve immediately.

Top each serving of soup with bacon bits for your carnivorous friends!

BRISKET STEW IN A SOURDOUGH BREAD BOWL

BBQ LONGHORN RANCH HANDS

This hearty classic gets a zesty and savory kick from the onions, vinegar and lemon zest. Served in a bread bowl, it provides the perfect base for sopping up all the delicious sauce.

YIELD: 4 SERVINGS • COOK TIME: 3 HOURS

2¼ lb (1 kg) onions

2¼ lb (1 kg) beef brisket

1 cup (205 g) lard

1 tbsp (7 g) sweet paprika (or spicy if preferred)

Dash of vinegar

2 cups (475 ml) water

1 tbsp (15 g) salt

2 cloves garlic, finely chopped

Pinch of marjoram

Pinch of caraway

1 tbsp (16 g) tomato paste

1 cup (240 ml) beef injection (we like FAB B, a meat enhancer for beef and veal)

1 bell pepper, seeded and cut into ½" (1.3-cm) cubes

8 slices bacon

Sourdough buns, for serving, optional

Lemon zest

2 stalks celery, diced

Heat the smoker to 230°F (110°C).

Peel and finely chop the onions. Cut the beef brisket into ½-inch (1.3-cm) cubes. Place a 5-quart (4.7-L) Dutch oven directly on the hot charcoal, and let it heat up for about 10 minutes.

Melt the lard in the Dutch oven. Add the onions and let them roast, stirring carefully, until the onions are golden brown. Add the sweet paprika and stir it for just 3 seconds. Deglaze your pan with a dash of vinegar and the water.

Add the brisket, salt, garlic, spices, tomato paste and the FAB B marinade to the boiling stew.

Let the stew simmer, covered, for 2 to 3 hours in the smoker. Stir it from time to time until the color of the broth becomes a nice red-brownish, the meat gets tender and the liquid gets thicker. In the last half hour of cooking, add the bell pepper.

While the stew is cooking, place the bacon strips directly onto an oiled cooking grate. Cook using indirect heat for 60 to 90 minutes, or until the bacon turns brown and crispy. Remove the bacon from the smoker and allow to cool. Crumble and reserve.

For a nice touch, buy sourdough bread buns. Cut off the top, hollow out the buns and fill with stew to serve.

Garnish with the crumbled bacon, lemon zest and some chopped celery.

*See photo on page 180 (bottom left).

BREAKFAST BREAD BOWL

WILBUR'S REVENGE

Whip up a quick and savory breakfast with this easy bread bowl recipe. Filled with eggs, sausage, cheese and fresh vegetables, it not only smells good but tastes delicious and makes for a colorful presentation!

YIELD: 6 SERVINGS • COOK TIME: 50 MINUTES

6 breakfast sausages

4 eggs

4 oz (113 g) cheddar cheese, shredded

1 small onion, diced

4 oz (113 g) multicolored bell peppers, diced

2 oz (57 g) sliced mushrooms

Salt and pepper, as desired

12" (30-cm) sourdough bread roll

8 slices provolone cheese

Configure your grill for indirect cooking. Preheat to 350°F (177°C). Oil a piece of foil.

Oil the cooking grate. Place the breakfast sausages on the grill and cook for 3 to 4 minutes with the lid on. Remove the lid, flip the sausages and cook with the lid on for an additional 3 to 4 minutes, or to an internal temperature of 160°F (70°C).

Crack the eggs into a bowl and beat until fluffy. Add the cheddar, onion, peppers, mushrooms, salt and pepper and stir the mixture to combine.

Cut the top out of the bread roll and hollow the center out until the walls are 2 inches (5 cm) thick. Place the provolone slices on the bottom and sides of the bread bowl. Pour the egg mixture into the bread bowl. Evenly space and place the cooked sausage into the egg batter, leaning on the bread wall around the loaf. Place the bread on the oiled side of foil and set it on the cool side of the grill. Using indirect heat, bake for 45 minutes or until the eggs are set. Remove from the grill, slice into wedges and serve.

BUFFALO CHICKEN TATER TOT CASSEROLE

BIG UGLY'S BBQ TEAM

With a simple assembly of roasted chicken, a slather of sauce topped with bacon, tater tots and cheddar cheese, the end result is a delicious, hot and cheesy plate that's so good it'll make you feel like a kid!

YIELD: 6 SERVINGS • COOK TIME: 45 MINUTES

Nonstick cooking spray

½ roasted rotisserie chicken, skin removed and torn into small pieces

¼ cup (59 ml) Frank's RedHot Buffalo Sauce

1 cup (236 ml) Hidden Valley Ranch dressing

¼ cup (13 g) scallions, diced, divided, optional

½ cup (115 g) chopped cooked bacon, divided

1 (32-oz [905-g]) bag frozen tater tots

8 oz (227 g) Mexican-blend shredded cheese

Small bunch parsley, optional

Preheat your grill or smoker to 350°F (177°C). Coat a 9 x 13-inch (23 x 33-cm) aluminum half pan with nonstick cooking spray.

Cut up the chicken and spread the pieces across the bottom of the half pan. In a small bowl, combine the Frank's Buffalo Sauce and Hidden Valley Ranch dressing. Stir to mix well. Pour half of the sauce over the chicken pieces.

Toss half of the scallions (if using) and ¼ cup (55 g) of chopped bacon on top of the sauce-covered chicken. Layer the frozen tater tots in single rows on top of the bacon. Pour the remaining sauce over the tater tots. Add the rest of the scallions and chopped bacon.

Layer the top with the shredded cheese. Place it on the smoker and bake, using indirect heat at 350°F (177°C), for 45 minutes. Remove from the smoker and top with bits of parsley, if desired.

SAUSAGE CASSEROLE

DISCO PIGS

This hearty casserole can be made as spicy as you would like by substituting bulk hot sausage or pepper Jack cheese. It's easy to make it your own!

YIELD: 4–6 SERVINGS • COOK TIME: 60–75 MINUTES

2¼ cups (68 g) croutons

1½ lb (680 g) bulk sausage

4 eggs, beaten

2¼ cups (532 ml) milk

1 (10.5-oz [294-g]) can cream of mushroom soup, undiluted

1 (4-oz [113-g]) can sliced mushrooms, drained

¾ tsp dry mustard

2 cups (226 g) shredded cheddar cheese

Cherry tomatoes, optional, for garnish

Parsley, optional, for garnish

Spread the croutons in a lightly greased 9 x 13-inch (23 x 33-cm) pan or half pan and set aside. Heat a cast-iron skillet over medium heat. Brown the sausage, stirring often to break it apart, until the sausage is no longer pink, about 10 to 15 minutes. Remove the cooked sausage from the heat, crumble and drain well.

Cool the sausage for about 10 minutes, and then sprinkle it over the croutons. Combine the eggs, milk, soup, mushrooms and mustard in a medium mixing bowl. Mix well to incorporate the ingredients. Pour the mixture over the sausage and croutons. Cover and refrigerate for 8 hours or overnight.

Configure your smoker or grill for indirect cooking. Preheat your cooker to 325°F (163°C). Place the pan in the cooker and bake, uncovered, for 50 to 55 minutes. Sprinkle the cheese over top and bake an additional 5 minutes, or until the cheese melts.

Garnish with cherry tomatoes and parsley, if desired.

DIZZY CHILI

DIZZY PIG BBQ TEAM

Some people like chili over pasta, some like it over rice and some just like it in a bowl. Any way you serve it, you will enjoy it! One of the best things about chili is that it's always better a day or two after you make it and the flavors have time to meld.

YIELD: 4–6 SERVINGS • COOK TIME: 1½–2 HOURS

3 tbsp (42 g) Dizzy Pig Cow Lick or favorite rub, divided

1½ lb (680 g) ground beef

3 dried pasilla chiles

2 cloves garlic, or more

1 tbsp (6 g) whole cumin seeds, toasted

Olive oil, for browning

1 large sweet onion, coarsely chopped, or more

Salt

1 qt (946 ml) beef broth

2 (14.5-oz [410-g]) cans diced tomatoes

1 tbsp (8 g) ground New Mexico chile or other pure ground chiles to your heat preference (not a blended "chili powder")

2 (16-oz [455-g]) cans beans (mix and match kidney, black, pinto, red, white)

Masa flour, to thicken, if needed

3–4 small squares dark chocolate

Sugar, if needed

Shake about half the rub onto the beef and toss. Slice the chiles open and remove the seeds. Soak them in warm water until softened and rehydrated, about an hour.

Purée the soaked chiles and garlic in a blender or food processor. In a dry, heavy skillet over medium heat, toast the whole cumin seeds until fragrant, about 1 to 2 minutes. Remove from the heat. Use a mortar and pestle to grind the cumin into power.

Configure your grill for two-zone cooking, and preheat to 325 to 350°F (163 to 177°C). Place a 5-quart (4.7-L) Dutch oven (cast iron is best) directly over the hot charcoal. Allow the Dutch oven to warm up for 10 minutes with the lid on your grill.

Brown the ground beef with olive oil in the Dutch oven. Do small batches over high heat so that the meat actually browns, and don't stir until the meat starts to caramelize. Reserve the cooked meat from the Dutch oven, and then brown the next small batch. Allow 5 to 10 minutes per batch.

Remove the browned meat from the pan. It's okay to leave a few bits in the pan. Add the onion and a little salt and stir while scraping the brown bits from the pan. This "fond" is packed with flavor and is part of making a great pot of chili!

Once the onion is cooked soft, about 5 minutes, move the Dutch oven to the cool side of the grill. Add your browned beef back to the pan. Pour in your chile/garlic purée, the beef broth and tomatoes. Stir, and then add the cumin, pure ground chile and the remaining half of the rub. Stir well.

Bring to a simmer, uncovered, and cook for 30 to 60 minutes until the chili starts to thicken. Add the beans and stir well.

Cook another half hour or more until the desired thickness is achieved. If needed, thicken with a little masa flour, which also adds a pleasant corn tortilla flavor. Add the chocolate and stir. Add more Cow Lick rub if needed for a fresh peppery bite. Taste and add salt as needed; add sugar if it needs a tad of sweetness.

GRILLED CORN *AND* CRAB CHOWDER

PORK BARREL BBQ

Fresh corn and sweet crab make this chowder a can't-miss hit in the summer. In the winter, substitute frozen corn kernels for a hearty soup that will keep you warm while you're dreaming about summer!

YIELD: 6–8 SERVINGS • COOK TIME: 1 HOUR

8 ears corn (about 3 cups [433 g] of kernels)

½ lb (227 g) bacon, cut into ½" (1.3-cm) pieces

2 tbsp (30 ml) olive oil

2 tbsp (29 g) butter

2 cloves garlic, minced

5 red potatoes, diced

2 celery ribs, diced

1 medium yellow onion, diced

1 red bell pepper, seeded and diced

2 bay leaves, fresh or dried

1 tbsp (14 g) Pork Barrel BBQ All-American Spice Rub or favorite rub

3 tbsp (23 g) all-purpose flour

2 cups (473 ml) seafood or vegetable stock

3 cups (720 ml) milk

8 oz (227 g) lump crabmeat

Salt and pepper, to taste

Preheat your grill to medium-high at 350 to 400°F (177 to 204°C). Soak the corn, still in husks, in water for 15 minutes. Place the corn on your grill and cook with the grill lid down for 12 to 15 minutes, turning occasionally. Let the corn cool for 10 minutes. Peel the husk off each ear of corn. Hold each ear of corn upright on a cutting board and carefully cut downward, removing the kernels from the cob.

Heat a pot over medium-high heat. Place the bacon in the pot and cook for 5 to 7 minutes. Flip the bacon and continue to cook for 5 to 7 minutes or until the bacon curls and begins to crisp. Remove the cooked bacon from the pot and place it on a paper towel. Repeat the process, as needed, until all the bacon is cooked. Let the bacon cool; then crumble.

Pour out three-fourths of the bacon grease from the pot. Add the olive oil and butter and place the garlic, potatoes, celery, onion and bell pepper in the pot. Add the bay leaves and All-American Spice Rub; sauté for 7 minutes.

Sprinkle the flour over the vegetables and cook for an additional 3 minutes, stirring every 30 seconds.

Stir in the stock and milk and bring to a slow boil. Add the corn kernels and crabmeat to the pot. Simmer for 5 minutes. Add the bacon and simmer for an additional 5 minutes. Remove the bay leaves and season with salt and pepper, to taste, before serving.

MEXICAN LASAGNA

DISCO PIGS

This dish is delicious and holds the perfect amount of heat. Definitely a go-to dish that reheats well, but it's doubtful you will have any leftovers!

YIELD: 12 SERVINGS • COOK TIME: 40 MINUTES

1½ lb (680 g) ground beef (or leftover brisket or pork shoulder)

Salt and pepper

1 tbsp (8 g) chili powder

Spray oil

12 tortillas

1 (15-oz [425-g]) can chili beans, rinsed and drained

1 (16-oz [455-g]) can corn, drained

2 cups (241 g) shredded cheese, cheddar or your favorite blend, divided

1 (10.5-oz [294-g]) can cream of celery soup

1 (10-oz [285-g]) can diced Rotel

Preheat your smoker or grill to 350°F (177°C), indirect heat.

Heat a cast-iron skillet over medium heat. Place the beef in the pan. Cook the beef, stirring frequently and breaking into small pieces, until the meat is no longer pink, about 10 to 15 minutes. Season the meat with salt, pepper and chili powder.

Spray the bottom of a 12 x 10-inch (30 x 25-cm) pan with oil. Line the pan with tortillas, and cover with the meat mixture. Add the beans and corn and cover with half of the cheese. Add another layer of tortillas. Combine the soup and Rotel in a bowl and stir. Pour this mixture over the tortillas and top with the remaining cheese.

Bake the lasagna on the cool side of the grill for 30 minutes, or until the cheese is melted.

PORTUGUESE EGG BAKE

A MAZIE Q

Portuguese baked eggs are high on the comfort food list. Eggs baked over a bed of ricotta cheese in a spicy red pepper and tomato ragout, this dish is hearty and can be served at a brunch or dinner.

YIELD: 5–6 SERVINGS • COOK TIME: 50 MINUTES

RAGOUT

¼ cup (60 ml) olive oil

2 red bell peppers

1 large yellow Spanish onion

½ fresh jalapeño, sliced lengthwise and halved

1 (28-oz [794-g]) can whole tomatoes, preferably San Marzano

1¼ cups (292 g) piquillo peppers, halved, in their juice

5 whole basil leaves

1½ tbsp (5 g) chopped fresh oregano

½ tsp ground thyme or 1 tsp chopped fresh thyme

¾ cup (177 ml) chicken stock

1 tsp piment d'espelette

1 tsp paprika

8 cloves garlic

Salt and pepper

½ lb (227 g) or rounded ½ cup (227 g) linguica, sliced

BREAD DIP

½ cup (115 g) butter

1 cup (236 ml) water plus ¾ tbsp (11 g) chicken base or 1 cup (236 g) chicken stock

4 cloves garlic

2 tbsp (6 g) chopped oregano

1 tbsp (3 g) parsley

1 large baguette

RICOTTA NEST

16 oz (454 g) ricotta

½ cup (90 g) pecorino Romano or Parmesan-Romano blend

¾ cup (90 g) sharp white cheddar cheese

½ tbsp (3 g) oregano

Salt and pepper

5–6 eggs

Chives or scallions, for garnish

Heat your grill or smoker to 250 to 275°F (121 to 135°C) for medium-high heat.

To make the ragout, heat a cast-iron skillet over high heat (on a cooktop or grill). Add the olive oil, bell peppers, onion and jalapeño. Sauté until the veggies are tender, about 7 to 10 minutes; a little caramelization is ideal.

Break up the tomatoes with your fingers or a fork and add them to the ragout, along with the juice from the can.

Add the remaining ragout ingredients, except the linguica, and cook for 20 to 30 minutes, or until the liquid reduces by half. Stir occasionally to prevent items from burning. Taste the ragout as it cooks, and remove the jalapeño when the ragout contains the level of spiciness you prefer.

To make the bread dip, heat the butter, water with chicken base and garlic in a microwaveable bowl (or over the grill or on a stovetop). Once all the items are melted and hot, add the fresh herbs and stir. Let it bloom.

Slice the baguette into ½- to 1-inch (1.3- to 2.5-cm) thick slices. Coat both sides of each slice with the bread dip and set aside.

To prepare the ricotta nest, mix all the contents of the nest in a bowl and set aside.

Check the ragout as it cooks, and when it obtains the desired consistency, add the sliced linguica and remove the cast-iron skillet from the heat.

With a spoon, make shallow cavities for 5 or 6 eggs to be cooked in the skillet. The number of eggs you cook depends on what your pan can hold. After the cavities have been sectioned off, add enough ricotta to each pocket to form a "cup" for each egg so that the egg contents won't spill out to the rest of the pan. If you have any leftover white cheddar, feel free to add to the pockets. Carefully crack an egg into each ricotta nest.

Put the cast-iron pan in the smoker. After you put the pan on the smoker, you should have time to toast the dipped bread. This step can be done in advance of the recipe, but I like to toast the bread while the egg bake is cooking. Place the bread on the smoker or grill, close to the heat source. Toast the bread on each side to obtain a nice char, 3 to 5 minutes.

After 20 minutes, check the egg bake continuously until the desired yolk consistency is reached. I like over-medium consistency, which usually takes about 10 additional minutes of cook time. The egg yolk will be slightly firm but still oozing. The actual cook time will vary depending on the airflow of the smoker. Once the desired yolk consistency is reached, serve immediately with the toasted bread, and garnish with snipped chives or scallions.

ROASTED RED PEPPER, SAUSAGE ⅋ PORK FRITTATA

FIRE DOWN BELOW

Ed and Ginny Roach of Fire Down Below have come up with this easy frittata using chopped leftover pulled pork, hot sausage and bacon for a quick meal. It is made to serve eight people, but once you sink your teeth into this spicy and gooey cheese frittata, they're sure you will wish you had doubled the recipe!

YIELD: 6–8 SERVINGS • COOK TIME: 55 MINUTES

1 red pepper or ½ cup (116 g) chopped jarred pepper

½ lb (227 g) hot sausage, casings removed

4 slices bacon, chopped

½ cup (120 g) chopped shallots

3 cloves garlic, minced

½ lb (227 g) leftover pulled pork (page 44), chopped

½ cup (55 g) chopped, drained, oil-packed sun-dried tomatoes

3 tbsp (11 g) chopped fresh parsley, divided

5 large eggs

3 large egg yolks

1 cup (236 ml) whipping cream

1 cup (236 ml) half-and-half

2 cups (241 g) shredded Queso Chihuahua Rallado cheese, or your favorite cheese, divided

1 tsp salt

Configure the grill for two-zone cooking, and preheat the grill to 350°F (177°C).

Place the red pepper on the grill over direct heat. Cook the pepper, turning it as the skin blackens and chars, about 3 to 4 minutes each side. When the pepper is blackened on all sides, place it in a brown paper bag, close and let sit for 10 minutes. Remove the pepper from the bag. Using a small, sharp knife, carefully scrape away the charred skin. Cut the pepper in half and remove the seeds and membrane. Chop into small pieces.

Butter an 11-inch (28-cm) cast-iron skillet and add the sausage and bacon. Place the pan over direct heat and sauté the sausage and bacon until the sausage is brown and the bacon is crisp, breaking the sausage into small pieces, about 15 minutes. Add the shallots and garlic and sauté for 3 minutes. Add the pulled pork, roasted red pepper, sun-dried tomatoes and 2 tablespoons (7 g) of parsley. Stir for 1 minute and place on indirect heat, away from the coals.

Whisk the eggs, egg yolks, whipping cream, half-and-half, 1½ cups (181 g) of the cheese and salt in a large mixing bowl. Pour the egg mixture over the bacon and sausage mixture in the skillet. Sprinkle the remaining ½ cup (60 g) of cheese and 1 tablespoon (4 g) of parsley over the top. Cook over indirect heat until the top of the frittata is golden brown, about 35 to 40 minutes. Rotate the pan after 15 to 20 minutes to help ensure even cooking. Enjoy!

TEXAS BRISKET ENCHILADAS

407 BBQ

This smoky brisket enchilada dish has a corn tortilla, stuffed with a tender brisket filling and topped with a chile verde sauce. If you are lucky enough to have leftover brisket, this is a great dish to feed a crowd.

YIELD: 5 SERVINGS • COOK TIME: 25 MINUTES

1 (28-oz [794-g]) can green chile verde sauce

8 oz (227 g) sour cream

3 cups (405 g) chopped cooked brisket

½ cup (24 g) chopped cilantro

½ cup (76 g) finely chopped purple onion

2 cups (241 g) shredded Mexican cheese blend, divided

10 corn tortillas

Sliced jalapeños, to serve

Configure your smoker or grill for indirect cooking. Preheat your cooker to 350°F (177°C).

In a small mixing bowl, blend the chile verde sauce and sour cream. In a large bowl, combine the brisket, cilantro, onion, 1 cup (120 g) of the cheese and ½ cup (61 g) of the chile verde mixture. Mix well and set aside. Warm the tortillas in a tortilla warmer or wrapped in damp paper towels on a plate in the microwave.

Spray an 8 x 10-inch (20 x 25-cm) baking dish with cooking spray.

Fill each tortilla with approximately 1 heaping tablespoon (14 g) of the brisket filling. Roll the enchiladas, and lay them seam-side down in a baking dish.

Pour the remaining chile verde sauce mixture over the enchiladas until completely covered, and then top with the remaining 1 cup (120 g) of cheese. Bake for approximately 25 minutes until the cheese is melted and hot. Top with sliced jalapeño peppers to serve.

CHAPTER 7

APPETIZERS
AND SIDES

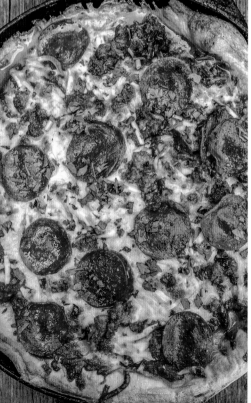

DISCOVER DELICIOUS AND EASY-TO-PREPARE appetizer recipes for your grill, and complete your meal with perfect sides for any dinner or get-together with friends and family.

Appetizers are small servings of food, usually intended to stir up your appetite. This chapter contains some real crowd-pleasers, including backyard takes on meatballs, various dips and salsas, stuffed mushrooms and numerous interpretations of smoked jalapeño poppers.

Side dishes accompany the main course. When you grill vegetables, the natural sugars in these foods caramelize, creating a new layer of flavor. The following pages contain recipes for grilled lettuce, variations on green beans, vegetable ratatouille and potato dishes, along with backyard classics such as cornbread and barbecue baked beans.

After you try some of these recipes, feel free to experiment a little bit. You can grill most vegetables, and the recipes in this chapter provide lots of seasoning combinations that just might inspire some of your own flavorful ideas.

ABIGAIL'S HAWAIIAN MEATBALL KABOBS

ABIGAIL RICHARDSON

Abigail Richardson won first place in the six- to eight-year-old age division of the Kids Que competition at Pork and Brew in Rio Rancho, New Mexico. Abby is six years old. She used a Weber kettle grill and Kingsford charcoal for her competition win. Great job, Abby—those kabobs sound delicious!

YIELD: 8 MEATBALLS • COOK TIME: 9–12 MINUTES

TERIYAKI SAUCE
½ cup (120 ml) soy sauce

⅓ cup (79 ml) honey

¼ cup (60 ml) sherry

1 clove garlic, smashed

¼ tsp ground ginger

MEATBALLS
1 lb (454 g) ground beef

1 cup (121 g) panko breadcrumbs

1 tbsp (10 g) garlic pepper

1 tbsp (7 g) onion powder

½ tsp salt

2 tbsp (28 g) brown sugar, packed

1 egg

4 wooden skewers

GARNISH
Pineapple chunks

Sweet peppers, sliced into ¾" (2-cm) pieces

To make the sauce, combine all of the ingredients in a small bowl and whisk them together until combined. Set the sauce aside.

For the meatballs, add all of the ingredients to a large bowl plus ½ cup (120 ml) of the teriyaki sauce. Mix until well combined. Roll the meatball mixture into approximately 2-inch (5-cm) balls. Allow the meatballs to rest for at least 20 minutes in the refrigerator.

While the meatballs are resting, prepare your grill for indirect cooking and heat to 350 to 400°F (176 to 204°C). Once the grill is hot, place the meatballs on the cool side of the grill, away from the heat. Turn the meatballs every 2 to 3 minutes until all sides are browned and the internal temperature is 165°F (74°C), 9 to 12 minutes total. You will know they are done when the juice runs clear.

Once the meatballs are cooked, take them off the grill and place them in a shallow bowl. Pour the remaining teriyaki sauce over the meatballs. Cover them with foil and allow them to rest for 5 minutes.

While the meatballs are resting, prepare the wooden skewers by cutting each in half. On each skewer, place 1 chunk of pineapple, 1 slice of sweet pepper and 1 meatball. Enjoy!

AMPED-UP CHILE CON QUESO

FIRE DOWN BELOW

Spicy roasted green chile and melted cheese make a creamy dip that can be eaten with tostadas or warm corn tortillas. If you like heat and prefer it spicier, then you can use Rotel (hot), or add a finely chopped jalapeño.

YIELD: 15 SERVINGS • COOK TIME: 25 MINUTES

¾ cup (172 g) unsalted butter, cut into cubes, plus more for greasing

1 lb (454 g) Jimmy Dean hot pork sausage

1½ lb (680 g) Velveeta brand cheese

½ lb (227 g) Monterey Jack cheese

1 (10-oz [284-g]) can Rotel (original) diced tomatoes and green chiles, juice reserved

1 onion, diced

1 (4.25-oz [120-g]) can diced green chiles, juice reserved

¾ cup (177 ml) heavy cream

Tortilla chips

Configure your grill for two-zone cooking. Build a pile of charcoal on one side and leave the other side empty. Preheat the grill to 350°F (177°C).

Grease a large cast-iron skillet with butter. Place the skillet over direct heat and brown the sausage for about 8 minutes, breaking the meat up as you go. Once browned, drain off the fat.

Chop the Velveeta and Monterey Jack into small cubes, and mix with the sausage. Add the diced tomatoes, onion and green chiles with juice. Stir and add the butter. Carefully move the skillet away from the hot charcoal and place it on the indirect side of the grill.

Slowly add the heavy cream, stirring frequently, until the mixture comes together, about 15 minutes. Remove the dip from the grill and serve with tortilla chips.

BACON-WRAPPED APRICOTS

RIBS WITHIN BBQ TEAM

These sweet morsels of love are wrapped in flavorful bacon and carry a little bit of heat at the back end. Bacon-wrapped apricots tend to be a hit at gatherings, so be sure to make a lot of them to satisfy your guests!

YIELD: 12–16 APRICOTS • COOK TIME: 34 MINUTES

12–16 dried apricots

1½ cups (355 ml) apple juice

1 cup (240 g) Ribs Within Rub 4 All, OR ½ cup (96 g) sugar, ¼ cup (60 g) salt, 2 tsp (5 g) chili powder, divided

6–8 slices applewood smoked bacon, regular sliced

Rehydrate the dried apricots in apple juice and ½ cup (120 g) of Ribs Within Rub 4 All for 1 to 2 hours. Reserve 2 teaspoons (9 g) of the rub to sprinkle on the bacon.

Remove the apricots from the liquid and place them on a paper plate. Let them sit for 5 minutes to dry.

Wrap each apricot in half a slice of bacon, using two toothpicks to keep it closed. Sprinkle the remaining rub on each wrapped apricot.

Configure your grill for two-zone cooking and preheat to 300°F (149°C). Put the wrapped apricots in a shallow aluminum pan and place them on the grill. Cook with indirect heat for 30 minutes. Remove the apricots from the pan and place them directly over the heat for 2 minutes a side, or until the bacon is crispy around the edges.

Remove the apricots from the grill and place them back in the pan or on a serving tray. Serve hot or at room temperature.

BRISKET-STUFFED JALAPEÑO POPPERS

BOOTYQUE BBQ TEAM

While there are many variations of stuffed peppers wrapped in bacon, stuffing them with brisket brings this recipe over the top! If you find yourself with leftover brisket, chop it up, mix it with your favorite sauce and grab some peppers—it's that simple. These peppers are so addictive that if you want any for yourself, you'll either need to make a double batch or hide some ahead of time!

YIELD: 24–30 SERVINGS • COOK TIME: 60 MINUTES

2 lb (907 g) cooked brisket, flat or point cut, chopped

8 oz (227 g) Monterey Jack cheese, shredded

1 medium purple onion, finely chopped

1 bunch cilantro, chopped

1 (8-oz [237-ml]) bottle your favorite BBQ sauce

12–15 jalapeño peppers

1–1½ lb (454–680 g) bacon

1 tbsp (15 g) Sweet Swine O' Mine rub or favorite rub

Combine the brisket, cheese, onion, cilantro and sauce in a bowl and set aside.

Cut the tops off the jalapeño peppers. Slice them lengthwise and remove the seeds and ribs.

Prepare your grill for indirect cooking, and preheat to 250°F (121°C).

Spoon the mixture into the peppers and wrap it with bacon. Secure the bacon with a toothpick. Apply the rub to the bacon and place it on the grill. Cook the poppers for 60 minutes or until the bacon becomes crispy. Remove them from the grill and enjoy.

BACON-WRAPPED PINEAPPLE TREATS

COUNTY LINE SMOKERS

These bacon-wrapped pineapple treats are a great dessert any time of the year. If you like heat, when you wrap the pineapple chunks, add grilled jalapeños or serrano chile strips between the fruit and the bacon!

YIELD: 30–35 SERVINGS • COOK TIME: 10 MINUTES

1 whole pineapple (3–4 lb [1–2 kg])

2 tbsp (30 g) Oakridge BBQ Dominator Sweet Rib Rub, divided

1 (1-lb [455-g]) package low-sodium bacon, thick sliced

¾ cup (177 ml) Smokey Kansas City Spicy BBQ Sauce from Burnt Finger BBQ

2 tbsp (30 ml) honey

Core the pineapple and cut it into 1½-inch (4-cm) chunks. Dust the pineapple chunks with half of the rub.

Cut the bacon in half. Wrap a half-piece of bacon around each pineapple chunk, using a toothpick to hold the bacon in place. Dust the outside of the bacon-wrapped pineapple chunks with the remaining rub. Let the rub sweat a little while the pineapple and bacon get to room temperature.

Configure your grill for direct cooking over medium-high heat (400 to 500°F [204 to 260°C]). Place the bacon-wrapped pineapple chunks on the grill, and let them cook for about 5 minutes. Flip them and cook for an additional 5 minutes.

Mix the spicy barbecue sauce with the honey to make a sweet and spicy glaze.

Brush the glaze onto the bacon-wrapped pineapple chunks at the end of the grilling process. Apply the glaze several times, but be careful to not let it burn, cooking for another minute or so.

CRISPY BACON-WRAPPED TAILGATING POPS

THE SHED BBQ TEAM

What better way to wrap up a tailgate than a win by your team?!? Try combining ground pork and ground beef with The Shed's deliciously sweet Southern BBQ sauce to get the juicy, spicy results you've been waiting for. Now go root your team on to victory fueled by these bacon-wrapped meatballs!

YIELD: 5–6 SERVINGS • COOK TIME: 16–20 MINUTES

8–10 wooden skewers

6 oz (170 g) pepper Jack cheese

¾ lb (340 g) ground beef

¼ lb (113 g) ground pork

3–4 fresh jalapeños, minced

1 small sweet onion, minced

Rack Attack rib rub or your favorite rub

1 lb (454 g) bacon

⅓ cup (79 ml) your favorite The Shed BBQ Sauce (we recommend Original Spicy Sweet) or your favorite BBQ sauce

Soak the wooden skewers for 30 minutes. Set up your grill for direct cooking and preheat to 350°F (176°C).

Cube the pepper Jack cheese.

Mix the beef, pork, jalapeños and onion together. Form the mixture into roughly 3-ounce (85-g) palm-size cigar shapes. As you form the meat, stuff a cube of pepper Jack cheese into the center of each one. After the cigars are formed, sprinkle with the Rack Attack rib rub as desired.

Wrap the meatballs with bacon; then slide each one onto a skewer.

Grill your meatballs on medium-high heat for 8 to 10 minutes. Rotate once and cook for an additional 8 to 10 minutes. Make sure the bacon is crispy on all sides.

In the final moments of cooking, baste with The Shed BBQ Sauce.

NOTES: Soak your wooden skewers in water to prevent burning; use two per pop to make it easier to rotate while cooking.

We prefer to use thin, meatier bacon.

Add red pepper flakes or substitute habañeros or ghost pepper to kick the heat into overtime.

When wrapping the meatball with bacon, rotate a quarter turn on each roll to cover evenly and tightly.

BLUE CHEESE ⊗ BACON GRILLED ROMAINE SALAD

GUADALUPE BBQ COMPANY

This grilled salad makes a great side dish to accompany any of your barbecued meals. It's quick and easy to put together, and cooks in minutes! You can also enjoy it for a speedy lunch.

YIELD: 4 SERVINGS • COOK TIME: 4 MINUTES

VINAIGRETTE DRESSING

½ cup (120 ml) extra-virgin olive oil

½ cup (120 ml) balsamic vinegar

1 clove garlic, minced

1 tsp ground mustard

Pinch of salt

Ground black pepper, to taste

SALAD

2 heads romaine lettuce, split lengthwise with outer leaves removed

3 tbsp (44 ml) olive oil

2 tbsp (20 g) granulated garlic or garlic powder

Coarse sea salt

Fresh cracked black pepper

½ cup (90 g) fresh Parmesan cheese, grated

½ cup (60 g) blue cheese crumbles

1 cup (112 g) crumbled bacon

Set up your grill for direct cooking. Get your grill hot at 400 to 550°F (204 to 288°C).

To make the dressing, mix together the olive oil in a bowl with the vinegar, garlic, mustard, salt and pepper.

To make the salad, drizzle the romaine halves with olive oil. Sprinkle on the garlic, then season with salt and pepper to taste.

Let the cooking grate heat up for 3 to 5 minutes. Brush your grill clean, and then apply olive oil to the grate. Place the romaine lettuce on the grill. Using direct heat, cook the romaine lettuce for 1 to 2 minutes per side, watching for grill marks and a slight wilt.

Remove the romaine lettuce from the grill. Sprinkle with Parmesan, blue cheese and bacon; then drizzle with the dressing and enjoy!

BUFFALO CHICKEN DIP RECIPE

COUNTY LINE SMOKERS

You want a crowd-pleaser, whether you're tailgating before the game or watching it in the comfort of your own home. This recipe delivers the punch of buffalo chicken wings in the form of a velvety dip! It's also a great way to use leftover chicken.

YIELD: 15 SERVINGS • COOK TIME: 20 MINUTES

9–12 oz (255–340 g) grilled chicken

2 (8-oz [227-g]) blocks of cream cheese

½ medium yellow onion, diced

2 cloves garlic, minced

½ cup (60 g) shredded cheddar cheese

2 cups (473 ml) Texas Pete's Wing Sauce or your favorite wing sauce

¼ cup (60 ml) ranch dressing, divided, optional

½ cup (60 g) blue cheese crumbles

1 scallion, chopped

Set up your grill for indirect cooking and heat to 325°F (163°C).

Chop up some leftover chicken. (You can use 3 to 4 chicken thighs or 1 to 2 chicken breasts.)

Bring the cream cheese to room temperature.

In a large bowl, mix together the chicken, onion, garlic, cream cheese and cheddar cheese. Add the wing sauce and half of the ranch dressing (to ensure it's not too runny) and continue to mix.

Spread the mixture into an 8 x 8-inch (20 x 20-cm) pan. Add the blue cheese crumbles to one half of the pan—many people do not like blue cheese, so this way not all of the dip will have it. Cook the dip at 325°F (163°C), using indirect heat, for 20 minutes or until it is bubbly all around the edges.

Garnish with the scallion and drizzle with the remaining ranch dressing.

CRISPY POTATO POUCHES

SMOKIN' ACES

Quick and easy to make, these foiled potatoes are arranged with slices of sweet onion and aromatic spices, and then baked until crisp. Keep this handy idea in mind the next time you need a side dish. You can use this versatile grilling method for other vegetables, too!

YIELD: 3 SERVINGS • COOK TIME: 45 MINUTES

3 russet potatoes

½ medium Vidalia onion

6 tbsp (86 g) butter, divided

⅜ tsp paprika

⅜ tsp salt

⅜ tsp black pepper

Configure your grill for two-zone cooking. Preheat your grill to 350°F (177°C).

Cut the potatoes and onion into thin slices, about ⅛ inch (3 mm) thick.

On a sheet of heavy-duty or nonstick foil, layer a third of the potatoes, a third of the onion and 2 tablespoons (29 g) of butter. Sprinkle on a third of the paprika, salt and pepper. Wrap the packet tightly, and then wrap it again in a second sheet of foil.

Repeat the process two more times using the remaining ingredients.

Place the potato pouches on the cool side of the grill, and cook using indirect heat for 45 minutes.

BUTTERMILK CORNBREAD

SMOKE ON WHEELS BBQ TEAM

This slightly sweet cornbread has a tender crumb thanks to the buttermilk. This Southern staple is best served with soups, stews or salads. Bake it just before your guests arrive so they can savor the aromas and enjoy the cornbread while it's hot.

YIELD: 1 LOAF • COOK TIME: 45 MINUTES

2 cups (341 g) cornmeal (white or yellow)

1 cup (125 g) all-purpose flour

1 cup (192 g) sugar

1 tsp baking soda

1 tsp salt

2 cups (473 ml) buttermilk

3 tbsp (44 ml) vegetable oil

Configure your grill for indirect cooking and heat to 350°F (177°C).

Combine the dry ingredients; then add the buttermilk and oil. Mix until integrated. Pour the mixture into a greased 9 x 5-inch (23 x 13-cm) loaf pan.

Place the loaf pan on the cool side of the grill, away from the hot charcoal. Place the lid on the grill and bake for 45 minutes, until golden.

CHORIZO-STUFFED JALAPEÑO POPPERS

PHIL THE GRILL

Warm and gooey, these jalapeño appetizers are sure to be delicious! With just one bite, you'll notice how the charred pepper adds to the depth of flavors these spicy stuffed poppers provide.

YIELD: 12 POPPERS • COOK TIME: 26 MINUTES

12 jalapeños, stems removed and hollowed out

2 tbsp (30 ml) olive oil, divided

1 shallot, diced

2 tbsp (19 g) minced garlic

Salt and freshly ground black pepper

¾ lb (340 g) chorizo sausage, finely chopped

1 cup (240 g) cream cheese, at room temperature

Configure your grill for two-zone cooking and preheat to 375°F (190°C), or medium-high.

Toss the jalapeños in 1 tablespoon (15 ml) of the olive oil. Place the peppers on the grill, directly over the heat source. Using tongs, turn the peppers constantly and allow the surface to char, about 3 minutes. Remove them from the grill and refrigerate. When cool enough to handle, peel the skins off the peppers.

Place a medium skillet directly over the heat source, and heat up for 5 minutes. Add the remaining 1 tablespoon (15 ml) olive oil. Add the shallot, garlic, salt and pepper to taste, along with the chorizo sausage. Cook for 2 to 3 minutes until nicely browned. Pour the contents of the skillet into a medium bowl, and allow it to cool slightly, about 5 minutes. Stir in the cream cheese and mix well.

Place the cream cheese mixture in a piping bag. Pipe the mixture into the peeled peppers. (Alternatively, you can make a piping bag by cutting one corner off of a plastic sandwich bag.)

Preheat your barbecue to 400°F (204°C) or high heat. Open the air vent if necessary. Using indirect heat, place the peppers on a cooking grate and allow the filling to get warm and gooey, about 20 minutes. Remove the poppers from the grill and allow them to cool slightly before serving.

CINDY'S MEXICAN STREET CORN BAKE

MOO COW

While this rich, creamy corn dish makes for a tasty side, we think it can stand out as a starring entrée, too. Give this one a try and see for yourself!

YIELD: 7 SERVINGS • COOK TIME: 38 MINUTES

1 (28.8-oz [817-g]) bag frozen corn, thawed

1 clove garlic, diced

½ cup (75 g) red onion, diced

1 medium bell pepper, finely diced (green or red)

1 (4.5-oz [127.6-g]) can chopped green chiles

¼ cup (12 g) chopped fresh cilantro

1 cup (122 g) crumbled cotija or queso fresco cheese, divided (substitute feta cheese if the others are unavailable)

Salt, to taste

1 cup (220 g) mayonnaise

½ cup (60 g) sour cream

Zest and juice of 1 lime

1 tsp chili powder

⅛ tsp cayenne pepper

Set up your grill for two-zone cooking and preheat to 350°F (177°C).

Place a cast-iron skillet on the hot side of the grill, and let it heat up for 8 minutes. Add the corn to the skillet. Heat the corn over direct heat for 6 to 8 minutes, or until the corn starts to char. Add the diced garlic during the last minute of the cook time. Remove the skillet from your grill and let the corn cool slightly.

In an aluminum quarter pan, mix together the corn and garlic, onion, bell pepper, green chiles, cilantro and half of the cheese. Add salt to taste.

Mix together the mayonnaise, sour cream, lime zest and juice, chili powder and cayenne pepper. Add this to the corn mixture and combine.

Top with the remaining ½ cup (61 g) cheese.

Cover and bake over indirect heat for approximately 30 minutes, or until warm. Uncover and cook for an additional 8 minutes to add a special depth of flavor from your grill. Remove and serve.

CRISPY PARMESAN-COATED GRILLED ASPARAGUS

STICKS-N-CHICKS BBQ TEAM

Parmesan-covered asparagus will make the whole family happy! This simple asparagus dish, grilled with a little oil, steak seasoning and salt, gets topped with Parmesan cheese and a zesty squeeze of lemon to make it a sizzling summer side dish.

YIELD: 4 SERVINGS • COOK TIME: 15 MINUTES

1 bundle asparagus (approximately 1 lb [450 g])

1 tbsp (15 ml) olive oil

1½ tbsp (5 g) Montreal steak seasoning (or substitute with your favorite beef rub that has a peppercorn and salt combination)

2 oz (57 g) Parmesan cheese, shredded

1 lemon, halved

Prepare your grill for direct cooking. Preheat your grill to a medium temperature of 250 to 325°F (121 to 163°C).

Spread the asparagus out on a large piece of foil and drizzle with olive oil. Sprinkle the rub on the asparagus and mix around.

Place the foil on a grill grate (or place the asparagus in a veggie basket). Grill for 10 minutes, or until tender. Add the cheese and continue to cook for an additional 5 minutes. You want the asparagus to be crisp yet tender, and not mushy. Timing will vary depending on how hot the grill is.

Remove the asparagus from the heat and squeeze lemon juice over it right before serving.

DEEP-DISH PIZZA PIE

SON SEEKERS BBQ

Who doesn't love pizza? Cooking it on the grill in a cast-iron skillet is an easy way to bring a little more pizzazz to an already sought-after dish! This deep-dish pizza is packed with alluring pork flavors from the sausage, a mild caress of heat from the pepperoni and a sweet pizza sauce that will have your taste buds singing with every bite!

YIELD: 4 SERVINGS • COOK TIME: 30 MINUTES

1 lb (454 g) Italian sausage

2 (6.5-oz [184-g]) packages pizza crust mix, like Kroger

Cooking spray, butter flavor

Pinch of salt and pepper

1 (8-oz [225-g]) jar pizza sauce, divided

1 (6-oz [170-g]) package pepperoni

1 small yellow onion, chopped

1 green bell pepper, chopped

4 cups (452 g) shredded mozzarella cheese

Configure your grill for indirect cooking. Preheat to 350 to 400°F (177 to 204°C). Cook the sausage for 6 to 8 minutes.

Mix the pizza crust according to the instructions on the package, and let the dough rise. Roll it out to the size of your skillet.

Spray a large 10- to 12-inch (25- to 30-cm) cast-iron skillet with butter-flavored cooking spray. Place the crust in the skillet, forming it up the sides. Using a fork, poke holes into the crust. Lightly salt and pepper the crust. Place the skillet on the grill and cook for 3 to 5 minutes, until the crust is slightly browned.

Spread half the jar of pizza sauce onto the crust. Add a layer of sausage, pepperoni, onion and green pepper. Spoon on a little more pizza sauce, and then top off with shredded cheese. Return to the grill and cook for 6 to 8 minutes. Rotate your skillet and continue to cook for 6 to 8 additional minutes, or until the cheese is golden brown.

Remove the pizza from the skillet (it should slide right out) and place it on a cooling rack. Let the pizza rest for 5 to 10 minutes before slicing.

OPERATION BBQ RELIEF IN ACTION

Son Seekers BBQ Team's involvement in OBR actually predates OBR, because it started out as an organization that cooked for returning troops. It was referred to as Operation BBQ.

We were asked by Lynn Entrekin if we would like to go to Fort Campbell in 2009 and cook for some returning troops. Our team, along with three other BBQ teams, went down and cooked a bunch of food for approximately 800 folks (soldiers and family members). During the next few years we returned to Fort Campbell and cooked for returning troops on two or three different occasions.

The commanding officer presented each of our teams with a plaque and an Airborne Flag to thank us for supporting our troops. We have proudly displayed these items in our cooking trailer ever since.

To this day when considering all of the wonderful things we have been able to do through BBQ, going to Fort Campbell and cooking for our troops has been our greatest honor.

—JOHNNY SPEIGHT AND JIM HERRENBRUCK,
Son Seekers BBQ

DIVA Q'S GRILLED PANZANELLA SALAD

DIVA Q, AKA DANIELLE BENNETT

This classic Tuscan salad is a popular summer dish that uses tomatoes and basil fresh from the garden! This Italian bread and tomato salad manages to be light and refreshing, yet it's still hearty enough to eat for supper or lunch.

YIELD: 4 SERVINGS • COOK TIME: 15 MINUTES

PANZANELLA SALAD

½ cup (120 ml) extra-virgin olive oil

2 French bread loaves, cut into 1" (2.5-cm) slices, total of 12 slices

Salt and pepper

2 lb (907 g) cherry tomatoes

2 red onions, sliced in half, cores intact

BASIL PESTO

1 bunch basil leaves

¾ cup (177 ml) extra-virgin olive oil

½ cup (70 g) pine nuts

½ cup (90 g) shredded Parmesan cheese

2 cloves smoked garlic

½ tsp kosher salt

½ tsp freshly ground black pepper

Salt and pepper, to taste

¼ cup (45 g) shredded Parmesan cheese

10 basil leaves

To make the salad, brush the olive oil on the French loaf slices. Season the bread slices with salt and pepper. Thread the cherry tomatoes onto metal skewers. Preheat your grill for medium-high heat, 375 to 450°F (190 to 232°C).

Grill the bread slices and tomatoes 2 to 3 minutes per side, or until lightly charred. Grill the onions 6 to 7 minutes, until charred and softened. Remove them from the grill.

Cut the bread slices and onions into bite-size pieces and place them into a large bowl. Add the tomatoes and mix.

To make the pesto, add all of the pesto ingredients to a food processor and pulse until smooth. Toss the pesto with the bread mixture. Season your salad with salt and pepper, and add the Parmesan cheese and basil leaves.

NUKE-SEARED SQUID *WITH* BOMBAY CURRY-ISH HOISIN KETCHUP

CHRIS CAPELL, DIZZY PIG BBQ TEAM

Years ago Chris began cooking fresh squid against the will of all the folks who think of squid as fish bait. He learned two tricks for cooking squid: cook it super-hot-and-fast, and use a small, tender squid. When properly cooked, the texture is amazing, and it's a surprisingly light and refreshing dish that can act as an appetizer, be served in a salad or turned into a side.

YIELD: 3–4 SERVINGS • COOK TIME: 2 MINUTES

8–10 fresh whole squid (6" [15-cm] long bodies are the most tender)

MARINADE

2 tsp (9 g) fresh grated ginger

1–2 cloves garlic, smashed

1 tbsp (15 ml) sesame oil

2 tbsp (30 ml) vegetable, peanut or other oil

¼ cup (60 ml) soy sauce

1 tsp Dizzy Pig Cow Lick rub or your favorite rub

SAUCE

¼ cup (61 g) ketchup

1 tbsp (15 ml) hoisin sauce

1 tsp sesame oil

1 tsp Dizzy Pig Bombay Curry-ish or your favorite curry blend

Select fresh squid without a strong fishy smell. Asian markets often have fresh squid on ice. Long fat squid are tougher, shorter thin squid are the most tender. For the best results, target a 6- to 7-inch (15- to 18-cm) body length.

Clean the squid under cold running water. Gently pull on the tentacles to remove most of the entrails from the body. Remove the stiff, clear cartilage, which looks like a piece of plastic, and any remaining innards. Cut the tentacles off just above the "eye" where the squid ink is, and reserve. (The body has a thin membrane that should be removed, and this can be done simply by pulling it off with your fingers.)

To make the marinade, combine all the ingredients in a bowl. Place the tentacles in the marinade. Store in the fridge for a minimum of 1 hour (or as long as overnight).

To make the sauce, combine the ingredients in a bowl and reserve.

Prepare your grill for direct grilling over a VERY hot fire, 500 to 600°F (260 to 316°C). When you cannot get your hands anywhere near the fire, it is hot enough. To prevent the squid from falling through the cooking grate, use a perforated pan, or use two cooking grates rotated perpendicular to each other.

Using long tongs and gloves, sear the squid bodies and tentacles for approximately 30 to 45 seconds per side. Sizzling, popping and whistling is normal—enjoy the music!

Sauce each side, cooking an additional 15 to 20 seconds per side to char the sauce.

Remove, slice into thin rings and serve immediately.

DUTCH OVEN BBQ BEANS

SMOKE ON WHEELS BBQ TEAM

Homemade BBQ beans can be a magical delight! The sweetness of barbecue sauce, brown sugar, honey and molasses contrast the hot sauce, so these beans will make your palate sing! During the last hour of cooking, these savory, flavorful beans pick up the perfect amount of smokiness. You tuning up those vocal chords yet?

YIELD: 10–12 SERVINGS • COOK TIME: 6 HOURS

2 qt (2 L) water

2 tbsp (32 g) kosher salt

1 lb (454 g) small dried beans, such as great northern or pinto beans

½ lb (227 g) bacon, sliced into ½" (1.3-cm) strips

1 large sweet onion, diced

½ yellow bell pepper, finely diced

1 large jalapeño, finely diced

4 cloves garlic, pressed

5 cups (1 L) chicken stock or pork stock

1½ cups (355 ml) your favorite BBQ sauce

⅔ cup (147 g) dark brown sugar

⅓ cup (79 ml) honey

¼ cup (60 ml) molasses

¼ cup (60 g) yellow mustard

1 tbsp (15 ml) apple cider vinegar

1 tbsp (14 g) your favorite barbecue rub

1 tbsp (15 ml) hot sauce

In a large container, whisk together the water and salt until the salt has dissolved. Add the beans, cover and let stand overnight at room temperature. Drain and rinse the beans.

Place a large Dutch oven on the stovetop over medium-high heat. Add the bacon and cook until the fat has rendered and the bacon becomes crispy, about 7 to 10 minutes. Transfer the bacon to a paper towel–lined plate, leaving as much fat in your Dutch oven as possible.

Add the onion to your Dutch oven and cook, stirring occasionally, until the onion softens. Stir in the yellow pepper, jalapeño and garlic, and continue cooking for 4 to 5 minutes. Stir in the chicken (or pork) stock with the reserved bacon and beans. Bring to a boil, and then reduce the heat to low and simmer for an hour.

Preheat your grill to 300°F (149°C) while the beans are simmering.

After simmering the beans for 1 hour, stir in the BBQ sauce, brown sugar, honey, molasses, mustard, vinegar, barbecue rub and hot sauce. Cover and transfer to your grill. Cook the beans for 4 hours, stirring occasionally. Remove the cover and cook until the beans are tender throughout and the sauce has thickened, about 1 hour longer.

EASY GRILLED SWEET POTATOES

SWAMP BOYS BBQ TEAM

Many fruits and vegetables are great on the grill. Pineapple, peaches, tomatoes, squash, zucchini, green beans, corn on the cob, cabbage, eggplant, peppers, asparagus, onions, potatoes and sweet potatoes are just a few of my favorites that taste great with a little lovin' from a live fire. Grilling is a simple way to showcase the flavor of what you're cooking. You can use your microwave to speed up the cook time on this by about an hour.

YIELD: 4 SERVINGS · COOK TIME: 8 MINUTES

4 sweet potatoes, 1 per person

1 tbsp (15 ml) extra-virgin olive oil

¼ tsp kosher salt, divided

⅛ tsp fresh cracked black pepper, divided

Set up your grill for direct cooking. Preheat your grill to 400 to 450°F (204 to 232°C).

Wash the sweet potatoes and pierce them several times with a fork. Microwave on high for 5 minutes, flip and cook for 2 more minutes, until the potatoes begin to feel soft. Remove the potatoes from the microwave. Apply a light coating of olive oil to the outside skin of each potato. Apply a sprinkle of kosher salt. Use half the salt to cover the outside skin of each potato. Cut each potato lengthwise, and then cut in half again to create quarter wedges. Lightly oil the orange flesh, and then season with the remaining kosher salt and pepper.

Place the potato wedges on the grill, flesh-side down. Cook for 3 to 4 minutes on each side to add caramelization, grill marks and smoke flavor. You can use GrillGrates to make it easier.

These sweet potato wedges are great eaten straight off the grill. Or for a sweet and savory version, top with some cinnamon butter.

FIRE-ROASTED VEGGIE DIP

THE SHED BBQ TEAM

Turn your next party into a fiesta with this fire-roasted corn and veggie dip! A combination of corn, bell peppers, jalapeños, onions and cheese, this deeply satisfying recipe leaves room to play with flavors of the dip. Try adding some jalapeño seeds and red pepper flakes for the heat lovers out there!

YIELD: 3 SERVINGS • COOK TIME: 10 MINUTES

3 ears fresh, sweet corn

3 tbsp (44 g) mayonnaise, divided

5 tbsp (74 g) The Shed "Cluckin' Awesome" Rub, divided (available in Bass Pro Shops nationwide)

1 medium red onion

1 red bell pepper

1 orange bell pepper

1 yellow bell pepper

3 tbsp (45 ml) vegetable oil (or PAM high-heat grilling nonstick spray)

3 fresh jalapeños

4 oz (113 g) cream cheese, softened

3 tbsp (45 ml) heavy whipping cream

½ tbsp (7 ml) olive oil

Black pepper and sea salt, to taste

Prepare your grill for direct cooking and preheat to 400°F (204°C).

Remove the husk and silk from each ear of corn. Evenly coat each ear of corn with 1 tablespoon (15 g) of mayonnaise and 1 tablespoon (15 g) of rub. Slice the onion and bell peppers into rings, and coat lightly with oil or nonstick spray.

Grill the corn, onion, bell peppers and jalapeños (whole) over high heat for about 10 minutes, or until tender. Flip the vegetables every 2 to 3 minutes to obtain a flavorful char on all sides. Once the vegetables are grilled to your liking, remove them from the grill and place them on the counter to cool to room temperature.

Mix together the cream cheese, whipping cream, olive oil and remaining 2 tablespoons (30 g) of rub. Slice the kernels off the cob, and then use the back side of your knife to "milk" the corn cob by scraping from top to bottom. This releases small, sweet corn seeds and creamy milk from the corn cob—use it all!

Dice the remaining veggies and combine all the ingredients, adding salt and pepper to taste.

GREEN MOUNTAIN APPLE BACON *AND* SAUSAGE BBQ PIZZA

SWEET BREATHE BBQ TEAM

Bacon, sausage, apples and onions, cooked with a hint of maple syrup, top off this sweet and savory mountain of a pizza. While maple and apple are flavors of New England, you can use your favorite barbecue sauce to give this pizza some flavor of your own.

YIELD: 2 PIZZAS • COOK TIME: 25–30 MINUTES

16 oz (454 g) pizza dough, prepared or homemade

1 lb (454 g) ground bulk sausage

8 thick slices smoked bacon

1 sweet onion, peeled and thinly sliced

2 apples, peeled, cored and thinly sliced

Salt and pepper

2 tbsp (30 ml) maple syrup

½ tsp ground cinnamon

Flour or cornmeal

1 cup (236 ml) your favorite BBQ sauce, divided

12 oz (340 g) cheddar cheese, shredded (we prefer extra sharp), divided

Remove the dough from the refrigerator and let it come to room temperature.

In a cast-iron skillet on the stovetop over medium heat, cook the sausage for 6 to 8 minutes, or until browned. Remove from the heat, drain the grease and let cool on a plate. Place the bacon in the same skillet and cook for 5 to 6 minutes on each side, then remove it from the pan and chop it into ½-inch (1.3-cm) pieces.

Reduce the heat to medium-low and add the sliced onion and apples to the pan. Add salt and pepper to taste. Cook in the bacon fat until softened, about 5 minutes. Add the maple syrup and cinnamon, and cook for 2 minutes.

Prepare your grill for direct high-heat cooking (400 to 500°F [204 to 260°C]).

Cut the pizza dough in half. Working with one half at a time, shape the dough and flatten it on a lightly floured surface. Stretch the dough by hand, or use a rolling pin, and form it to the desired thickness and shape, about 7 to 8 inches (18 to 20 cm) in diameter. Using a knife or fork, poke a few holes in the dough. This helps prevent pockets of air from forming while the dough is cooking. Repeat the process with the second piece of dough.

Using a pizza peel that is lightly coated with flour or cornmeal, slide the dough onto the hot grate and let it cook for 2 to 3 minutes, until the dough is lightly browned. Using a pizza peel or spatula, remove the dough from the grill and place it grilled-side up.

Brush on ½ cup (120 ml) of the BBQ sauce. Sprinkle on half of each topping: cheddar cheese, crumbled sausage, bacon bits, apples and onions.

Slide the pizza back onto the grill. Close the lid and cook for 2 to 3 minutes, until the bottom is browned and the cheese is melted. Using a pizza peel, remove your pizza from the grill and let it rest for a couple of minutes before slicing. Repeat to make the second pizza.

GRILLED BRUSCHETTA

A MAZIE Q

What could be more summery than fresh plum tomatoes heaped on toasted bread that's slathered with garlic and cheese? Absolutely nothing! This versatile recipe works as a first course, a side or even a whole meal.

YIELD: 6–8 SERVINGS • COOK TIME: 7 MINUTES

TOMATO MIXTURE

7 plum tomatoes, seeded

2–4 cloves garlic, chopped, to taste

¼ cup (60 ml) olive oil (the greener the better, so look for cold pressed)

⅓ cup (79 ml) balsamic vinegar

½ cup (21 g) basil, chiffonade or chopped

A generous amount of salt and freshly cracked black pepper (approximatly ½ tsp each)

BREAD DIP

½ cup (120 ml) water with ¾ tbsp (11 g) chicken base, or ½ cup (120 ml) chicken stock

¼ cup (57 g) butter

½ tbsp (6 g) Italian seasoning or fresh herbs, such as rosemary, thyme and marjoram

4 cloves garlic

1 baguette

Shredded or sliced cheese of choice, or blend of mozzarella, provolone and fontina

To make the tomato mixture, cut and seed the plum tomatoes, and then place them in a large bowl. Chop the garlic and add it to the tomatoes. Go with 4 cloves if you enjoy the taste of garlic, but adjust this to your preference. Try to use fresh garlic, instead of the chopped garlic in a jar, as fresh ingredients are more pungent and aromatic. Add the remaining ingredients and refrigerate for at least an hour.

To make the bread dip, combine all the ingredients in a pot on the stove. Heat until the butter is melted and the contents are warm. Do not let the mixture come to a boil. Let it stand for a few minutes to allow the flavors to bloom.

Heat your grill to low (250 to 275°F [121 to 135°C]) and build the hot charcoal on one side of the grill.

Slice the baguette in half lengthwise and brush generously with the bread dip. Place the baguette on your grill, directly over the hot charcoal, with the side containing the bread dip facing down. Let it toast for 1 to 2 minutes.

Flip the baguette over and move it away from the hot charcoals. Allow the heat to toast it for 3 to 4 minutes.

Add the cheese and place the lid on top of the grill. Cook until the cheese is melted and bubbly, about 5 to 7 minutes. Remove it from the heat, add the tomato mixture and serve.

NOTE: It is important to seed your tomatoes. Skipping seeding will water down the marinade and weaken both flavor and texture. Please remember to salt and pepper on the heavy side. Salt and pepper amounts can fluctuate based off of the integrity of the ingredients in your area. Lastly, always taste the tomatoes when you remove them from the fridge. Refrigerating marinated tomatoes allows full flavor to come through and sometimes adjustments to seasonings are necessary.

GRILLED JALAPEÑO CREAMED CORN

GUADALUPE BBQ COMPANY

Grilling corn adds another depth of flavor to this cream corn recipe. You'll love the spicy and savory flavor combos of this creamy, cheesy dish. Get ready to shout "YUM!"

YIELD: 4 CUPS (940 G) • COOK TIME: 25 MINUTES

6 ears fresh corn, husks on

1 (8-oz [225-g]) block cream cheese, softened and cubed

3 fresh jalapeño peppers, cored, seeded and minced

¼ cup (57 g) butter, softened

Salt and pepper, to taste

Minced chives, for garnish, optional

Submerge the corn in a container of water for 20 minutes prior to grilling.

Configure your grill for direct cooking, and let the grill get hot at 350 to 450°F (177 to 232°C).

Remove the corn from the water, and shake out any excess water.

Put the corn, still in wet husks, directly on the grill. Cook for 15 to 20 minutes. Turn occasionally, about every 4 to 5 minutes, until the outer husks appear charred and dried.

Remove the corn from its husk and cut the kernels off the cob. Immediately place the corn kernels in a cast-iron pot or pan that is grill safe. Add the cream cheese, minced jalapeño and butter. Season to your preference.

Place the pan on the grill. Cook for about 5 minutes and stir to incorporate all the ingredients. Garnish with chives if desired. Serve and enjoy.

GRILLED SMOKED CAULIFLOWER RICE

RIBS WITHIN BBQ TEAM

It's nice to substitute a vegetable in place of a starch, and this cauliflower rice is a healthy protein and fiber-packed alternative to white rice. It's also a great way to squeeze more servings of vegetables into your day. Adding your choice of rub helps makes this smoky dish all your own.

YIELD: 4–6 SERVINGS • COOK TIME: 30 MINUTES

1 head cauliflower

1 tbsp (15 ml) olive oil, plus more for finishing

½ cup (112 g) Ribs Within Secret Rub or your favorite BBQ rub

1 cup (90 g) applewood chips, or a small applewood chunk

Butter, optional

Parsley

Sea salt, to taste

Configure your grill for two-zone cooking. Ideally, you want medium-high heat 350 to 375°F (177 to 191°C).

Rinse the head of cauliflower, remove any green leaves and then cut off the stem. Rub the cauliflower with a tablespoon (15 ml) of olive oil and your favorite rub. Make sure you apply the rub to the top and bottom of the cauliflower.

Place the smoking chips over high heat and the cauliflower on the indirect side of the grill. Smoke for 20 minutes. Move the cauliflower to the direct cooking zone. Grill directly, top-side up, for 10 minutes. Flip and continue to cook over direct heat with the top of the cauliflower facing down, for an additional 5 minutes. Cool for 5 minutes. Cut the cauliflower in chunks and put it in a food processor. Pulse until it looks like rice grains; then add butter (if using), olive oil, parsley and salt to taste.

Serve as a healthy BBQ side.

GRILLED PEACH SMOKJITO

PORK BARREL BBQ

Savor some sweet and juicy peaches this summer with a recipe to showcase a favorite seasonal fruit. We consider a good drink an essential side for any barbecue. This one is perfect for outdoor gatherings or just kicking back on the porch, so you'll want to make a whole batch of these peachy smokjitos.

YIELD: 4 SERVINGS • COOK TIME: 7 MINUTES

8 ripe peaches

1 tbsp (6 g) grated lime peel

1 cup (236 ml) fresh lime juice (about 4 large limes)

¾ cup (144 g) sugar

½ cup (14 g) packed mint leaves

4 cups (946 ml) lemon-lime soda, chilled

2 cups (473 ml) white rum

Crushed ice

Mint sprigs

Preheat your grill to medium-high at 350 to 400°F (177 to 204°C). Cut the peaches in half and place them on the grill, cut-side down. Grill them with the lid on for 5 to 7 minutes, until the peaches are lightly browned. Remove the peaches from the grill and cool for 10 minutes.

Remove the skin from 7 of the peaches and cut them into 1-inch (2.5-cm) pieces. Place them in a blender or food processor and process until smooth. Pour the peach purée through a strainer into a bowl and throw away the solids. Cut the remaining peach into wedges.

In a large pitcher, combine the lime peel, lime juice, sugar and mint leaves. Crush well using a muddler. Add the peach purée, lemon-lime soda and rum. Stir until the sugar dissolves.

Fill the glasses with crushed ice and pour your peach mojito mixture over the ice. Garnish with mint sprigs and grilled peach wedges.

GRILLED STUFFED SHRIMP MUSHROOMS

BABEÉ BLUE'S BBQ

Mushrooms, grilled to perfection and stuffed with shrimp—that'll make your taste buds jump!

The mixture of pepper and earthy seasonings shines through after you incorporate it into the cheese filling. Sprinkle it onto the shrimp prior to grilling and watch what happens. Serve these mushrooms at your next gathering and we're sure your guests will agree with the judges that this recipe is a winner!

YIELD: 12 MUSHROOMS • COOK TIME: 15 MINUTES

12 large mushrooms

8 oz (227 g) pepper Jack cheese, grated

4 oz (113 g) cream cheese, softened

Weber Carne Asada Seasoning or favorite steak seasoning

4 wooden skewers, soaked in water for 30 minutes

12 medium shrimp, peeled and deveined

1 tbsp (15 ml) cooking oil

2–3 tbsp (6–9 g) chives, for garnish

Remove the mushroom stems and clean the mushrooms. In a mixing bowl, combine the pepper Jack and cream cheese. Season the cheese to your liking with the Weber Carne Asada Seasoning or your favorite steak seasoning. Stuff the mushrooms with the mixture, and then set them aside.

Skewer 3 shrimp per wooden skewer and brush with oil. Apply a light coating of Carne Asada Seasoning.

Grill the mushrooms at medium to low heat on a gas grill, or 325°F (163°C) indirect heat over charcoal, for about 8 to 10 minutes.

Grill the shrimp over direct, medium heat for 2 to 3 minutes. Flip the shrimp and cook for an additional 2 to 3 minutes. Remove the shrimp from the skewers. Place one shrimp on each mushroom and garnish with chives to serve!

GRILLED VEGETABLE RATATOUILLE

PORK BARREL BBQ

Want a vegetable dish that even the reddest of meat eaters will love? This French classic, kicked up on the grill, offers a great side dish for a grilled steak or smoked ribs. You can easily turn this recipe into a pasta salad or serve it as a vegetarian entrée. Equally great served hot or at room temperature, this is a versatile dish you'll want in your repertoire.

YIELD: 12 SERVINGS • COOK TIME: 8 MINUTES

1 zucchini, quartered lengthwise

1 yellow squash, quartered lengthwise

1 eggplant, cut into ½" (1.3-cm) thick rounds

1 red onion, cut into ½" (1.3-cm) thick rounds

1 red bell pepper, quartered and seeded

1 yellow bell pepper, quartered and seeded

2 (8-oz [227-g]) packages baby portobello mushrooms

1 pint (300 g) cherry tomatoes

⅔ cup (158 ml) extra-virgin olive oil, divided

2 tbsp (28 g) Pork Barrel BBQ All-American Spice Rub or your favorite rub

2 tbsp (30 ml) balsamic vinegar

¼ cup (10 g) finely chopped fresh basil leaves

2 tbsp (6 g) finely chopped fresh oregano leaves

¼ tsp kosher salt

4 cloves garlic, minced

Configure your grill for direct cooking and preheat to medium-high at 350 to 400°F (177 to 204°C). Toss the vegetables and ½ cup (120 ml) of olive oil in a large mixing bowl. Sprinkle with Pork Barrel BBQ All-American Spice Rub and toss to coat.

Grill the cut vegetables and mushrooms, covered with a grill lid, 4 minutes on each side or until tender. Grill the tomatoes for 4 minutes, turning occasionally.

Remove the vegetables from the grill, coarsely chop and place them in a large bowl. Combine the remaining olive oil with the vinegar, basil, oregano, salt and garlic; toss gently. Serve at room temperature.

CRISPY CRUST JALAPEÑO POPPER PIZZA

FEEDING FRIENDZ

This jalapeño popper pizza is one of Tim and Wendy's specialty dishes that's always a hit at their backyard barbecue gatherings or at barbecue contests when friends gather to socialize. A prepared pizza crust, topped with marinara sauce, cream cheese, jalapeño slices, bacon pieces and shredded cheese is baked until golden brown. Plan on making more than one, because this smoky pile of deliciousness goes fast!

YIELD: 6 SERVINGS • COOK TIME: 15 MINUTES

1 (1-lb [454-g]) package prepared pizza dough

4 oz (113 g) cream cheese, softened

2 tsp (7 g) minced garlic

2 scallions, white and green parts, finely chopped

1 tbsp (3 g) taco seasoning

¼ cup (30 g) panko breadcrumbs, plus more for dusting

1 tbsp (15 ml) olive oil, divided

1 cup (237 ml) marinara sauce

1 cup (130 g) shredded Monterey Jack cheese

4 jalapeño peppers, cored, seeded and thinly sliced

1 cup (130 g) shredded pepper Jack cheese

3–4 slices bacon, cooked and crumbled

Prepare a hot grill, 400 to 450°F (204 to 232°C).

Roll out the dough as thin or thick as you prefer to fit a grill pan.

In a medium bowl, combine the cream cheese, garlic, scallions and taco seasoning; then set aside. In a small bowl, toss the panko with half of the olive oil, and set aside.

Spread the marinara sauce over the pizza dough. Dust the outer edges with the panko crumbs.

Sprinkle the Monterey Jack cheese over the sauce, and then top generously with the sliced jalapeños.

Scatter small dollops of the cream cheese mixture over the pizza. Sprinkle with the pepper Jack cheese and bacon pieces. Drizzle the remaining ½ tablespoon (7 ml) of olive oil over the top.

Place the pan on the grill, close the lid and bake for 10 to 15 minutes, or until the cheese is melted and the crust browned.

KANSAS CAVIAR

SLAUGHTERHOUSE FIVE BBQ TEAM

This dish, aptly named Kansas Caviar, serves as a tribute to some of the Kansas-grown crops featured in the dish: corn and edamame. It's a nice complement to the smoke, salt, vinegar and fat of a good barbecue plate, but it makes a great side dish for just about any entrée you are serving.

YIELD: 15 SERVINGS • COOK TIME: 40 MINUTES

VEGETABLES

1 lb (454 g) frozen corn kernels, thawed

1 lb (454 g) frozen edamame, shelled

1 tsp salt

½ cup (120 ml) water

1 lb (454 g) red bell peppers, stemmed, roasted, peeled and diced ¼" (6 mm) thick

½ lb (227 g) shredded carrot

1 bunch cilantro leaves, chopped

HONEY LIME DRESSING

1 tbsp (18 g) kosher salt

¼ tsp ground mustard powder

1 cup (236 ml) fresh lime juice

1 tbsp (8 g) chopped pickled jalapeño

3 tbsp (44 ml) honey

1 cup (236 ml) canola oil

PICKLED RED ONIONS

3 medium red onions, diced into ¼" (6-mm) cubes

4 cups (946 ml) water, divided

½ cup (144 g) kosher salt

½ cup (96 g) sugar

2 cups (473 ml) apple cider vinegar

Heat a skillet on a medium-high grill, 400 to 450°F (204 to 232°C). Let the skillet get very hot, which should take about 2 minutes.

To make the vegetables, add the corn to the skillet and char, stirring when the corn begins to pop in the skillet. Add the edamame, salt and water. Continue to cook over medium-high heat until the edamame is cooked through and the water evaporates. Remove the skillet from the heat and pour the corn and edamame mixture into a mixing bowl. Place it in the refrigerator, uncovered, and let the mixture cool until thoroughly chilled.

To make the dressing, in a small bowl, mix the kosher salt and ground mustard powder. Stir to blend. In a blender, purée the lime juice, pickled jalapeño and honey. With the blender running on medium speed, sprinkle in the mustard and salt mixture, and blend for 30 seconds. Slowly drizzle in the oil to emulsify the dressing. Store in an airtight container, refrigerated, until ready to use. Reserve ½ cup (120 ml) for this recipe and save the rest for another use.

To make the pickled onions, place the red onions in a large Tupperware container. In a 2-quart (2-L) saucepot, bring 3 cups (710 ml) of the water to a boil and then pour it over the onions. After a minute, drain in a fine-mesh strainer. Place the poached onions back in the Tupperware container.

Using the same 2-quart (2-L) pot, bring the kosher salt, sugar and apple cider vinegar to a boil and pour over the onions. Add the remaining 1 cup (236 ml) water and cover the container. Let the contents cool to room temperature and then place in the refrigerator. Keep refrigerated until ready to use. Reserve ½ pound (227 g) for this recipe and save the rest for another use.

Once the corn-edamame mixture is chilled, add the peppers, carrot and cilantro and stir to combine. Cover the bowl and refrigerate for 30 minutes. When you're ready, stir the reserved dressing into the corn mixture, and serve with a side of the pickled onions.

MESQUITE-GRILLED SHRIMP ᴬᴺᴰ AVOCADO SALAD

LOOT N' BOOTY BBQ TEAM

Loot N' Booty BBQ's zesty stuffed avocado, loaded with fresh vegetables and roasted corn, will certainly refresh you on a hot day! Mesquite shrimp with lime wedges tops it off, adding to the revivification! We like to cook this dish on a Weber charcoal grill, but you can certainly prepare it on any smoker or grill.

YIELD: 4 SERVINGS • COOK TIME: 15 MINUTES

1 small chunk mesquite wood

1 ear of corn, husked

2¼ tsp (7 g) Loot N' Booty BBQ Everything Rub or your favorite rub, divided

16 medium-to-large raw shrimp, shelled and deveined

1 tsp Loot N' Booty BBQ Gold Star Chicken Rub or favorite rub, divided

4 wood skewers, soaked in water for 20 minutes

Avocado oil

GUACAMOLE

2 ripe avocados

⅛ cup (19 g) red onion, diced

¼ cup (40 g) Roma tomatoes, diced

1 tsp jalapeño, diced

⅛ cup (6 g) cilantro, diced

2 cups (681 g) shredded red cabbage

2 limes, halved and cut into wedges

½ tsp sesame oil

Fill a charcoal chimney about three-fourths full of Kingsford mesquite charcoal and ignite with a Weber lighter cube. While the coals are getting ready, season your corn with 1 teaspoon of Loot N' Booty Everything Rub.

When the coals have "grayed over" (this takes about 15 to 20 minutes), dump them into the bottom of the Weber grill, and then spread them into an even layer. Put the small chunk of mesquite wood in the center of the coals, and then place the cooking grate and lid on the grill. Make sure the top and bottom vents are fully open.

After approximately 15 minutes, or until you see a light blue smoke coming from the top vent, place the corn cob on the grill. Cook for 8 to 10 minutes, rotating occasionally, until the corn has caramelized and has turned golden brown. Remove the corn and set aside.

Skewer 4 shrimp, one at a time, on each skewer, leaving space between each shrimp. Season the shrimp with ¼ teaspoon of Loot N' Booty BBQ Everything Rub and ¼ teaspoon of Loot N' Booty BBQ Gold Star Chicken Rub per skewer. Lightly coat the shrimp with avocado oil, about ¼ teaspoon per skewer.

Place the shrimp skewers evenly on the cooking grate. After 1 to 1½ minutes, flip the skewers and cook for another 1 to 1½ minutes. When the shrimp are pink and no longer gray, they are done. Remove the shrimp and let them rest at room temperature.

To make the guacamole, halve the avocados and remove the pits. Scrape out the avocado and set the empty shells aside. Mash the avocado into a smooth yet chunky texture. Add the onion, tomatoes, jalapeño, cilantro and cabbage; stir to combine.

(continued)

Cut the corn kernels off the cob and add them to the avocado mixture. Squeeze the juice from ½ a lime into the avocado mixture and add ¼ teaspoon of Loot N' Booty BBQ Everything Rub. Stir to combine. Drizzle the sesame oil over the avocado mixture and stir to combine.

Fill each avocado shell with a quarter of the avocado mixture and top each with 4 shrimp. Garnish the tops of the shrimp with any leftover cilantro and onion. Serve with a lime wedge.

OPERATION BBQ RELIEF IN ACTION

One of the amazing things that I love about BBQ is the people I get to meet throughout the country. I have competed at the best and biggest competitions in the world and met so many people who share my passion for BBQ. I met Mark Lambert several years ago at one of those competitions when Operation BBQ Relief was just gaining momentum. He explained OBR's mission and values and I knew that I wanted to help and give back in any way I could.

—STERLING SMITH, *Loot N' Booty BBQ*

MEXICAN CORN DIP

HERE PIGGY PIGGY BBQ

Smoking this dip adds another flavor dimension to the cheese, but you can also enjoy this dish without smoking it. This dip holds just the right combination of heat from the jalapeños, sweetness from the corn and enticing zip from the rest of the ingredients that'll keep you dipping over and over and over until it's gone.

YIELD: 6 SERVINGS • COOK TIME: 30–60 MINUTES

3 (8-oz [227-g]) blocks of cream cheese

Applewood chips, optional

1 (11-oz [312-g]) can Mexican corn, drained

1 (6-oz [170-g]) can black olives, drained and chopped

1 red bell pepper, seeded and chopped

½ (12-oz [340-g]) jar jalapeños, drained

1 (1-oz [28-g]) envelope Hidden Valley Ranch dressing

Tortilla chips or crackers, for serving

Prepare your smoker for a cold smoke, no higher than 90°F (32°C).

Remove the cream cheese from the refrigerator and allow it to come up to room temperature, about 30 minutes.

Unwrap the blocks of cream cheese, and place them in an aluminum half pan. Put the pan on the smoker.

A handful of applewood chips gives the soft cheese a nice flavor, but you don't need much smoke. The cheese will pick up some smoke flavor from the charcoal, so if you use wood, 8 or 10 small chips should suffice. Allow the cheese to cold smoke for 30 to 60 minutes, depending on how much smoke flavor you want to infuse, and then remove it from the smoker.

Place all the remaining ingredients into the half pan. Stir the contents and serve with your favorite tortilla chips or crackers.

PEACH BACON BRISKET SMOKED BEANS

YES, DEAR BBQ

This medley of rubs and spices combines heat from ground cayenne with the sweet flavors and textures of sliced peaches! Add in some smoked brisket, along with chopped bacon, and this baked bean recipe becomes so sexy it's irresistible!

YIELD: 4 SERVINGS • COOK TIME: 2½ HOURS

2 cups (310 g) fresh or frozen peach slices

⅓ cup (64 g) granulated sugar

½ tsp ground cinnamon

4 slices bacon

1 red bell pepper, seeded and diced

1 green bell pepper, seeded and diced

1 yellow bell pepper, seeded and diced

2 tbsp (30 ml) apple juice or water

1 (15-oz [425-g]) can black beans, drained

1 (15-oz [425-g]) can red beans, drained

1 (28-oz [794-g]) can Bush's Original baked beans

1 (28-oz [794-g]) can Bush's Country Style baked beans

1 cup (135 g) leftover chopped brisket (or leftover meat of choice)

1 cup (220 g) brown sugar

4 oz (113 g) yellow mustard

1¼ cups (296 ml) sweet BBQ sauce (preferably Yes, Dear BBQ Red Sauce)

½ cup (112 g) all-purpose BBQ rub

3 tbsp (42 g) spicy BBQ rub

1 tsp chipotle powder

1 tsp cayenne powder

Place the peach slices, granulated sugar and cinnamon into a medium bowl and mix. Set it aside and stir occasionally to release the peach juices, about 30 minutes.

Meanwhile, in a large frying pan, cook the bacon over medium heat until it's well browned and the fat has rendered, about 8 minutes. Remove the bacon from the pan, crumble and set aside. Place the diced peppers into the pan and sauté for 2 to 3 minutes until slightly tender. Pour the apple juice or water into the pan and stir with a wooden spoon to scrape up any brown bits from the bottom.

Pour all the remaining ingredients, along with the cooked bacon, peaches and peach juice, into the pan and stir to combine. Stir occasionally until warmed through, 5 to 10 minutes.

Pour the contents of the pan into a disposable aluminum pan and place it on a preheated smoker set to 250°F (121°C). Cook on the smoker for 1 to 2 hours, stirring occasionally until the beans have thickened slightly.

Remove the beans from your smoker and enjoy.

SMOKED PIG CANDY BACON NUTS

CAN U SMELL MY PITS

These nuts—sweet and salty with a touch of heat, and with bits of pig candy—tend to be a real crowd-pleaser. At one barbecue contest, numerous competition cooks gnawed a batch of smoked pig candy bacon nuts down to nothing but the aluminum tray! This dish is great for parties, and is a nice holiday gift idea.

YIELD: 6–8 SERVINGS • COOK TIME: 10 MINUTES

1½ lb (680 g) thick-cut bacon

2 cups (473 ml) water

1¼ cups (240 g) turbinado sugar

1 lb (454 g) cashews, roasted and unsalted

10 oz (284 g) walnuts

10 oz (284 g) pecans

10 oz (284 g) almonds

1 tsp ground cinnamon

1 tsp allspice

½ tsp cayenne pepper

Prepare your grill for direct grilling and heat to 400 to 450°F (204 to 230°C). A 22-inch (56-cm) Discada plow disc grill fits perfectly in a Weber Kettle. A cast-iron skillet that is 12 inches (30 cm) or bigger will also work just fine, but you will have to cook in two batches. Place the pan on the cooking grate.

Cut the bacon into ¾-inch (2-cm) pieces. Heat the pan on the grill and partially cook the bacon pieces until they start to crisp, about 3 to 5 minutes. You want to leave some of the fat not rendered (it will render more in the next step, adding bacon salty goodness to the nuts). Drain and set aside.

This step will go really fast! Place the pan back on the grill and get it really hot (400°F [204°C]). Add the water, sugar, nuts and bacon. Stir continuously, constantly scraping the bottom of the pan and turning the nuts (they will burn if not constantly moving). Continue to stir until all the water evaporates and the sugar starts to caramelize, about 5 minutes.

Once the sugar has caramelized and the nuts are glazed and shiny, there should be very little sugar at the bottom of the pan. Remove the nuts from the heat and dust with the cinnamon, allspice and cayenne pepper (if you add spices too soon, they will burn). Mix well and pour the nuts onto a sheet pan. Spread the nuts out, let them cool for 5 minutes and enjoy.

CREAMY POLENTA ᴡɪᴛʜ WILD MUSHROOM MEDLEY

DISCO PIGS

This creamy polenta dish is one that mushroom lovers will enjoy! Spoon the sautéed mushrooms over smooth, cheesy polenta for a recipe that is delicious enough for your next dinner party.

YIELD: 6 SERVINGS • COOK TIME: 45–50 MINUTES

POLENTA

4 cups (946 ml) chicken stock

1 cup (170 g) stone-ground instant Italian cornmeal

2 tbsp (29 g) butter

½ lb (227 g) fontina cheese

½ cup (120 ml) heavy whipping cream

Salt and pepper, to taste

GORGONZOLA AND MUSHROOM SAUCE

8 wild mushrooms, such as porcini and baby portobellos

1 tbsp (14 g) butter

¼ cup (60 ml) Marsala wine

1 pint (473 ml) heavy whipping cream

½ cup (115 g) gorgonzola cheese

Sprigs of fresh rosemary

Prepare your grill or smoker for medium-high heat, about 400°F (204°C).

To make the polenta, bring the chicken stock to a boil in a 3-quart (2.8-L) pot. Add the cornmeal and cook for 5 to 6 minutes, until it's the consistency of porridge. Whisk in the butter, cheese and cream. Then season with salt and pepper and remove from the heat.

To make the mushroom sauce, sauté the mushrooms with the butter in a medium skillet, until they start to wilt and change color, about 6 to 7 minutes. Reduce with the Marsala wine. Add the cream and whisk in the gorgonzola. Cook until creamy and blended, about 10 minutes. Serve over the polenta and top with fresh rosemary.

PORK LOVER'S NACHOS

FIRE DOWN BELOW

Ed and Ginny Roach of Fire Down Below have made a big hit on the competition circuit, winning 1st place in pulled pork at the Jack Daniel's World Championship Invitational Barbecue contest. This nacho dish mixes their award-winning pulled pork with their chile con queso sauce atop tortilla chips. Add in their sweet and spicy barbecue sauce and you will have your friends and family begging for more!

YIELD: 10 SERVINGS • COOK TIME: 30 MINUTES

FIRE DOWN BELOW'S BBQ SAUCE

1½ cups (368 g) ketchup

¼ cup (60 ml) molasses

¼ cup (55 g) dark brown sugar

3 tbsp (44 ml) maple syrup

2 tbsp (31 g) prepared yellow mustard

2 tbsp (30 ml) apple cider vinegar

1 tbsp (15 ml) Worcestershire sauce

1 tbsp (15 ml) soy sauce

1 tbsp (15 ml) Heinz 57 Sauce

1 tbsp (15 ml) liquid smoke

1 tsp onion powder

1 tsp garlic powder

½ tsp kosher salt

½ tsp black pepper

½ tsp cayenne pepper

NACHOS

1 (10-oz [284-g]) bag your favorite tortilla chips, such as Tostitos scoops

2 cups (400 g) prepared BBQ pulled pork (page 44)

2 cups (500 g) Fire Down Below Amped-Up Chile Con Queso (page 207), heated, or your favorite cheese sauce

1 cup (90 g) sliced pickled jalapeños

Build a two-zone fire in a charcoal grill by situating the coals on one side, leaving the other side empty. Preheat the grill to 350°F (177°C).

To make the sauce, combine all the ingredients in a pan and heat over medium heat until blended, about 15 to 20 minutes. Store in the refrigerator until ready to use.

To make the nachos, spread the chips out in a cast-iron skillet or a baking sheet lined with foil. Place the pulled pork over the chips, pour on the chile con queso and then drizzle with the Fire Down Below BBQ sauce (or your favorite BBQ sauce). Top with the jalapeños.

Cook the nachos over indirect heat, away from the coals, for about 8 to 10 minutes, and serve.

CHEESY RANCHERO POTATOES

DISCO PIGS

These super creamy and cheesy potatoes are great to serve with brunch or dinner. The red and green bell pepper rings create a visual presentation that'll lure your guests over to the food table. Using your favorite barbecue sauce is a quick and simple way to control the level of spiciness these potatoes deliver.

YIELD: 6 SERVINGS • COOK TIME: 50 MINUTES

6 cups (1 kg) potatoes, peeled and sliced (about 5–6 medium potatoes)

¼ cup (57 g) butter

¼ cup (31 g) all-purpose flour

2 cups (473 ml) milk

1 tsp salt

¼ tsp black pepper

¾ cup (37 g) chopped scallions

8 oz (227 g) shredded sharp cheddar cheese

1 red bell pepper

1 green bell pepper

½–¾ cup (118–177 ml) your favorite BBQ sauce

Heat your grill or smoker to 350°F (177°C).

Boil the potatoes for about 20 minutes, or until al dente, and then set them aside. In a small saucepan, make a paste with the butter and flour over medium heat. Add the milk, salt and pepper, and cook, stirring until the mixture thickens. Stir in the scallions and cheese and remove from the heat.

Cut the stems from the bell peppers, and then remove the seeds from the cavity. Cut the peppers into rings, roughly ¼ inch (6 mm) thick.

Place half of the potatoes in a 13 x 9-inch (33 x 23-cm) pan or half pan. Pour half of the cheese mixture over the potatoes. Add the remaining half of the potatoes and top with the remaining cheese mixture. Lay the peppers on the top and drizzle with the BBQ sauce. Bake on the grill for 30 minutes, until the potatoes are tender and the cheese has melted.

RIBILICIOUS RIB TIPS

FAMOUS DAVE'S BBQ

Rib tips are inexpensive pieces of meat that have been trimmed off of spareribs, usually at the chine bone. Rib tips are very meaty and have a lot of fat running throughout. After the fat has been rendered out through the long smoking process, the remaining meat is succulent, juicy, flavorful and tender. When properly cooked, rib tips are a wonderful finger food or appetizer.

YIELD: 10 SERVINGS • COOK TIME: 5 HOURS

10 lb (5 kg) rib tips

2 cups (400 g) your favorite barbecue rub

Hickory wood chunks

Your favorite BBQ sauce

Have your butcher reserve 10 pounds (5 kg) of rib tips. Season all sides of the rib tips with your favorite barbecue rub.

Preheat your grill/smoker to 200 to 220°F (93 to 104°C) indirect with hickory wood chunks. Add more charcoal and hickory chunks every hour as needed. Keep the internal temperature of the grill at 200 to 225°F (93 to 107°C).

Place the ribs bone-side down but not directly over the hot coals. After 3 hours, remove the ribs from the grill and wrap them in aluminum foil. Hold them in the covered grill at 180 to 200°F (82 to 93°C) for 1½ to 2 hours, or until fork tender.

Build a real hot bed of coals over the entire bottom of the grill. Remove the ribs from the foil and place them back on the grill to add a char flavor. When the meat becomes bubbly, it is done, about 3 to 5 minutes.

Make sure to char off the bone-side membrane until it becomes papery and disintegrates. Then, slather the meat with BBQ sauce and let the heat caramelize the sauce. This caramelizing, along with the charring and slow cooking, is the secret to tender smoky ribs.

Using a cleaver and butcher block, chop the rib tips into bite-size pieces and serve warm.

SAUSAGE & CHEESE-STUFFED MUSHROOMS

UNCLE KENNY'S BBQ

These stuffed mushrooms are rich, creamy and inexpensive to make, but that doesn't mean they're not delicious! The cheese in the stuffing mixture picks up a hint of smoke, imbibing flavor. You can use your choice of mild, regular or hot sausage to make the stuffing mixture match your mood.

YIELD: ABOUT 40 MUSHROOMS • COOK TIME: 1 HOUR AND 15 MINUTES

1 (16-oz [454-g]) pack of Jimmy Dean Sage Sausage

Garlic salt, to your liking

1 (8-oz [227-g]) pack of cream cheese

1 (6-oz [170-g]) bag of Parmesan cheese

2 (16-oz [454-g]) packs of mushrooms

Fresh breadcrumbs

Olive oil

Set up your grill or smoker for indirect cooking. Uncle Kenny's choice is Southern Q Smokers.

Cook the sausage over medium heat for 10 to 15 minutes, or until the meat reaches an internal temperature of 160°F (71°C). Drain the meat and transfer to a bowl. Season with garlic salt and mix in the cream cheese. Add the Parmesan cheese, and stir until melted.

Rinse the mushrooms. Pop the stems out of each mushroom, and fill them with the stuffing mix.

Sprinkle the breadcrumbs over the top and then drizzle with olive oil. Cook the mushrooms at 240°F (116°C) for 1 hour.

OPERATION BBQ RELIEF IN ACTION

I started cooking BBQ in November 2004. After several years on the BBQ circuit, we made our first trip to the World Series of BBQ in 2012, where we were next to OBR. After spending a weekend around these guys, I began to follow them and loved what they were doing. Every year since then I would go and support OBR at the Royal. In 2016, I became the Florida State Lead and went on my first deployment to Nitro, West Virginia. Ever since then I want to help do more, and it's great to be a part of such a growing organization that is there for people in a time of need to help lift people with great food. But that is our BBQ family—always there for one another.

—KENNY NADEAU, *Uncle Kenny's BBQ & Catering*

SAUSAGE, BEAN & SPINACH HOT DIP

MOO COW

This smoky medley of hot ground sausage, pinto beans, cream cheese and Parmesan infused with wine and herbs turns this recipe into the ultimate spinach dip! Hearty enough to be a main dish, it is an appetizer that won't disappoint.

YIELD: 16 SERVINGS • COOK TIME: 35 MINUTES

1 sweet onion, diced

1 red bell pepper, diced

1 lb (454 g) hot ground pork sausage

2 cloves garlic, minced

1 tsp chopped fresh thyme

½ cup (120 ml) dry white wine

1 (8-oz [227-g]) package cream cheese, softened

1 (6-oz [170-g]) package fresh baby spinach, coarsely chopped

¼ tsp salt

1 (15-oz [425-g]) can pinto beans, drained and rinsed

½ cup (90 g) shredded Parmesan cheese

Corn chips, bell peppers and pretzel rods, for serving

Preheat a smoker or grill to 375°F (191°C).

Cook the diced onion, bell pepper and ground pork in a large cast-iron skillet on the stove over medium-high heat. Cook for 8 to 10 minutes, stirring often, or until the meat crumbles and is no longer pink. Drain. Stir in the garlic and thyme; cook for 1 minute. Stir in the wine; cook for 2 minutes or until the liquid has almost completely evaporated.

Add the cream cheese and cook, stirring constantly, for 2 minutes or until the cream cheese is melted. Stir in the spinach and salt and cook, stirring constantly, for 2 minutes or until the spinach is wilted. Gently stir in the beans.

Sprinkle with the Parmesan cheese, and place the skillet on your smoker. Bake for 18 to 20 minutes, or until the dip is golden brown.

Serve with corn chip scoops, bell pepper strips and pretzel rods.

SAVORY GRILLED BRUSSELS SPROUTS

KIM PERRY, BEHIND BBQ

Even if you don't like Brussels sprouts, we think you'll like this recipe! Coated with a seasoned oil and then grilled, they're a quick and easy side dish for barbecue gatherings. Give them a taste, and notice how the grill brings out the natural sweetness of these lovely little cabbages.

YIELD: 5 SERVINGS • COOK TIME: 10 MINUTES

SEASONED OIL MIX

¼ cup (60 ml) regular olive oil (not extra-virgin)

1 tsp kosher salt

½ tsp black pepper

1 tsp garlic powder

½ tsp onion powder

20 (or so) small Brussels sprouts, bottoms trimmed and cut in half

1 tbsp (15 ml) balsamic vinegar

Chimichurri Sauce (page 39), optional

To make the seasoned oil, combine all the ingredients in a large bowl. Add the sprouts and toss to combine.

Using a slotted spoon or tongs, place the sprouts in a perforated grill pan on a medium-hot grill, 400 to 500°F (204 to 260°C), reserving the excess seasoned oil. Don't let too much oil get in the grill pan or you'll get flare-ups.

Grill the Brussels sprouts, turning and flipping, until browned and tender, about 10 minutes. Toss in the reserved oil and the balsamic vinegar, and then serve. For an interesting twist, toss the sprouts with a little chimichurri sauce.

OPERATION BBQ RELIEF IN ACTION

I am honored to support the spectacular work that OBR does. I was introduced to OBR by my BBQ buddy Neil Gallagher of Too Sauced to Pork, who has served as an on-site volunteer and who has also helped spread the word about OBR here in the Northeast. Bringing hot, delicious food to people who need it most and bringing real comfort in a time of crisis is an incredible effort with real rewards for everyone involved. I am so glad to see OBR going strong.

—KIM PERRY, *Behind BBQ*

SMOKED CABBAGE

SWAMP BOYS BBQ TEAM

Melted butter, smoke and barbecue rub will wrap this green vegetable in a velvety cape of delicious! What really makes the dish wonderful are its simplicity and its versatility. You can add additional ingredients to this smoked cabbage dish to make it your own. Crispy crumbled bacon, sliced jalapeño peppers, chunks of ham or pulled pork—the possibilities end only when your taste buds get bored!

YIELD: 6 SERVINGS • COOK TIME: 2½ HOURS

1 large head cabbage

1 cup (230 g) unsalted butter, softened

4 tbsp (56 g) Swamp Boys Original Rub or your favorite rub

½ cup (120 ml) Swamp Boys Original BBQ Sauce for a sweeter flavor, or Swamp Boys Bootleg Red BBQ Sauce for a tangy vinegar flavor, or your favorite BBQ sauce

Using a sharp paring knife, core out the center of the cabbage.

Make the hole about 2 to 3 inches (5 to 8 cm) wide. Be careful NOT to go all the way through on the bottom.

Smash the butter and the rub together to form a compound butter. Use your hands to work the butter mixture into the cored area, pushing it into the nooks and crannies wherever you can.

Stand the cabbage up in a disposable half pan. Use a 2- to 3-foot (61- to 91-cm) piece of foil twisted into a "rope" to wrap around the bottom to help hold it upright. Place the pan into a 300°F (149°C) smoker for 2½ hours, or until tender.

Pour your sauce of choice over the top, so it works its way down between the leaves. Cook for 5 minutes more. Remove from the smoker and serve.

SMOKED GARLIC WHIPPED POTATOES

KEN HESS, BIG BOB GIBSON BAR-B-Q

Comfort food gets an upscale makeover in this rich and creamy smoked garlic whipped potato dish. These whipped potatoes have the light sweetness of roasted garlic and a rich smokiness, making them the perfect side for the holidays—or any day!

YIELD: 4–8 SERVINGS • COOK TIME: 50 MINUTES

SMOKED GARLIC

1 head garlic

1 tbsp (15 ml) olive oil

½ tsp kosher salt

¼ tsp black pepper

WHIPPED POTATOES

1–2 lb (454–907 g) russet potatoes, peeled and chopped

1 tbsp (18 g) kosher salt, plus more to taste

½ cup (115 g) unsalted butter

1 cup (235 ml) heavy cream

2 tsp (6 g) ground white pepper

Configure your grill for indirect cooking and heat to 350 to 400°F (177 to 204°C).

To make the smoked garlic, cut the top off the head of garlic. Place the head of garlic on a small square of aluminum foil. Drizzle the garlic with the olive oil. Sprinkle the salt and pepper over the cut part of the garlic. Wrap the garlic in the foil so it is sealed.

Place the garlic on the grill. Smoke until the garlic is soft and pliable, about 30 minutes. The garlic should be able to be squeezed from its skin. This can be done a week ahead of time and stored in the fridge.

To make the whipped potatoes, first place the potatoes in a pot, cover with water and add the kosher salt. Bring the potatoes to a simmer on the stove and cook them until tender, about 20 minutes. While the potatoes are cooking, set the butter out and allow it to warm to room temperature. Heat the cream in a pot. Be careful: cream can boil over as you are heating it.

Once the potatoes are cooked, drain them. Set up a stand mixer with the whisk attachment. Pour in half of the cream and place the butter into the mixer bowl. Squeeze half of the roasted garlic into the bowl. Place the drained potatoes on top of the cream and garlic. Mix on medium speed until incorporated. Add salt and pepper to taste. Similarly, you may also want to add more of the heated cream and smoked garlic. Serve the whipped potatoes while hot, and watch your guests enjoy!

SMOKED CHEESE *with* BELL PEPPER RELISH

SAFFRON HODGSON, BUSH KITCHEN BBQ

Cooking this smoked cheese with pepper relish is Pitmaster Saffron Hodgson's favorite way to end a long day of cooking at a BBQ competition or family gathering. When the day's work is done, you can simply place the cheese on the smoker as it's cooling down, to make this wonderful appetizer. It's also a nice addition for an end-of-meal cheese platter. To make things easier, the relish can be made a day ahead of time.

YIELD: 4–5 SERVINGS • COOK TIME: 95 MINUTES

BELL PEPPER RELISH

2 tbsp (29 g) butter

4 red bell peppers, finely diced

½ small brown onion, finely diced

1 small chile, to preferred heat, finely diced

1 clove garlic, minced

2 small sprigs thyme, leaves roughly chopped, to taste

4 tbsp (60 ml) apple cider vinegar

4 tbsp (55 g) brown sugar

½ tsp salt

2 tbsp (30 ml) water

SMOKED CHEESE

1 round Brie or Camembert

1 sprig rosemary

1 clove garlic, thinly sliced

1 dash olive oil

Bread or crackers, for serving

To make the relish, in a skillet over medium heat, melt the butter and add the diced bell pepper, onion, chile, garlic and chopped thyme to taste. When the bell pepper and onion have softened but not browned, about 15 minutes, add the vinegar and let it simmer another 15 minutes. Stir regularly and add water if required to keep it moist. Add the sugar, salt and water, and cook gently for 45 minutes, until the bell pepper has softened and formed into a chunky jam.

To make the cheese, using a small knife, poke slots into the cheese. Do not go all the way through the cheese. Press a small sprig of rosemary, consisting of only a few leaves, and a piece of thinly sliced garlic into each slot. Drizzle the olive oil over the cheese. Place the cheese on a small plank or pizza stone and smoke in a cool pit, about 200°F (93°C), until the cheese is soft but not so hot it starts to collapse, about 20 minutes.

To serve, place the cheese on a larger serving tray, top with the bell pepper relish and enjoy with bread or crackers.

SMOKED CREAM CHEESE AND JALAPEÑO PINWHEEL

COUNTY LINE SMOKERS

Smoked cream cheese is the bomb, and it's great on a cracker! Try it once, and we have no doubt that you will be hooked. You can adapt this idea for and use it with your favorite pinwheel recipe by smoking blocks of cream cheese and using them to transform your old recipe into something new and more flavorful.

YIELD: 4 WRAPS WITH 14–16 SLICES EACH • COOK TIME: 40 MINUTES

Fruit wood, for smoking

2 (8-oz [227-g]) packages cream cheese

3–4 slices bacon

1 sweet onion

Olive oil

2–3 jalapeño peppers

Salt and pepper, to taste

4 of your favorite wraps, like sun-dried tomato wraps

A couple dashes of chipotle sauce, optional

Scallions and/or your favorite barbecue sauce, optional

Configure your grill for two-zone cooking and heat to 300°F (149°C).

Smoke the cream cheese using a couple of chunks of fruit wood, such as apple or peach. Starting with cold cream cheese right out of the refrigerator, place the cream cheese in a half pan. Take another half pan and fill it halfway with ice. Insert the pan containing the cream cheese on top of the pan containing the ice. Place this on the indirect side of the grill and smoke for 20 to 30 minutes. Flip the cream cheese every few minutes to get smoke on all sides of the blocks. The color of the cream cheese should darken during the smoking process.

Place the bacon into a cast-iron pan. Cook over direct heat until the bacon darkens in color and begins to curl, about 5 minutes per side.

Cut the onion into slices and drizzle with olive oil. Briefly place these on the grill over direct heat, just to char. Core and halve the jalapeños. Grill the jalapeños over direct heat until softened, about 1 to 2 minutes per side.

Remove the bacon from the pan. Chop up the grilled onion and jalapeños, and place in a cast-iron pan. Cook until the onion softens. Remove from the grill and add the chopped bacon. Mix the cooked ingredients with the smoked cream cheese. Add salt and pepper to taste. Let it set and remix several times to get the flavors blended throughout the cream cheese.

Smear the cheese onto the wraps, and then roll them up like burritos. Place the rolled wraps on a plate. Cover with plastic wrap, and refrigerate. For best results, let them sit overnight in the fridge.

Remove the plate from the fridge and cut the wraps into ½-inch (1.3-cm) pinwheel segments. Insert a toothpick into each segment to hold it together. The remaining ends that you don't serve are what we call the chef's snacks. Serve with chipotle sauce and scallions or barbecue sauce.

SMOKED SNACK MIX

BOO BOO QUED BBQ TEAM

Spicy, sweet and salty, with some crunch! This smoked snack mix brings a bit of all the flavors you love to really wow your pallet. Be cautious—this tasty snack is so addicting it's scary!

YIELD: 16 SERVINGS • COOK TIME: 3 HOURS

1 lb (454 g) each of four different nuts, such as walnuts, almonds, pecans and peanuts

2 lb (907 g) sesame sticks

½ cup (120 ml) honey

1 cup (230 g) butter

2–4 tbsp (28–55 g) dark brown sugar

4 tbsp (29 g) paprika

¼ tsp ground cinnamon

2 tbsp (16 g) chili powder

2 tbsp (8 g) red pepper flakes, plus more to taste

4 tbsp (72 g) coarse sea salt, divided

Oak, hickory, apple or cherry smoke wood

Confectioners' sugar, optional

Mix the nuts together with the sesame sticks, and then separate into two half pans.

In a saucepan, add the honey, butter, brown sugar, paprika, cinnamon, chili powder, pepper flakes and a teaspoon of salt. Place the pan over medium heat and stir until the butter melts and the ingredients combine.

Once combined, taste and add more pepper flakes if needed. Divide the blended mixture over the nut mixture in the two pans, and mix well. When well combined, place the half pans into the smoker, preheated to 240°F (116°C). Add your preference of smoke wood, such as oak, hickory, apple or cherry.

During the smoking process, stir the contents of each pan about every 40 minutes. Smoke for 2 to 3 hours, until the mixture starts drying. Remove the pans from the smoker and sprinkle the remaining sea salt over the mixture. Stir occasionally while the mixture cools. If it's sticky after cooling, you can sprinkle a small amount of confectioners' sugar over the mixture, but don't use too much.

MAC *AND* CHEESE

SMOKIN' ACES

Toasty cracker crumbs give this spaghetti and cheese dish a crispy top in just minutes! The sharp cheddar cheese delivers bold flavors to the sauce.

YIELD: 9 SERVINGS • COOK TIME: 60 MINUTES

1 (3.4-oz [95-g]) sleeve Ritz crackers

1 (4-oz [112-g]) sleeve saltine crackers

6 tbsp (86 g) butter, plus more for greasing

1 lb (454 g) thin spaghetti, cooked and drained

12 oz (340 g) sharp white cheddar cheese, diced into small cubes

Salt and pepper, to taste

1½ cups (355 ml) milk

Use a 9-inch (23-cm) square pan with 3-inch (7.5-cm) sides, or a disposable half pan.

Put the crackers in a ziplock bag and crush with a rolling pin. Butter or spray the sides and bottom of the pan, and then put one layer of spaghetti into the bottom of the pan. Add a layer of crackers and then a layer of cheese. Sprinkle with salt and pepper.

Repeat the layering process two times. Arrange the topmost layer so it's a mix of cheese and crackers. Dot the layer with the butter and drizzle the milk over the whole pan.

Cook uncovered for 45 to 60 minutes at 325°F (163°C), using indirect heat.

The mac and cheese is done when it is golden brown. Let it sit a few minutes before cutting into nine 3-inch (7.5-cm) squares for a side dish. For an appetizer size, cut into thirty-six 1½-inch (3.8-cm) squares. Leftovers reheat well.

APPLE PIE BAKED BEANS

MOO COW

This deliciously sweet side-dish recipe has been borrowed, tweaked and changed until fit for crowds of hungry carnivores. For extra flavor, cook your half pan of beans under a smokin' pork butt because there is nothing better than smoke and pork drippings added to beans!

YIELD: 12 SERVINGS • COOK TIME: 1½ HOURS

3–4 slices bacon, diced

1 medium onion, chopped

2 (28-oz [794-g]) cans Bush's baked beans, slightly drained of liquid (leave a little)

½ cup (120 ml) BBQ sauce (use your favorite Kansas City style—sweet and spicy works well)

1 lb (454 g) leftover smoked pulled pork

1 (21-oz [595-g]) can apple pie filling (apple pieces need to be cut into smaller chunks)

½ cup (110 g) brown sugar

2 tbsp (30 ml) Worcestershire sauce

2 tbsp (31 g) prepared mustard

1 tbsp (14 g) barbecue rub (use your favorite)

Heat the smoker to 325°F (163°C).

Brown the bacon in a large pan or Dutch oven on the stove. Cook until the bacon changes color and begins to curl, about 6 to 8 minutes. Remove it from the pan. Sauté the chopped onion in the bacon grease until the onion turns translucent and soft, about 6 to 8 minutes.

Mix all the ingredients in an aluminum half pan and place in the smoker. Cook, uncovered, until browned, about 1 to 1½ hours.

SPICY BUFFALO CHICKEN DIP

UNCLE KENNY'S BBQ

A few simple ingredients make this a creamy, cheesy and zesty hot dip that tastes just like Buffalo chicken wings! It's best served hot with crackers, chips, bread cubes or celery sticks. No matter what you serve it with, each time it's served, everyone seems to love the results!

YIELD: 24 SERVINGS • COOK TIME: 20 MINUTES

1 (8-oz [227-g]) block cream cheese, softened

½ cup (120 ml) Uncle Kenny's Spicy BBQ Sauce or your favorite BBQ sauce

½ cup (120 ml) blue cheese or ranch dressing

2 cups (280 g) shredded cooked chicken

½ cup (60 g) blue cheese, crumbled (or your favorite shredded cheese)

Crackers, chips or cubed bread, for serving

Set up your smoker or grill to cook using indirect heat at 350°F (177°C).

In a medium bowl, thoroughly mix all the ingredients until well combined. Place in an aluminum half pan. Bake for 20 minutes until the cheese is melted and the dip is bubbly. Enjoy with crackers, chips or cubed bread.

SPINACH 〰 FETA-STUFFED BREAD

FEEDING FRIENDZ

Easy to put together, this stuffed bread recipe is a great go-to meal that can easily be doubled to feed a crowd. The ranch dressing adds lots of flavor to the baked bread, and the feta cheese is a creamy accompaniment to the chopped chorizo and spinach leaves.

YIELD: 4 SERVINGS • COOK TIME: 40 MINUTES

1 lb (454 g) frozen bread dough, thawed

½ cup (120 ml) ranch dressing

1 lb (454 g) baby spinach leaves

8 oz (227 g) feta cheese, crumbled

1 chorizo link, sliced and cut into small pieces

Configure your smoker or grill for indirect cooking and preheat to 350°F (177°C).

Roll the dough on a lightly floured surface into a 12-inch (30-cm) circle. Pour the ranch dressing on the dough and spread across using the back of a spoon. Cover the dressing with the baby spinach—the more the better since it will reduce as it bakes. Top with the feta cheese and chorizo pieces.

Roll the dough into a log, turning in the side edges as you roll. (Don't be afraid to stretch the dough to make everything fit.) Wet the edges with water and pinch together to seal it. Shape it by hand to finish forming into a log.

Spray a foil pan with nonstick cooking spray and place the bread log into it. Cover and cook for about 30 minutes. Remove the cover and cook until the top is golden brown, about 5 to 10 minutes. Remove from the cooker and let it cool for about 10 minutes before slicing.

NOTE: This is also awesome stuffed with cooked shaved steak and cheddar or pepper Jack cheese.

SPICY CHORIZO-STUFFED MHROOMS ~WITH~ SMOKED PROVOLONE

THREE MEN AND A BABYBACK BBQ TEAM

So simple and inviting, you've got to make this savory appetizer for your next gathering! Spicy chorizo sausage and creamy, melted provolone provide the perfect meaty blend to the marinated mushrooms in this dish.

YIELD: 12 MUSHROOMS • COOK TIME: 45 MINUTES

BASIC MARINADE

1 small onion, diced

3 cloves garlic, minced

½ cup (120 ml) olive oil

¼ cup (60 ml) white wine vinegar

2 tbsp (30 ml) Worcestershire sauce

2 tsp (8 g) sugar

1 tsp salt

1 tsp black pepper

MUSHROOMS

12 medium cremini mushrooms

Salt and pepper

1 lb (454 g) chorizo sausage meat, casings removed

6–8 slices smoked provolone, or any good melting cheese of your choice

To make the marinade, combine all the ingredients in a bowl.

To make the mushrooms, remove the stem from each mushroom, and then rinse the mushrooms.

Configure your grill for two-zone cooking, and let it heat up to 400 to 450°F (204 to 232°C). Generously baste each mushroom cap with ½ cup (120 ml) of the marinade, season with salt and pepper and let sit for 10 minutes. Grill each side of the mushroom for 1 to 2 minutes over direct heat, just to "mark" and sear the mushrooms. Remove them from the grill and set them aside to cool slightly.

Stuff each mushroom with about a tablespoon (15 g) of chorizo and season again with salt and pepper. Place the mushrooms on a sheet pan or baking pan, and place the pan on the indirect side of the grill (with no charcoal under the pan). Shut the lid and allow to slow cook for 40 minutes.

Cut the provolone into small squares or circles the size of the mushrooms. Open the lid and place a piece of cheese over each mushroom. Cook for another 5 minutes, until the cheese is melted and bubbly; then remove from the grill. Let the mushrooms rest for a few minutes before serving.

OPERATION BBQ RELIEF IN ACTION

In September of 2017, I was asked to deploy and cook with Operation BBQ Relief. I jumped on a plane and went to Fort Myers after Hurricane Irma destroyed southwest Florida. I spent five days cooking with the most amazing people on the planet. These people are absolutely incredible and all they care about is helping people. They work day and night, nonstop, to fulfill the needs of thousands of people. It's people helping people. I met a lot of great people while I was in southwest Florida, however there is one person that I will never forget. It was a little girl that showed up to our cooking site by accident with her mom and her brother. They were evacuated from their home in Bonita Springs. The cooking site where we were set up had previously been used as a shelter during the hurricane but had recently been evacuated prior to us arriving there. This family had heard that there was food, water and shelter at the arena where we were, so they showed up in a small Prius filled with their only possessions (a TV, some pillows, a stereo and some other random stuff). They lost everything in the hurricane. They came to me looking for food and water, and even though our site was not set up for individual meal service, we NEVER turn anyone away. I looked at the little girl and asked her if she liked mashed potatoes. She looked up at me with a big smile and said, "Yes, I haven't eaten in two days." My heart dropped to my stomach and I almost broke down in tears. Her mom looked at me with the saddest face and said "Well, she did have a cookie this morning." I immediately thought of my three daughters and, holding back tears, I began to gather supplies for these people. I gave them water, ice, sliced pork loin, mashed potatoes, veggies and some snacks that we had lying around. I asked them if there was anything I could do for them, but the mother told me that they were on their way to a relative's house near Tampa and that they would be OK. She thanked me for my generosity, and they were on their way. It all happened so fast that I never got a chance to get their names or their story. But I will never forget the face of that little girl when I gave her some mashed potatoes and some ice cold water to drink. It wasn't much, but it warmed her heart for that one moment in her life—and that's what OBR is all about. If we can provide a warm meal to people who may not have eaten in a few days due to a disaster, and it puts a smile on their face just for that one moment, we have done our job.

Needless to say, when I went back to the house I was staying in that night, with all the day's emotions built up inside me, I broke down in tears while in the shower. I couldn't help but think about that little girl and how much I missed my family.

—**MARC MANGANO,** *Three Men and a Babyback*

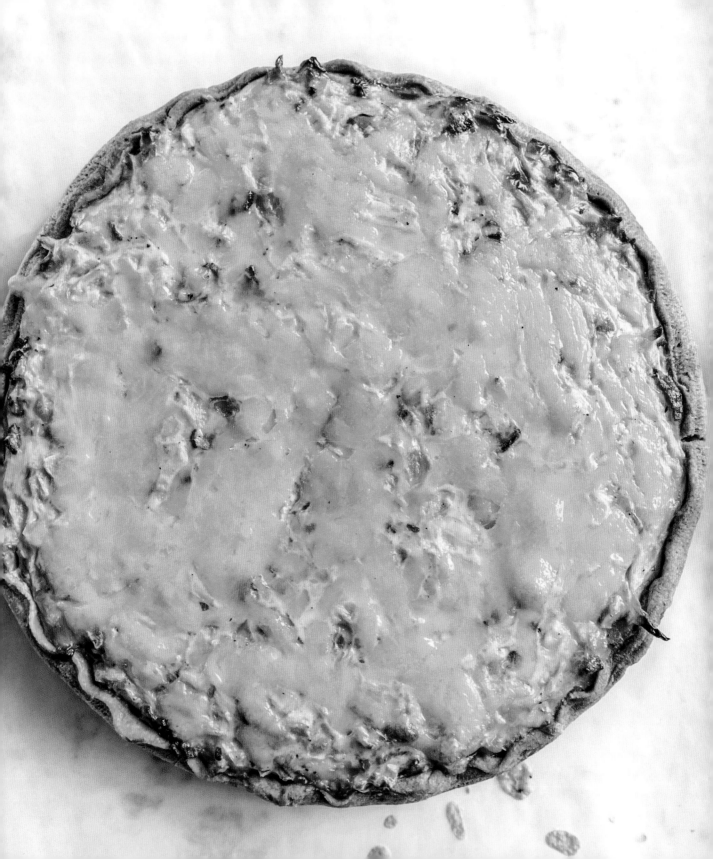

SWEET ONION PIE

SWAMP BOYS BBQ TEAM

Chock-full of sweet onions, this creamy pie is a great side dish that goes well with any barbecue meal. It also makes a scrumptious addition to a potluck dinner or brunch buffet!

YIELD: 6–8 SERVINGS • COOK TIME: 40 MINUTES

2 lb (907 g) sweet onions, thinly sliced

2 tbsp (29 g) butter

3 eggs

1 cup (130 g) grated pepper Jack cheese

½ tsp salt

1 tsp white pepper

1 cup (121 g) sour cream

4 slices bacon, fried and crumbled

1 (9″ [23-cm]) frozen pie shell

1 cup (121 g) grated sharp cheddar cheese

2 splashes (or to taste) your favorite hot sauce

Prepare your cooker for an indirect cook at 375°F (191°C).

In a skillet over medium heat, sauté the sliced onions in the butter until they soften and begin to caramelize. Let them stand and cool.

Beat the eggs and add the pepper Jack cheese, salt, pepper, sour cream and bacon to the eggs. Mix well.

Pour onions and egg mixture into the frozen pie shell, add the cheddar cheese on top, and bake using indirect heat for 40 minutes. Let it cool, and serve with hot sauce.

SWEET SLAW *for* A CROWD

SMOKE ON WHEELS BBQ TEAM

This must-have item for pulled pork sandwiches is also a great side dish with almost any food you grill! It's perfect for potluck dinners or any outdoor gathering, because there is no need to keep it refrigerated.

YIELD: 32 SERVINGS • COOK TIME: 1 MINUTE

SLAW

2 heads cabbage

1 large red onion

2 cups (383 g) sugar

DRESSING

1 cup (236 ml) apple cider vinegar

1 cup (236 ml) vegetable oil

2 tbsp (30 g) salt

3 tbsp (47 g) yellow mustard

1 tbsp (7 g) celery salt

To make the slaw, shred the cabbage and red onion. Place it in a large bowl and mix. Sprinkle with the sugar and let it sit for 2 hours.

To make the dressing, after 2 hours, place all of the dressing ingredients in a saucepan and boil for 1 minute. Pour the dressing evenly over the cabbage mixture—don't stir. Cover and let it sit for 24 hours; then stir and serve.

TEJAS POTATO TARTE

LONESTAR SMOKE RANGERS BBQ TEAM

The smooth texture of the potatoes in this creamy tarte makes it great for a luncheon or supper. Adjust the spices and add heat to your preference, but we think it's fantastic just the way it's written!

YIELD: 8 SERVINGS • COOK TIME: 1 HOUR 25 MINUTES

1 lb (454 g) bacon

2 cups (241 g) crème fraîche

2 tbsp (31 g) Dijon mustard

6 lb (3 kg) golden potatoes, divided

2 shallots

¼ cup (12 g) cilantro

1 jalapeño

1 lb (454 g) Polish sausage

½ tsp salt

½ tbsp (2 g) chopped fresh thyme

½ tbsp (2 g) chopped fresh rosemary

½ tsp white pepper

½ tsp cumin

1 tbsp (10 g) roasted garlic

¼ cup (57 g) butter, melted, divided

1 tsp paprika-based BBQ rub

Prepare your cooker for two-zone cooking, and preheat to 400°F (204°C).

Crisp the bacon in a skillet over medium heat. Drain on paper towels, then chop and set aside. Set aside the bacon fat that is left over. Combine the crème fraîche and Dijon mustard in a bowl and chill. Rinse and peel 3 pounds (1.5 kg) of the potatoes. Slice into thin, round medallions, approximately ⅛ inch (3 mm) thick. Dice and chop the shallots, cilantro and jalapeño. Slice the Polish sausage into thin, round slices no thicker than ¼ inch (6 mm).

In a large saucepan, bring water to a rolling boil. Reduce the heat to medium-low. Place the remaining 3 pounds (1.5 kg) of potatoes in the pan and boil until tender, about 15 to 20 minutes. Mash the potatoes with the skins on.

In the bacon fat left in the skillet, sauté the shallots, cilantro and jalapeño along with the salt, thyme, rosemary, white pepper, cumin and roasted garlic for about 5 minutes over medium heat. Blend the mashed potatoes and chopped, crisped bacon with the sauté.

Line a glass 3-quart (2.8-L) casserole dish with parchment paper. Brush the parchment paper with half of the melted butter. Dredge the potato and sausage slices in the crème fraîche and Dijon mixture. Layer the bottom and sides of the dish with half of the potato slices and sausage medallions. Carefully fold the mashed potato sauté over the potato slices and sausage medallions. Spread evenly.

Take the remaining potato and sausage slices you dredged through the crème fraîche mixture, and arrange them ornately across the top of the mashed potato mixture. Lightly brush with the remaining melted butter. Cover with parchment paper and place a second dish on top of the pie to act as a weight.

Bake using indirect heat until the top layer is tender, approximately 45 minutes to 1 hour. Remove the pan you inserted as a weight and the top layer of parchment paper. Dust the surface with the rub and cook for 5 minutes to crisp the top layer of the pie. Let it cool before slicing.

TENDER-CRISP GREEN BEANS

SMOKE ON WHEELS BBQ TEAM

Riesling may well be the most accommodating wine for pairing with challenging flavors and spice profiles. Whether it's sweet or dry, we think it pairs well with the vegetables, bacon and seasonings in this tasty side dish!

YIELD: 8–10 SERVINGS • COOK TIME: 30–40 MINUTES

½ lb (240 g) bacon

1 pint (145 g) cremini mushrooms, cleaned and sliced

1 small Vidalia onion, chopped

2 lb (907 g) fresh green beans

¼ cup (60 ml) Riesling wine, sweet or dry, per your taste preference

Cattleman's Grill California Tri-Tip Rub and Seasoning or your favorite rub

Cook the bacon in a large skillet over medium heat until crisp. Drain on paper towels and then crumble into a bowl, reserving the grease in the skillet.

In the reserved bacon grease, sauté the mushrooms and onion until the onion is translucent, about 10 minutes. Toss in the green beans and the crumbled bacon; then place the mixture in an aluminum half pan. Add the Riesling and stir gently until combined.

Place in a 350°F (177°C) cooker and cook until the green beans begin to soften, about 10 to 15 minutes. The mushrooms will be well wilted. Remove from the cooker and season with Cattleman's Grill California Tri-Tip Rub and Seasoning to serve.

TEXAS CAVIAR

COUNTY LINE SMOKERS

Texas Caviar is a refreshing Southern salsa. It's tasty on hot summer days, but this zesty side is great any time of year.

YIELD: 20 SERVINGS • COOK TIME: 15 MINUTES

2 (15-oz [425-g]) cans black-eyed peas

1 (11-oz [312-g]) can super sweet corn

½ medium red onion

1–2 jalapeño peppers

2–3 Roma tomatoes

1 cup (50 g) chopped cilantro

1 tbsp (9 g) minced roasted garlic

1 bottle zesty Italian salad dressing

1–2 limes, divided

Salt and pepper, to taste

Olive oil, optional

Drain the black-eyed peas. Rinse and drain the corn.

Dice the red onion. Slice the jalapeños lengthwise (remove the seeds and veins for a milder salsa), and then dice. Seed and then dice the Roma tomatoes.

In a large bowl, mix all the ingredients together. Add approximately 1½ cups (355 ml) of the zesty Italian dressing. Juice 1 lime and add it to the mixture. Add salt and pepper to taste. If needed, add more lime. If you feel like you have too much lime, just add some olive oil to the mix to help offset the citrus fruit's acid.

Refrigerate for a couple of hours, or overnight, and then serve.

TOMATO, ARUGULA AND AMARENA CHERRY PIZZA

JOHN DELPHA, IQUE BBQ

John keeps his Amarena cherries recipe handy to add to his pizza, and also to his cocktails. Once you try them, I am sure you will decide to do the same. The sweetness of the cherries on your pizza will have you wanting to grill up seconds in no time.

YIELD: 10 MEDIUM PIZZAS • COOK TIME: 6–8 MINUTES PER PIZZA

PIZZA DOUGH

2¼ cups (532 ml) warm water (100°F [38°C])

4 tsp (13 g) yeast

1 tbsp (12 g) sugar

2 tbsp (30 ml) extra-virgin olive oil

5 cups (625 g) all-purpose flour

½ cup (88 g) semolina

1 tbsp (15 g) salt

TOMATO SAUCE

4 cloves garlic, peeled and finely minced

2 tbsp (30 ml) extra-virgin olive oil

2 (28-oz [794-g]) cans whole, peeled tomatoes in heavy purée

2 tsp (12 g) kosher salt

JOHN DELPHA'S AMARENA CHERRIES

2 cups (240 g) dried cherries

1 cup (236 ml) dry red wine

2 cups (383 g) granulated sugar

½ cup (120 ml) water

¾ cup (177 ml) amaretto

JOHN DELPHA'S PIZZA CHEESE BLEND

1 lb (454 g) cheddar cheese, shredded

½ lb (227 g) Parmesan cheese, grated

½ lb (227 g) Pecorino Romano cheese, grated

PIZZA

Extra-virgin olive oil

¾ cup (84 g) Pizza Cheese Blend (recipe provided)

2 oz (59 g) fresh mozzarella, torn into small pieces

¾ cup (177 ml) basic Tomato Sauce (recipe provided)

1 tbsp (10 g) Amarena Cherries, drained (recipe provided)

1 tbsp (15 ml) Amarena cherry syrup

½ cup (10 g) loosely packed baby arugula

4 medium basil leaves, torn into pieces

To make the dough, place the water, yeast and sugar in the bowl of a stand mixer. Let it sit for 5 minutes until the yeast is activated (bubbly). Add the oil and then add the dry ingredients. Place a dough hook on a mixer and turn to medium-low. Mix for approximately 5 minutes, until a smooth ball appears. Turn to medium-high and knead for approximately 2 minutes, until the ball obtains a light shine. The dough can be placed in a bag and refrigerated for use within 3 days or frozen for up to a month. This dough yields approximately 10 (5-ounce [142-g]) portions, which makes it a great go-to recipe when you have a crowd in attendance for your next pizza party.

To make the sauce, sauté the garlic in olive oil over medium-high heat until the garlic is translucent, about 1 to 2 minutes. Remove from the heat. Empty the tomatoes into a small mixing bowl and crush into small chunks by hand. Add the garlic, oil and salt. Mix well and reserve until needed.

To make the cherries, place all the ingredients in a medium saucepan over medium heat and reduce by a third. Remove them from the heat, cool and store in a sealed container in the refrigerator until needed.

To make the cheese blend, combine all the ingredients in a small bowl. This is a simple cheese for a majority of your pizzas. Feel free to experiment with your own favorites and substitutes.

Now, to make your pizzas, prepare your grill for two-zone cooking and heat to 400°F (204°C).

Lightly grease a metal work surface and the palms of your hands. Place the dough ball in the center of the surface and press down evenly with the palm of your hand. Working with both hands, start in the middle and spread the dough out with your palms while stretching the outer edges with your fingers. You should have an approximately 12 x 8-inch (30 x 20-cm) rectangle.

Lift up the edge further from yourself and slide your fingers under the dough. Move to the direct zone of your grill and place the bottom edge of the dough at the furthest point from you and pull the dough toward you to place on the grill. Gently lift up one edge of the dough with the tongs to check for color. When you see some color setting in, lift the dough and give it a quarter turn with the peel. When the dough is sufficiently browned on the bottom, but not charred, remove it from the direct zone and flip it over onto the indirect zone.

Drizzle olive oil on the crust and brush evenly. Sprinkle the cheese blend all over, add the mozzarella and spoon dollops of the tomato sauce all over. Scatter the cherries and drizzle the syrup around. Move the pizza to the direct side of the grill and rotate every 15 to 30 seconds to crisp the bottom. When the bottom is crispy, add the arugula, drizzle with olive oil, sprinkle the basil around, slice and serve. Repeat with the remaining dough balls, tomato sauce, cherries, cheese blend and toppings to make 9 more pizzas.

VTPB (VERMONT PEPPER BOMBS)

SWEET BREATHE BBQ

These are not your average pepper bombs. The addition of sweet or tart apples to the mix brings the taste of New England to these spicy treats!

YIELD: 24 PEPPER BOMBS • COOK TIME: 2–3 HOURS

1 lb (454 g) bulk sausage

2 apples, peeled and sliced

1 onion, peeled and sliced

Salt and pepper

8 oz (227 g) cheddar cheese, preferably extra sharp

12 jalapeños, halved lengthwise and seeds removed

12 slices bacon, sliced in half

¼ cup (60 ml) your favorite BBQ sauce

Heat your smoker to 225°F (107°C).

Brown the sausage on the stove over medium-high heat until fully cooked, about 6 to 8 minutes. Remove the sausage with a slotted spoon and put it into a food processor.

Drain the grease from the pan, leaving 2 tablespoons (30 ml) to cook the apples and onion until softened, about 3 to 5 minutes. Season the mixture with salt and pepper to your liking.

Add the cooked onions, apples and cheddar cheese to your food processor. Pulse until all the ingredients are mixed well.

Using a spoon, stuff the pepper halves with the mixture until slightly rounded. Wrap a half-slice of bacon around each pepper and use a toothpick to hold the bacon in place. Repeat this process for the remaining peppers.

Place them on the smoker until the bacon is browned, about 2 to 3 hours.

Brush on your favorite BBQ sauce during the last 5 minutes of cooking. Remove from the grill and serve.

WHITE LIGHTNING ROASTED FINGERLING POTATOES

BOOTYQUE BBQ TEAM

Whether cooking for a crowd or just a few people, carefully choose your quantities for these flavorful potatoes and be prepared for NO leftovers. Quick and convenient, this is the simplest—and tastiest—side dish you will ever make!

YIELD: 4 SERVINGS • COOK TIME: 30 MINUTES

1 lb (454 g) fingerling potatoes

1 tbsp (15 ml) olive oil

1 large onion, chopped

Granulated garlic, to taste

Ground black pepper, to taste

Boar's Night Out White Lightning Rub or your favorite rub

Dry ranch dressing mix or cheese, optional

Preheat your grill to 350 to 400°F (177 to 204°C). Heat a cast-iron skillet on the grill for 15 minutes.

Rinse and dry the potatoes.

Place the potatoes in a medium bowl with the olive oil and chopped onion. Sprinkle generously with granulated garlic, black pepper and Boar's Night Out White Lightning Rub. Toss the potatoes to coat with the ingredients.

Arrange the potatoes in a single layer in the preheated cast-iron skillet. Roast until they are golden on the outside and tender when pierced with a sharp knife, 25 to 30 minutes, or to your desired tenderness.

Remove from the grill, and serve hot with some additional rub on the side. You can also sprinkle dry ranch dressing mix for added flavor, or add cheese to the cooked potatoes until melted.

GRANDMA FRANCES W'S CALICO BEANS

FERGOLICIOUS BBQ TEAM

This is a great recipe when you need a fast side dish to accompany your meal. Combine your favorite variety of beans to make this smoky dish. It's a great complement to brisket or pork butt, and is savory enough to eat just as it is.

YIELD: 12 SERVINGS • COOK TIME: 30 MINUTES

½ lb (227 g) bacon, sliced into small pieces

½ cup (75 g) onion, diced

½ lb (227 g) ground chuck

½ cup (122 g) ketchup

1 tsp yellow mustard

½ cup (110 g) brown sugar

1 tbsp (15 ml) cider vinegar

1 (20-oz [560-g]) can pork and beans

1 (20-oz [560-g]) can kidney beans, rinsed and drained

1 (20-oz [560-g]) can lima beans, rinsed and drained

Set up your grill or smoker for 350°F (177°C), indirect heat.

Place a Dutch oven directly on the hot charcoal. Allow it to heat up for 10 minutes.

In the bottom of the Dutch oven, fry the bacon with the diced onion for 4 to 5 minutes, stirring frequently. Add the beef and cook until the beef is browned, about 5 minutes. Drain the fat and add the remaining ingredients to the pan, stirring well.

Place the uncovered Dutch oven on the indirect section of your grill or smoker. Place the lid on the cooker and bake for 30 minutes, or to the desired consistency. Rotate the Dutch oven after 15 minutes to help ensure even cooking.

Remove the Dutch oven from your smoker and serve (we like to present them in bell pepper cups).

OPERATION BBQ RELIEF IN ACTION

Fergolicious BBQ got involved with Operation BBQ Relief in 2016 when they approached us about being apart of an upcoming cookbook. We were honored to be included in this amazing project and excited to contribute to the OBR mission. As competition cooks, we travel across the country doing our best to provide excellent BBQ entries to the judges. While winning and rankings drive our desire to compete, our ultimate goal—much like that of the Operation BBQ Relief—is to make a positive impact on those we come in contact with along the way.

—**RICH FERGOLA,** *Fergolicious BBQ*

CHAPTER 8

DESSERTS

AHHH, THE FONDNESS OF SWEET MEMORIES. Make room on the grill for some of these desserts and you'll have a collection of sinful sweets guaranteed to keep people talking about happy times.

Toasted and baked. Candied and caramelized. Sticky and sweet. This chapter of irresistible desserts features creative takes by competition cooks on some classic ideas you already know and love.

From rich, chocolaty cake to refreshing cantaloupe pie, your backyard smoker or grill is the perfect cooking device to create a sweet finish to a hearty barbecue gathering.

APPLE CARAMEL SALTED GALETTE

DIVA Q, AKA DANIELLE BENNETT

This is one of the easiest ways to prepare apple pie on the grill. This galette is quick to assemble, and the salted caramel puts it over the top. You may want to make two while you are at it, just to guarantee seconds for everyone!

YIELD: 6–8 SERVINGS • COOK TIME: 40 MINUTES

1 (18–21-oz [510–595-g]) can apple pie filling

½ tsp ground cinnamon, plus more for dusting

1 (8-oz [227-g]) package cream cheese, softened

⅓ cup (64 g) granulated sugar

1 egg

2 tbsp (19 g) cornstarch

2 tbsp (30 ml) heavy whipping cream

½ tsp pure vanilla extract

1 (9" [23-cm]) store-bought frozen piecrust, thawed

2 tsp (5 g) all-purpose flour, for dusting

½ cup (120 ml) caramel topping, mixed with ½ tsp sea salt, divided

1 egg beaten with 2 tbsp (30 ml) water, for egg wash

2 tbsp (24 g) turbinado sugar

Preheat the grill by turning one burner on high and leaving the remaining burners off. Place a baking sheet or pizza stone on the unlit side. Toss the apples with the cinnamon in a medium bowl and set aside.

Using a mixer, whip the cream cheese and the sugar until fluffy. Add the egg, cornstarch, whipping cream and vanilla. Then continue to beat the cream cheese mixture until smooth.

Roll out the piecrust on a floured piece of parchment paper until it is a flat circle.

Using a spatula, spread half of the cream cheese filling on the pie, leaving a 2-inch (5-cm) space around the perimeter. Drizzle ¼ cup (60 ml) of the salted caramel onto the cream cheese layer. Spread the apples and cinnamon on top of the cream cheese. Spread the remaining cream cheese mixture around the perimeter, letting the apples peek through in the center. Dust with cinnamon. Fold over the edge of the crust all around the pie. Brush the pie edge with the egg wash and sprinkle with turbinado sugar.

Place the galette on the pizza stone, leaving the pie on the parchment paper. Close the grill lid. After 15 minutes, open the lid and rotate the pie a third of a turn. After an additional 15 minutes, open the lid and rotate the pie again. This helps ensure the pie has a nicely browned crust all around its edges. Bake on the grill another 10 minutes, or until the apples are bubbling and the crust is nicely browned. Remove it from the grill and cool slightly. Drizzle with the remaining ¼ cup (60 ml) of caramel and sprinkle with additional sea salt if desired.

APPLE PIE BAKED IN AN APPLE

BIG UGLY'S BBQ TEAM

A sticky, sweet and tart Granny Smith apple pie filling is poured into a hollowed apple and topped with an easy lattice piecrust. This makes for a tender baked apple dessert that is easy to make and sure to impress!

YIELD: 4 SERVINGS • COOK TIME: 45 MINUTES

5–6 Granny Smith apples (make sure they can stand on their own), divided

1 tbsp (8 g) ground cinnamon

¼ cup (48 g) granulated sugar

1 tbsp (14 g) brown sugar

Piecrust (homemade or premade)

Preheat the cooker to 375°F (191°C).

Cut off the top of 4 apples and discard the tops. Carefully remove the inside of each apple with a spoon or melon baller. Do not puncture the apple peel. If you're a skilled interior apple excavator, salvage as much as you can so you can use the fruit in the next step. Remove the skin from the remaining apple(s) and slice very thinly. These apple pieces will give you the additional filling needed to fill the 4 apples you are baking.

In a bowl, mix the sliced apples with the cinnamon and sugars. Taste the sliced apples and adjust the cinnamon and/or sugar to your preference. Scoop the sliced apples into the hollow apples.

Roll out the piecrust and slice into ¼-inch (6-mm) strips. You can also add a strip of pastry inside the top of the apple almost like a liner to add a little more texture and sweetness. Cover the top of the apple in a lattice pattern with piecrust strips.

Place the apples in an 8 x 8-inch (20 x 20-cm) pan. Add just enough water to cover the bottom of the pan. Cover with foil and bake on the cooker using indirect heat for 20 to 25 minutes. Remove the foil and bake for an additional 20 minutes, or until the crust is golden brown and the sliced apples are soft.

BAILEY'S *and* BROWNIE PARFAITS

DISCO PIGS

These parfaits are simple to make and oh so yummy! If you are a fan of Bailey's Irish Cream, as well as brownies, then this dessert is for you! For an interesting substitute, use your favorite Bailey's flavor in place of the original liqueur, or try the Bailey's Mint Chocolate and use chopped Andes Mints for another refreshing twist.

YIELD: 10–12 SERVINGS • COOK TIME: 30–45 MINUTES

2 (18.5-oz [524-g]) boxes your favorite brownie mix, plus ingredients according to package directions

8 oz (227 g) semisweet chocolate, roughly chopped

2 tsp (2 g) instant coffee granules

1 cup (236 ml) milk

4 cups (946 ml) heavy whipping cream, really cold

⅔ cup (158 ml) Bailey's Original or any flavor, chilled

½ cup (65 g) confectioners' sugar

Set up your smoker for an indirect cook at 325 to 350°F (163 to 177°C).

Mix both boxes of brownies together and prepare according to package directions. Spray a half pan (12¾ x 10 inches [32 x 25 cm]) with oil. Line with parchment paper, and then spray the top of the parchment paper with oil. Carefully pour the batter into the pan and bake approximately 30 to 40 minutes. Remove from the smoker and place on a wire rack to cool completely.

Place the chopped semisweet chocolate in a small bowl. Sprinkle the instant coffee granules over the chocolate. Heat the milk over medium heat. Watch carefully, and when you see small bubbles form along the edge of the pan, reduce the heat to low. Stir constantly for 2 to 3 minutes, and then pour over the chocolate. Let it sit for 2 to 3 minutes, and then stir. If any chunks of chocolate remain, put it back on the heat until all the chocolate has melted. The resulting mixture will be a liquid, with a consistency similar to chocolate milk. Set the mixture aside and let it cool to room temperature.

Place the cooked and cooled brownies on a cutting board. Cut off the crunchy sides and ends, and reserve for a topping. Cut about half of the brownie into 1-inch (2.5-cm) strips. Use your fingers and crumble. You will probably have leftovers.

Using a mixer, combine the heavy cream, Bailey's and confectioners' sugar. Beat on high until stiff peaks form, about 5 to 7 minutes. Divide the cream mixture in half. The first half of the whipped cream will be used as it is in the parfait. The second half will be mixed with the chocolate. Slowly add the chocolate mixture over half of the whipped cream, gently folding them together until completely mixed.

Using a pastry bag (or just a spoon), add layers of the chocolate cream on the bottom of a parfait glass. Using another pastry bag or a spoon, top with the plain cream. Sprinkle with crumbled brownie as you see fit. Repeat the layers. Finish with crunchy brownie edge crumbles on top. Parfaits can be served immediately. If you'd like the chocolate layer to be firmer, chill the parfaits for 2 to 3 hours before serving.

SPICY BROWN SUGAR–GRILLED PEACHES *with* WHITE CHOCOLATE

RIBS WITHIN BBQ TEAM

After you finish off a great backyard meal, and the charcoal is burning down, sometimes you want a little something sweet. In this dish, the heat from the grill helps caramelize the peach's natural sugars, and you can whip it up in about 10 minutes!

YIELD: 4 SERVINGS • COOK TIME: 10 MINUTES

¼ cup (57 ml) salted butter, melted

2 tbsp (28 g) Ribs Within Rub 4 All, 1 tbsp (14 g) brown sugar and ½ tsp ground cinnamon OR 2 tbsp (28 g) brown sugar, 1 tsp salt, ¾ tsp ground cinnamon and ¼ tsp ground chile pepper

4 medium peaches, halved and pitted

Cooking oil

⅓ cup (60 g) white baking chocolate, chopped

3 tbsp (23 g) chopped pecans, optional

Whipped cream, optional

Heat the grill to medium heat, 300 to 400°F (149 to 204°C).

In a small bowl, combine the butter and rub. Divide the mixture in half. Using one half of the butter mixture, toss the peaches and coat them. Reserve the remaining butter mixture.

Moisten a paper towel with cooking oil, and using long-handled tongs, lightly coat the grill rack with oil.

Place the peaches, cut-side down, on the grill rack. Cover the grill and cook for 5 minutes. Flip the peaches and fill them with the white chocolate. Drizzle with the reserved butter mixture. Close the cover. Grill the peaches for 4 to 5 minutes or until the chocolate melts and begins to caramelize (a little longer if the peaches are not tender).

Sprinkle the peaches with pecans and serve with whipped cream, if desired.

CHOCOLATE GOOEY SKILLET CAKE

NAUGHTY NURSES BBQ

Intrigued by a chocolate cake that is intensely rich, fudgy and baked to gooey perfection? Top it off with a layer of ice cream, caramel sauce and whipped cream for a sweet finish on a warm summer evening. Another topping choice to finish it off is crushed graham cracker pieces and toasted mini marshmallows. No matter which topping you choose, this dessert ushers in some happy times!

YIELD: 6–8 SERVINGS • COOK TIME: 20 MINUTES

CAKE

1 cup (125 g) all-purpose flour

½ tsp baking soda

1 cup (192 g) sugar

Dash of salt

¼ cup (57 g) butter

¼ cup (60 ml) vegetable oil

2 tbsp (14 g) cocoa powder

½ cup (120 ml) water

¼ cup (60 ml) buttermilk

1 egg

½ tsp vanilla extract

FROSTING

¼ cup (57 g) butter

2 tbsp (14 g) cocoa powder

3–4 tbsp (44–60 ml) milk, as needed for consistency

2 cups (440 g) confectioners' sugar

½ cup (60 g) pecans, chopped

½ tsp vanilla extract

FOR SERVING

Vanilla bean ice cream

Caramel sauce

Whipped cream

Preheat your cooker to 350°F (177°C), indirect heat.

To make the cake, whisk together the flour, baking soda, sugar and salt in a large bowl. Then set it aside.

In a 10-inch (25-cm) cast-iron skillet, bring the butter, vegetable oil, cocoa powder and water to a boil. Remove it from the heat, and then whisk in the dry ingredients. Whisk until well incorporated. Mix in the buttermilk, egg and vanilla. Bake the skillet cake on a high rack at 350°F (177°C) for 15 to 20 minutes. You should be able to insert a toothpick in the center of the cake, and when you remove it there should only be a few moist crumbs.

Remove the cake from the cooker and set aside to cool. While the cake cools, make the frosting.

To make the frosting, bring the butter, cocoa and milk to a boil in a medium saucepan. Remove from the heat and add the confectioners' sugar, pecans and vanilla. Stir to combine. Pour over the warm cake, spread with a spatula and serve with vanilla bean ice cream, caramel sauce and whipped cream.

CARAMEL BACON STICKY BUNS

A MAZIE Q

These sticky buns are an insanely delicious treat. The soft, buttery dough is brushed with a bacon smear, rolled up with brown sugar and bacon and then baked in a gooey maple-caramel sauce with crunchy bacon bits. You can serve them immediately or at room temperature. Yummy either way you choose, just make sure you have some napkins handy!

YIELD: 20 SERVINGS • COOK TIME: 45 MINUTES

DOUGH

⅔ cup (158 ml) water or milk

1 (¼-oz [7-g]) package active dry yeast

⅓ cup (64 g) granulated sugar

¼ cup (55 g) brown sugar

2 eggs

½ tsp salt

3¼ cups (406 g) all-purpose flour

¾ cup (172 g) butter, cut into cubes, softened

2 lb (907 g) bacon

CARAMEL

½ cup (115 g) butter

¾ cup (144 g) granulated sugar

½ cup (110 g) brown sugar

½ cup (120 ml) rum

½ cup (120 ml) pure maple syrup

1½ cups (355 ml) heavy cream

BACON SMEAR

1 cup (230 g) butter, softened

¼ cup (55 g) brown sugar

¼ cup (49 g) granulated sugar

¼ cup (49 g) maple sugar (if you can't find it, just use granulated sugar)

1 tbsp (8 g) ground cinnamon

¼ cup (60 ml) rum

Pinch of ground nutmeg

To make the dough, warm the water or milk in a microwave-safe bowl, or over the stove. Do not boil. It should be just warm to the touch. Add this to a mixer or bowl with a dough hook attachment. Add the yeast and granulated sugar to the warm water or milk. Wait for the yeast to start to grow and form little clusters; it should take 5 to 10 minutes. If your liquid is too hot, it will kill the yeast.

Add the brown sugar, eggs, salt and flour. Mix until uniform. Please note that the dough will be extremely sticky; this is OK.

Slowly add the butter until all of it is incorporated. You may have to add more flour, but add no more than ½ cup (62 g). The stickier you can keep the dough without adding more flour, the better your overall result will be. The dough will also come together more after it proofs.

You will now need to proof your dough. Cover with plastic wrap and let it sit until the dough has doubled in size, about 1 to 2 hours, depending on the temperature in your house.

While the dough is proofing, cook the bacon until crispy, and crumble once cooled.

To make the caramel, melt the butter in a deep pot and add the sugars. This should form a thick paste. Cook for a few minutes just until the mixture bubbles and has darkened slightly in color. Remove from the heat and carefully add the rum. This will bubble aggressively, and will be scalding hot, so be careful! Add the maple syrup and cream. You will probably have hard, pebble-like sugar particles—do not worry, you will cook this smooth. Let the mixture cook on a slight simmer until the particles are gone. The longer you cook this, the thicker it will be when cooled. Set aside.

To make the bacon smear, combine the ingredients in a mixing bowl. Beat together until all the ingredients just start to mix. The mixture should be a tan color.

Once the dough is ready, remix. The dough will still be sticky.

Turn the dough over on a floured surface. Roll with your hands until you can form a ball. Dust any areas that seem sticky with flour. The dough will be soft and fragile.

On a floured surface, roll the dough into a rectangle about 12 inches wide by 30 inches long (30.5 by 76 cm). Spread the smear on the dough and take half the bacon and sprinkle it all over the smear. Your rectangle will probably be long, so start to roll like a pinwheel a section at a time, until a long log is formed. Reserve the remaining bacon aside.

Cut the log into 1½-inch (4-cm) thick slices. The log should yield about 20 slices.

Find a large baking pan and add about ½ cup (120 ml) of caramel to it. Now add the sticky bun slices. The caramel should rise as you add the slices to the pan. Allow it to come up to about a quarter to one-half the height of the cinnamon bun.

Allow for another hour to proof or until the buns almost double in size.

Adjust the temperature on your smoker to 325°F (165°C) and cook for about 45 minutes, or until the tops are golden brown.

Remove from the smoker and remove from the pan, flipping over so the caramel-cooked side is now on top. Add the remaining caramel if desired along with the remaining crumbled bacon.

CHOCOLATE TRUFFLE STOUT CAKE ~WITH~ SMOKED CARAMEL PEARS

A MAZIE Q

Bake with your booze. Could there be a better backyard combination than this?!? The secret to this moist, rich cake is a healthy dose of your favorite stout in the batter. This decadent chocolate cake is covered with smoky caramel pears for flavors you'll never forget.

YIELD: 8–10 SERVINGS • COOK TIME: 30 MINUTES

SMOKED PEARS

8 pears

2 tbsp (29 g) butter, softened

Cayenne pepper, optional

CARAMEL

¼ cup (57 g) butter

1½ cups (288 g) granulated sugar

½ cup (110 g) light brown sugar

1 cup (236 ml) pear/apple brandy

1½ cups (355 ml) pear juice

STOUT GLAZE

5 (12-oz [340-g]) bottles stout beer

½ cup (96 g) granulated sugar

CAKE

6 eggs, room temperature

1 cup (192 g) sugar

8 oz (227 g) bittersweet chocolate

4 oz (113 g) unsweetened chocolate

2 oz (57 g) semisweet chocolate

1 cup (230 g) butter

¾ tsp salt

½ tsp vanilla bean paste, or vanilla extract

¾ cup (177 ml) Stout Glaze (recipe provided)

¼ cup (60 ml) stout (uncooked)

2½ tbsp (20 g) all-purpose flour

Heat your smoker to 250°F (121°C).

To make the smoked pears, cut the pears in half lengthwise, seed and remove the stem. Spread the butter in a baking pan and place the pears on top, then dust with cayenne (if using). Place the pan of pears in your smoker for an hour. Depending on the size and seasonal freshness of your pears, check for doneness at half-hour intervals. The pears are done once a knife can easily slide through and they have shrunk in size.

To make the caramel, while the pears are cooking or have been removed from the smoker, melt the butter and then add the sugars. This will form a thick paste. Cook for 2 to 3 minutes or until the mixture is hot. Slowly add the liquids to the paste. Be cautious, as sugar can get to high temperatures and will forcefully bubble when you add the liquids. Cook until the mixture is reduced by a quarter or until the caramel's bubbles become larger, approximately 5 to 7 minutes. The color and consistency of the caramel will intensify. As the caramel thickens, it will cling to and coat the back of a spoon. If you test the flavor at this point, please be sure to test with a metal spoon on a plate and taste only when the caramel is cooled—the caramel will be extremely hot.

Add the pears, remove from the heat and refrigerate. This will start to "candy" the pears. The pears are best if they're made at least a day in advance.

To make the glaze, place the stout and the granulated sugar in a pan and bring to a simmer. Reduce until a syrup forms. Once the syrup forms, remove from the heat immediately. This should take no more than 20 minutes depending on your heat and pan.

Prepare your smoker for 250 to 350°F (121 to 177°C) and butter a 9- or 10-inch (23- or 25-cm) cake pan or springform pan.

To make the cake, in a standing mixer or a bowl with handheld mixer, whip the eggs and sugar until thick and pale. The eggs should almost triple in size.

While the eggs are whipping, melt all the chocolate and butter in a large glass or metal bowl over a heated water bath. For the water bath, fill a medium saucepan halfway with water. Bring to a simmer, and gently rest the bowl containing the butter and chocolate atop the saucepan. Stir the contents until completely melted.

Remove the melted chocolate from the stove and add the salt, vanilla, stout glaze and ¼ cup (60 ml) of the uncooked stout. Using a rubber spatula, fold in the egg mixture in three intervals, adding one-third of the mixture each time. In the second interval, add the flour.

Pour the mixture into the cake pan, and place the pan in the smoker. After a half hour, check for doneness by inserting a toothpick or by pressing on the top. When you press down, and the cake is done, it will not bounce back and will be firm. When the cake is done, remove from the smoker.

Remove the pears from your refrigerator, and slice with a sharp knife. Place the sliced pears on top of the cake. Drizzle some of the remaining stout syrup on top of the cake and serve. You can store any leftover syrup in your refrigerator—it's also a great ice cream topping!

> **NOTE:** Cayenne is optional on the pears. If you prefer, you can add a dash of cayenne to the cake itself. The pears are exquisite, and they can be heated and used as a topping for ice cream or other desserts.

GRILLED POUND CAKE *AND* PEACHES *WITH* BOURBON-INFUSED WHIPPED CREAM

COUNTY LINE SMOKERS

The toasty flavor of lightly grilled pound cake makes the perfect accompaniment to sweet, grilled peaches. Top off with bourbon whipping cream for a delightful finish to your next backyard meal.

YIELD: 4–6 SERVINGS • COOK TIME: 15 MINUTES

2–4 tbsp (30–60 ml) bourbon, depending on how pronounced you want the bourbon flavor

1 (16-oz [455-g]) container whipped cream

Dash of vanilla extract

1 cup (230 g) butter

4–5 peaches (you could use pineapple or nectarines, etc.)

½ cup (110 g) brown sugar

1 store-bought pound cake, sliced

For this dessert, it's best to make the whipped cream a day in advance. You can make your own whipped cream or purchase it at the store. Chill the bourbon ahead of time. Mix 2 tablespoons (30 ml) of bourbon (or more if desired) into 16 ounces (455 g) of whipped cream. Add a dash of vanilla, whip together and chill in the refrigerator.

In a small saucepan, melt the butter over medium heat and set aside.

On a gas grill set to high, 500 to 600°F (260 to 316°C), preheat a cast-iron skillet.

Cut the peaches in half and remove the pits. Brush the cut side of the peaches with the butter and place them on the grill, skin-side down, and cook for 1 minute. Brush the skin side with the butter and cook for 1 minute on high heat. After 1 minute, rotate the peaches a quarter turn. After another minute, turn the heat down to low, flip to the skin side and close the lid.

Let the peaches cook for 2 to 3 minutes, open the lid and brush with butter. Sprinkle the brown sugar over the peaches.

Lay out the slices of pound cake. Brush both sides of each slice with a generous coating of butter.

Melt a little butter in the cast-iron skillet. Place the slices of pound cake in the skillet, and cook until golden brown, about 3 to 5 minutes. Flip, and cook for an additional 3 to 5 minutes. Remove from the grill.

Remove the peaches from the grill. Cut them into approximately 7 to 8 slices.

Place 2 slices of pound cake on a plate. Add peach slices and finish with a dollop of the bourbon whipped cream.

HOMEMADE CHOCOLATE BUNDT CAKE WITH RASPBERRY GLAZE

BBQ GURU

Chocolate and raspberry are a match made in dessert heaven. This pairing is featured beautifully in this rich chocolate cake filled with chocolate chips and drizzled with a fresh raspberry glaze.

YIELD: 12–16 SERVINGS • COOK TIME: 70 MINUTES

CAKE

½ cup (43 g) unsweetened cocoa powder (plus 2 tbsp [11 g] for dusting)

3 cups (375 g) all-purpose flour

½ tsp baking powder

½ tsp salt

1 cup (230 g) butter, softened

½ cup (109 g) shortening

3 cups (575 g) granulated sugar

1 tsp vanilla extract

5 eggs

1 cup (236 ml) milk

1 cup (180 g) dark chocolate chips

GLAZE

2 tbsp (40 g) raspberry preserves

1 tbsp (14 g) butter

1 pint (246 g) fresh raspberries

Preheat your cooker to 325°F (163°C), indirect heat. Grease a 10-inch (25-cm) Bundt pan. Dust the pan using cocoa powder to avoid white spots on your finished product.

To make the cake, sift together the cocoa, flour, baking powder and salt. Set aside.

In a large mixing bowl, cream the butter, shortening, sugar and vanilla until light and fluffy. Add the eggs one at a time, beating well after each egg is added. Add the flour mixture alternately with the milk and mix well. Fold in the dark chocolate chips.

Pour into the prepared Bundt pan. Bake for 70 minutes, or until a toothpick inserted into the cake comes out clean when it is removed. Let the cake cool for 10 minutes in the pan. Flip the pan onto a wire rack, carefully remove the cake from the pan and allow the cake to cool completely.

To make the glaze, melt the raspberry preserves and butter in a small saucepan, add the fresh raspberries and set aside.

Slice the cake, drizzle with raspberry glaze and serve.

LIGHT AS A FEATHER CANTALOUPE PIE

OLD VIRGINIA SMOKE BBQ TEAM

This pie is a wonderfully refreshing dessert on warm, summery barbecue evenings! It's not your normal, everyday pie. Instead, it's a light, flavorful pie made with fresh cantaloupe and orange juice-flavored gelatin. This dessert is a real crowd-pleaser, especially after a heavy barbecue meal.

YIELD: 6–8 SERVINGS • COOK TIME: 15 MINUTES

2 Keebler Shortbread Crusts (NOT graham cracker) or you can make your own crusts (see below)

SHORTBREAD CRUST

2 cups (250 g) all-purpose flour

⅔ cup (85 g) confectioners' sugar, or icing sugar

¼ tsp salt

1 cup (225 g) unsalted butter, cold and cut into small chunks

FILLING

1 ripe cantaloupe (3 cups [710 ml] purée)

½ cup (120 ml) orange juice, freshly squeezed

3 envelopes unflavored gelatin

¼–½ cup (48–96 g) sugar, depending on the sweetness of the cantaloupe

1 (8- or 9-oz [227- or 255-g]) container Cool Whip, in the blue container ONLY, plus more for serving

Lightly butter or spray an 8- or 9-inch (20- or 23-cm) tart or pie pan with nonstick vegetable spray.

To make the crust, in your food processor, place the flour, sugar and salt, and process to combine. Add the cold butter and pulse until the pastry starts to come together and form clumps. Transfer the pastry to the prepared pan and evenly press it onto the bottom and up the sides of the pan. To prevent the pastry crust from puffing up while it bakes, pierce the bottom of the crust with the tines of a fork.

Cover and place the pastry crust in the freezer for 15 minutes to chill. This will help prevent the crust from shrinking while it bakes.

Preheat your smoker to 425°F (218°C) with an indirect setup.

Place the pan on a larger baking sheet and bake the crust indirectly until golden brown, about 13 to 15 minutes. Remove the pan and place on a wire rack to cool. It is now ready to be filled.

To make the filling, cut the cantaloupe in half, and remove the seeds and rind. Cut off a few thin slices of melon, and reserve them for garnish. Cut the remaining melon into chunks and purée in an electric blender or food processor. You need 3 cups (710 ml) of purée.

Pour the orange juice into a small saucepan, sprinkle the gelatin on the orange juice, and then sprinkle sugar on top of the gelatin and let it stand for several minutes. Cook over medium heat, stirring constantly, until the sugar and gelatin dissolve. In a large bowl, pour in the melon purée and fold in the whipped topping.

Using a wire whisk, drizzle the orange juice mixture in and blend thoroughly. Pour it into the pie shell and place in the refrigerator.

Let it cool until the mixture is firmly set, at least 2 hours.

Garnish with the melon slices and serve with more whipped topping.

MYRON'S BLACKBERRY COBBLER

MYRON MIXON

When blackberries are in season, you will often find Myron carrying pints of them to snack on as he checks his smoker and pit temperature. He also enjoys the tart flavors and the sweetness of the blackberries in his cobbler, but you can substitute other fruits to your preference.

YIELD: 6–8 SERVINGS • COOK TIME: 1½ HOURS

2 pints (576 g) fresh or frozen blackberries

¾ cup (144 g) granulated sugar, divided

½ cup (110 g) firmly packed brown sugar

1 tbsp plus ½ cup (70 g) all-purpose flour, divided

1 tbsp (15 ml) apple cider vinegar

1 tsp ground cinnamon

1 tsp baking powder

½ tsp kosher salt

½ cup (120 ml) buttermilk or whole milk

¼ cup (55 g) lard or vegetable shortening

Vanilla ice cream, for serving

Set up your smoker for indirect cooking at 250°F (121°C).

In a medium nonreactive bowl, stir together the blackberries, ¼ cup (48 g) of the granulated sugar, brown sugar, 1 tablespoon (8 g) of the flour, the vinegar and cinnamon. Set aside.

In another medium nonreactive bowl, sift together the remaining ½ cup (62 g) of flour, the remaining ½ cup (96 g) of granulated sugar, the baking powder and the salt. Pour in the buttermilk and use a wooden spoon to stir and combine. The batter should be the consistency of pancake batter. It is fine if there are a few lumps. Set aside.

In a 10-inch (25-cm) cast-iron skillet, melt the lard over medium heat until it starts to brown around the edge and foam. You should hear it sizzling. When you hear the lard start to brown and sizzle, pour the batter into the hot skillet. Do not stir it. Pour the fruit mixture right on top of the batter. Remove the skillet from the heat.

Transfer the skillet into the pit that you have been steadily maintaining at 250°F (121°C). Smoke the cobbler until the crust is golden and crisp-edged, about 1½ hours. Serve warm, topped with vanilla ice cream.

PEANUT BUTTER SHEET CAKE

NAUGHTY NURSES BBQ

This wonderfully moist peanut butter sheet cake is large enough to serve at most gatherings. With even more peanut butter love in the frosting, this cake will leave peanut butter lovers feeling giddy!

YIELD: 35 SERVINGS • COOK TIME: 15–20 MINUTES

CAKE

1 cup (230 g) butter

½ cup (90 g) peanut butter

1 cup (236 ml) water

2 cups (250 g) all-purpose flour

2 cups (383 g) sugar

½ cup (120 ml) buttermilk

½ tsp salt

1 tsp baking soda

1 tsp vanilla extract

2 eggs

FROSTING

½ cup (90 g) peanut butter

⅓ cup (79 ml) milk, plus more as needed

½ cup (115 g) butter

1 tsp vanilla extract

4 cups (520 g) confectioners' sugar

Configure your smoker for indirect cooking, and let the temperature stabilize at 350°F (177°C).

To make the cake, in a saucepan, bring the butter, peanut butter and water to a light boil.

Meanwhile, in a mixing bowl, combine the flour, sugar, buttermilk, salt, baking soda and vanilla.

When the peanut butter mixture comes to a light boil, stir it into the flour mixture. Then add the eggs and mix until combined.

Pour the batter into a greased 12 x 17-inch (30 x 43-cm) sheet pan. Place in the smoker and bake for 15 to 20 minutes.

To make the frosting, in a saucepan, bring the peanut butter, milk, butter and vanilla to a boil; then add the confectioners' sugar. If the frosting is thick, add more milk, a tablespoon (15 ml) at a time, until smooth and of thinner consistency. Frost the cake when it is still warm.

PINEAPPLE HEAD PUMPKIN CAKE DOUGHNUTS

DIZZY PIG BBQ TEAM

These moist pumpkin doughnuts, with hints of spice throughout, are quick and simple to make. Leftover doughnuts can be kept in an airtight container for up to 3 days. Although this has yet to be put to the test, because these doughnuts tend to disappear rather abruptly.

YIELD: 12 DOUGHNUTS • COOK TIME: 15–18 MINUTES

PINEAPPLE HEAD AND CINNAMON-SUGAR MIXTURE

1½ tsp (4 g) ground cinnamon

1½ tsp (7 g) Dizzy Pig Pineapple Head seasoning

½ cup (96 g) sugar

CAKE

3 large eggs

1½ cups (288 g) sugar

1 tsp ground cinnamon

1½ tsp (8 g) salt

1 tbsp (14 g) Dizzy Pig Pineapple Head seasoning

1½ tsp (6 g) baking powder

1½ cups (355 ml) Libby's pure pumpkin purée

½ cup (120 ml) vegetable oil

1¾ cups plus 2 tbsp (235 g) unbleached all-purpose flour

Preheat your smoker to 350°F (177°C), indirect heat.

To make the sugar mixture, combine the cinnamon, Pineapple Head seasoning and sugar in a gallon-size (3.8-L) ziplock bag.

To make the cake, in a large bowl, beat the eggs and sugar together, until thoroughly mixed. Add the cinnamon, salt, Pineapple Head seasoning and baking powder and mix thoroughly. Add the pumpkin purée and vegetable oil, and mix until smooth. Slowly add the flour and mix until smooth.

Fill the pan indentations (doughnut or doughnut hole–shaped) three-fourths of the way up the sides. Bake for 15 to 18 minutes, or until a toothpick inserted into the center comes out clean.

Let cool 5 to 10 minutes. Remove from the baking pan and add to the bag with the Pineapple Head and cinnamon-sugar mixture, tossing to coat.

PUMPKIN CRUNCH

HERE PIGGY PIGGY BBQ

If you're looking for an easy pumpkin crunch recipe, this is a great choice! This pumpkin crunch is nicely spiced. While you can adjust the cinnamon to your liking, substituting it altogether using pumpkin pie spice works well, too. If you're not sure which choice to make, then simply serve both!

YIELD: 12 SERVINGS • COOK TIME: 55 MINUTES

1 (15-oz [425-g]) can pumpkin

1 (12-oz [340-g]) can evaporated milk

3 eggs

1½ cups (288 g) sugar

1 tsp ground cinnamon

½ tsp salt

1 (16.25-oz [460-g]) box yellow cake mix

½ cup (60 g) chopped pecans

1 cup (230 g) butter, melted

Whipped topping, for serving

Preheat your smoker to 350°F (177°C) for indirect cooking.

Grease the bottom of a round 9-inch (23-cm) cake pan. Combine the pumpkin, evaporated milk, eggs, sugar, cinnamon and salt in a large bowl. Pour it into the prepared pan. Sprinkle the dry cake mix evenly over the pumpkin mixture and top with the chopped pecans. Drizzle the butter over the pecans.

Bake indirectly for 50 to 55 minutes, or until golden brown. Cool and serve chilled, topped with the whipped topping before serving.

SALTED CARAMEL CHOCOLATE MINI CHEESECAKES

LORI-ANN, BARK BROTHERS BBQ

These mini cheesecakes are a crowd favorite. They're dense, New York–style tiny cheesecakes, perfect for any dessert table, or any occasion your sweet tooth desires. The combination of salted caramel, creamy cheesecake and chocolate ganache makes one highly addictive dessert!

YIELD: 12 SERVINGS • COOK TIME: 45 MINUTES

Solid coconut oil, for greasing the pan

CRUST

1 sleeve of chocolate graham crackers, crushed

4 tbsp (57 g) unsalted butter, melted and cooled

¼–½ tsp salt

SALTED CARAMEL CHEESECAKE FILLING

12 oz (340 g) cream cheese, room temperature

½ cup (110 g) brown sugar

2 eggs, room temperature

½ cup (120 ml) heavy whipping cream

2 tbsp (30 ml) salted caramel-flavored syrup

CARAMEL SAUCE

¼ cup (57 g) butter

¾ cup (165 g) packed brown sugar

1 tbsp (15 ml) salted caramel-flavored syrup

½ cup (120 ml) heavy whipping cream

DARK CHOCOLATE GANACHE

½ cup (120 ml) heavy whipping cream

½ cup (90 g) dark chocolate chips

WHIPPED CREAM

1 cup (236 ml) heavy whipping cream

1 tbsp (15 ml) vanilla extract

1 tbsp (18 g) flaked sea salt, for serving

Grease a 12-cup mini cheesecake pan with a removable bottom. I use solid coconut oil. Ensure the entire pan well is covered with a light coating.

Cook's tip: Wear disposable gloves for this next step. To make the crust, combine the crushed graham crackers with the melted butter and salt until all the crumbs are moistened. Add 1½ tablespoons (8 g) of moistened graham crackers to each well. Push the crumbs down until packed into the well of the pan. (If it's not packed well, pieces of the graham cracker crumbs will float up into the cheesecakes.)

While you prepare the filling, preheat your smoker to 325°F (163°C) for indirect cooking.

To make the filling, beat the cream cheese and brown sugar, using the paddle attachment on your stand mixer. Add the eggs, one at a time, and mix until smooth before adding the second egg. Then add the whipping cream and syrup. Beat until well blended, about 5 minutes.

(continued)

Spoon 1½ tablespoons (20 ml) of filling into each well, over the graham cracker crust. Let it sit for a few minutes to settle. You want the wells almost full, with room for ganache after cooling.

Set the mini cheesecake pan in a jellyroll pan or a similar pan with high sides that can hold at least ½ inch (1.3 cm) of water. Put in the smoker. Using a measuring cup with a pour spout, add enough water to cover the bottom of the mini cheesecake pan. Bake for 15 minutes or until the tops of the cheesecakes gently bounce back when you touch them. Remove and allow the cheesecakes to come to room temperature, about 20 to 30 minutes. The edges should be pulling away slightly from the cake well.

To make the caramel sauce, melt the butter in a saucepan on low to medium heat. Add the brown sugar and salted caramel syrup. Bring to a bubbling simmer, allowing the sugars to dissolve, about 2 minutes for light caramel or 4 minutes for dark caramel. Remove from the heat, and then stir in ½ cup (120 ml) of heavy whipping cream. Be careful, as the hot liquid can scald! Return to a simmer, stir 1 to 2 minutes and then allow to cool for 30 minutes. Put into a squeeze bottle when it's cool and squeeze a few drops to cover the cheesecakes. Wrap and refrigerate while making the ganache.

To make the ganache, combine the heavy whipping cream and dark chocolate chips in a small bowl. Microwave for 2 minutes on high, stirring every 30 seconds. Whisk after the chocolate is melted and combined with the heavy cream, and let it cool for about 10 minutes.

Add 1½ tablespoons (20 ml) of dark chocolate ganache to each of the cooled cheesecakes. Refrigerate and allow them to set overnight.

To make the whipped cream, place the heavy whipping cream and vanilla in a stand mixer fitted with the whisk attachment, or use a handheld mixer, and whisk until stiff peaks form, 3 to 4 minutes.

To serve, push the cheesecakes up through the bottom of the pan, and slide off the circular base using a sharp knife. Add a drizzle of caramel sauce and flaked sea salt, and top the cheesecakes with whipped cream.

OPERATION BBQ RELIEF IN ACTION

Our team, Bark Brothers BBQ, got involved with OBR after mutual friends on the competition trail told us about it. They actually went to cook in Moscow, Ohio, after a tornado ripped through in 2012. We, being competition cooks, thought it was an excellent idea and a great charity to support, so we try to promote it whenever possible. We have not been on a deployment yet, but if the need calls in our area we will rise to the occasion.

—TODD WERNICKE, *Bark Brothers BBQ*

SMOKED PEAR-APPLE CRISP *WITH* BACON–BROWN SUGAR CRUMBLE

PORK BARREL BBQ

Few things go with apples better than pork, and we all know that the best form of pork is bacon—so why not let what wants to be together come together? This is a great fall dessert, when apples and pears are at their peak.

YIELD: 12 SERVINGS • COOK TIME: 55 MINUTES

FILLING

¾ cup (90 g) pecans

¼ cup (57 g) unsalted butter, cut into ¼" (6-mm) pieces

4 Braeburn apples, peeled, cored and cut into ¼" (6-mm) slices

3 Comice pears, peeled, cored and cut into ¼" (6-mm) slices

½ tsp ground cinnamon

6 tbsp (72 g) granulated sugar

3 tbsp (44 ml) pear brandy

1 tbsp (15 ml) Grand Marnier

TOPPING

10 slices applewood smoked bacon, cut into 1" (2.5-cm) pieces

½ cup (110 g) tightly packed light brown sugar, divided

½ cup (62 g) all-purpose flour

4 tbsp (48 g) granulated sugar

½ cup (115 g) unsalted butter, cut into ¼" (6-mm) pieces

Vanilla ice cream, for serving

Preheat your grill to medium-high at 350 to 400°F (177 to 204°C).

To make the filling, toast the pecans on the grill by spreading them out on a small cookie sheet and baking for 10 to 15 minutes, stirring occasionally.

In a medium cast-iron skillet, melt the butter and add the apples, pears, cinnamon and sugar. Cook over medium heat. Bring the mixture to a boil, reduce the heat to medium-low and simmer. Stir occasionally, until the apples and pears are tender, about 7 minutes.

Butter a disposable aluminum half pan (10 x 12-inch [25.4 x 30.5-cm]). Remove the apple-pear mixture from the heat and add the brandy and Grand Marnier. Stir to mix and then add to the buttered aluminum pan.

To make the topping, in a medium cast-iron skillet, cook the bacon pieces over medium-low heat until crispy, 3 to 4 minutes. Transfer the cooked bacon to a paper towel to drain. Drain the bacon grease from the skillet and then return the bacon to the skillet. Sprinkle the bacon with ¼ cup (55 g) of brown sugar. Cook until the sugar has coated the bacon, about 3 minutes. Transfer the bacon to a cutting board, cool slightly, 2 to 3 minutes, and then chop the bacon into small bits.

In a bowl, combine the flour, granulated sugar and remaining ¼ cup (55 g) of brown sugar. Add the butter and mix together with a fork until crumbly. Stir in the pecans and half of the bacon bits. Sprinkle the topping over the apple-pear mixture. Top with the remaining bacon bits.

Place the crisp on the grill, close the cover and cook until the top is lightly browned, about 30 minutes. Let it cool and serve warm with a scoop of vanilla ice cream.

SWEDISH BAKED CHOCOLATE PUDDING

SMOKE ON WHEELS BBQ TEAM

Swedish baked pudding is a delicious, chocolaty pudding that is wonderful served warm with a spoonful of whipped cream or a high-quality vanilla bean ice cream. This wonderful fudgy cake, similar to brownies, will make children and adults happy!

YIELD: 9 SERVINGS • COOK TIME: 40 MINUTES

PUDDING

1 cup (125 g) all-purpose flour

¼ tsp salt

¾ cup (144 g) sugar

2 tsp (7 g) baking powder

½ cup (60 g) pecans, chopped

2 tbsp (29 g) butter, melted

1 oz (28 g) square baking chocolate, melted

½ cup (120 ml) milk

1 tsp vanilla extract

TOPPING

½ cup (96 g) granulated sugar

½ cup (110 g) brown sugar, packed

4 rounded tbsp (28 g) cocoa powder, unsweetened

Whipped cream or high-quality vanilla bean ice cream, for serving

Prepare your cooker for 325°F (163°C), indirect heat.

To make the pudding, combine the flour, salt, sugar, baking powder and pecans in a bowl. In a separate bowl, melt the butter and chocolate together in a microwave or a double boiler and add the milk and vanilla. Add the liquid ingredients to the dry ingredients and mix to incorporate the batter. Place the batter into a greased or buttered 9 x 9-inch (23 x 23-cm) baking dish.

To make the topping, mix the ingredients in a small bowl. Using a sifter, sprinkle the topping over the batter in the pan. Pour 1 cup (236 ml) of water into a pan that is large enough to hold the pan containing the cake. Bake for 40 minutes or until the top of the cake is dry.

Serve with whipped cream or vanilla bean ice cream.

TEXAS BOURBON-GLAZED BREAD PUDDING

BRYAN MCLARTY

This delicious Texas bread pudding is luscious, with an out-of-this-world buttery bourbon glaze. Make sure you serve the bourbon sauce while it is slightly warm.

YIELD: 8–10 SERVINGS • COOK TIME: 70 MINUTES

BREAD PUDDING

3–4 cups (125–160 g) day-old cinnamon rolls, cut into ¾" (2-cm) cubes (Pillsbury Grands work well)

2 cups (473 ml) whole milk

2 eggs

1 cup (192 g) sugar

1 tbsp (15 ml) vanilla extract

½ tsp ground cinnamon

¼ tsp ground nutmeg

4 tbsp (57 g) butter, melted and slightly cooled

½ cup (76 g) raisins

TEXAS BOURBON SAUCE

2 egg yolks

½ cup (115 g) butter (not margarine)

1 cup (192 g) sugar

⅓ cup (79 ml) TX Whiskey

Preheat the cooker to 350°F (177°C), indirect heat. Grease a muffin pan or a 9 x 13-inch (23 x 33-cm) baking dish.

To make the bread pudding, place the cut-up cinnamon rolls in a large bowl with the milk. Mix together, lightly squeezing with your hands until the milk is well absorbed. Pour off any extra milk.

In a separate bowl, with an electric mixer on high speed, beat the eggs with the sugar until thick and pale, about 3 to 4 minutes. Stir the vanilla, cinnamon, nutmeg, butter and raisins into the egg mixture. Add the soaked bread pieces to the egg mixture and stir well. Let stand for 10 minutes. It is important to allow enough time for the bread to absorb the egg mixture or the bread will float to the top during baking, leaving a layer of custard on the bottom of the dish.

Transfer the mixture to the prepared pan. Place on the indirect side of the grates and bake until firm, or until a knife inserted in the middle comes out clean, about 45 to 50 minutes. Let it slightly cool in the dish.

Near the end of the baking time, make the sauce. To make the sauce, with an electric mixer, beat the egg yolks until thick and pale, about 4 to 5 minutes. In a saucepan, melt the butter and sugar until the sugar is dissolved. Pour the butter and sugar mixture over the egg yolks, in a slow, steady stream, while beating constantly with your mixer until well thickened, about 2 minutes. Stir in the TX Whiskey by hand until smooth.

Serve the pudding warm with the sauce drizzled over the top.

CINNAMON-Y SWEET POTATO CUPCAKES

FREDDY RAY'S BBQ

These cupcakes are very moist and the cream cheese frosting topping this cinnamon-y delight adds the perfect sweetness and creamy texture. These would make a great fall dessert or even something unexpected for the Thanksgiving table.

YIELD: 18 JUMBO OR 24 REGULAR CUPCAKES • COOK TIME: 20 MINUTES

CUPCAKES

2 cups (250 g) all-purpose flour

2 tsp (7 g) baking powder

1 tsp ground cinnamon

½ tsp baking soda

¼ tsp salt

1 cup (230 g) butter, softened

1½ cups (288 g) granulated sugar

3 eggs

2 cups (482 g) mashed sweet potatoes

½ tsp vanilla extract

CREAM CHEESE ICING

½ cup (115 g) butter, softened

1½ (8-oz [227-g]) packages cream cheese, softened

1 (16-oz [454-g]) package confectioners' sugar

1½ tsp (7 ml) vanilla extract

Preheat your smoker or grill to 350°F (177°C), indirect heat.

To make the cupcakes, in a large bowl, sift together the flour, baking powder, cinnamon, baking soda and salt. Set aside.

In a separate large bowl, beat the butter for 30 seconds. Add the sugar and beat for 2 minutes until light and fluffy. Add the eggs one at a time, beating on low speed. Add the sweet potatoes and vanilla, and mix until well combined. Add the flour mixture and mix well. Place cupcake liners into muffin tins. Fill the muffin tins about three-fourths full with batter and bake for 20 minutes. The tops should bounce back after you press your hand on them. Let them cool completely.

To make the icing, beat the butter and cream cheese in a large bowl at medium speed until creamy, about 3 minutes. Add the confectioners' sugar and vanilla and beat at high speed until smooth, about 3 additional minutes. Spread on the cooled cupcakes.

CARAMEL-TOPPED CHOCOLATE BREAD PUDDING

RI COOK TEAM

This is a fun recipe because the chocolate makes it different from traditional bread pudding. It's a rich, comforting dessert!

YIELD: 8 SERVINGS • COOK TIME: 45–60 MINUTES

2½ cups (590 ml) half-and-half

1 pack sugar-free chocolate cook-and-serve pudding mix

½ cup (96 g) sugar

7 cups (415 g) cubed French bread

3 large Snickers bars, chopped (or any candies you like)

¼–½ cup (60–120 ml) caramel sundae syrup

Vanilla ice cream, optional

Configure your grill or smoker for indirect cooking, and preheat to 350°F (177°C).

Coat a 12 x 10-inch (30.5 x 25-cm) pan with cooking spray.

Combine the half-and-half, pudding mix and sugar in a medium bowl. Whisk together well.

Stir in the bread cubes, until coated, and pour into the pan. Sprinkle the chopped candies on top.

Place it on the grill or smoker and cook using indirect heat for 45 minutes to an hour. Rotate the pan after 25 minutes to help ensure even cooking.

Serve with drizzled caramel on top and vanilla ice cream, if you like.

NOTE: One option is to pour half the coated bread mixture into the pan, drizzle with caramel and then add the rest of the bread mixture.

CHAPTER 9

RUBS, SAUCES & BRINES

THESE AWARD-WINNING BBQ RUBS AND SAUCES used by professional and backyard cooks are a great way to bring added flavor to the foods you prepare on your grill. Rubs provide aromatic flair to food and form a crust on the surface of meat that helps seal in moisture. Marinades and brines are liquid concoctions that infuse flavor into foods prior to cooking. Marinades also contain acids that can help soften the tough exterior of meat, creating a tender finished product. Sauces usually get applied in the final part of the cooking process, and they're one of the great joys of the barbecue community. If you're looking for ideas on how to up your flavor, you've come to the right place!

REMOULADE SAUCE

SMOKE ON WHEELS BBQ TEAM

Top your crab, shrimp, lobster, salmon dishes or seafood po' boy sandwiches with this wonderfully spicy sauce, which has its origins in France and was popularized in New Orleans. It is best used the next day, and can last several days in the refrigerator.

YIELD: ABOUT 2½ CUPS (590 ML) • PREP TIME: 30 SECONDS

¼ cup (60 ml) fresh lemon juice

¾ cup (177 ml) light olive oil

½ cup (76 g) chopped sweet onion

½ cup (25 g) chopped scallions

¼ cup (25 g) chopped celery heart

4 cloves garlic, pressed

2 tbsp (30 g) prepared horseradish

3 tbsp (47 g) whole-grain mustard

3 tbsp (47 g) prepared yellow mustard

3 tbsp (46 g) ketchup

3 tbsp (9 g) chopped flat parsley

1 tsp salt

¼ tsp cayenne pepper

⅛ tsp freshly ground black pepper

Combine all the ingredients in the bowl of a food processor and process for 30 seconds. This sauce will keep for several days in an airtight container in the refrigerator.

CAROLINA MUSTARD BBQ SAUCE

DIVA Q, AKA DANIELLE BENNETT

Mustard sauces are a great change from your everyday barbecue sauce. Diva Q's tangy mustard and vinegar sauce, with a sweet background, is fantastic served on pulled pork sandwiches, ribs, ham or pulled chicken.

YIELD: MAKES 3 CUPS (710 ML) • COOK TIME: 15 MINUTES

½ cup (125 g) yellow mustard

½ cup (120 ml) apple cider vinegar

½ cup (110 g) light brown sugar

¼ cup (50 g) finely minced onion

¼ cup (60 ml) clover honey

1 tbsp (15 ml) Worcestershire sauce

1 tsp finely minced garlic

1 tsp hot sauce

½ tsp kosher salt

½ tsp chipotle powder

Mix all the ingredients in a medium pot. Bring to a boil, and then simmer for 15 minutes. Serve on pulled pork, ribs, ham or pulled chicken.

FAMOUS DAVE'S CAJUN DYNAMITE DUST

FAMOUS DAVE ANDERSON

Famous Dave's Cajun Dynamite Dust blackening spice is great on ribs, chicken or fish. Alter this recipe to your taste. Kick it up if you like it spicy by adding more cayenne pepper, or eliminate the cayenne altogether if you prefer it mild. This rub is ideal for all your grilled blackened dishes.

YIELD: ABOUT 2 ⅓ CUPS (270 G) • COOK TIME: NONE

½ cup (58 g) paprika

6 tbsp (108 g) kosher salt

¼ cup (24 g) coarse ground black pepper

3 tbsp (5 g) dried basil

3 tbsp (30 g) filé powder

2 tbsp (20 g) garlic powder

2 tbsp (15 g) dry mustard

2 tbsp (14 g) onion powder

2 tbsp (11 g) dried oregano

2 tbsp (10 g) cayenne, or to taste

2 tbsp (14 g) ground white pepper

2 tbsp (9 g) dried thyme

Mix all the ingredients in a bowl and store in an airtight container. Use as a rub for blackened dishes.

FAMOUS DAVE'S SECRET FRIED CHICKEN MARINADE

FAMOUS DAVE ANDERSON

Dave Anderson uses a chicken base in his marinade. The longer the chicken marinates, the better the chicken turns out. It's very little work and adds tremendously to the finished flavor of your fried chicken dish.

YIELD: ABOUT 1 GALLON (3.8 L) • COOK TIME: 5 MINUTES

1 gal plus 2 cups (4.5 L) cold water, divided

6 tbsp (88 g) chicken base

2 tbsp (30 g) salt

2 tsp (5 g) finely ground black pepper

1 tsp cayenne

1 tbsp (15 ml) liquid hickory smoke

Prepare the marinade 2 days before frying the chicken. In a small pot, bring 2 cups (473 ml) of water to a boil. Add the chicken base and dry ingredients. Mix well and remove from the heat. Add the liquid hickory smoke, and then immediately combine with 1 gallon (4 L) of water. Let the marinade stand overnight before using.

GRILLED PINEAPPLE POBLANO SALSA

DIVA Q, AKA DANIELLE BENNETT

In this pineapple-poblano salsa combination, the sweetness of the pineapple is offset by the smokiness and spiciness of the peppers. Serve this salsa alongside your favorite chips or over steak, pork or chicken. It also works great in fish tacos and similar seafood dishes.

YIELD: ABOUT 6 CUPS (1.47 KG) • COOK TIME: 15 MINUTES

2 tsp (10 ml) canola oil, plus more for coating

1 large ripe pineapple, trimmed

1 large white sweet onion, halved

1 whole poblano pepper, seeded and halved

1 jalapeño pepper, seeded and finely minced

1 red bell pepper, finely minced

Juice and zest of 2 limes

¼ cup (50 g) finely minced red onion

1 small bunch cilantro, finely chopped

Salt and pepper, to taste

Prepare the grill for medium-high heat. Oil the grates with canola oil. Slice the pineapple into ½-inch (1.3-cm) thick slices.

Grill the pineapple slices directly, turning often until just tender and lightly charred, about 4 to 6 minutes. Grill the white onion and poblano, turning often, until softened and the skin has blistered, about 6 to 8 minutes.

Cube the grilled pineapple and chop the poblano and white onion into small pieces. Add the remaining ingredients and serve with chicken, pork or fish.

IQUE SAUCE V2.0

CHRIS HART, IQUE BBQ TEAM

Version 1.0, the sauce recipe that Chris Hart's team IQue used to help them win the 2009 Jack Daniel's World Championship, was delicious. But some of the ingredients were a pain to procure, and the team often wondered if it was worth it. Over time they transitioned to this recipe, which uses readily available pantry ingredients that presented a more familiar flavor profile to the KCBS judges. Feel free to get creative with the spice blend and finishing spice components of this recipe and make it your own.

YIELD: APPROXIMATELY 5 CUPS (1.2 L) • COOK TIME: 55 MINUTES

1 cup (220 g) packed light brown sugar

1 cup (236 ml) apple cider vinegar

¼ cup (60 ml) Worcestershire sauce

1 tbsp (10 g) garlic powder

1 tbsp (8 g) chili powder

1 tsp onion powder

1 tsp ground cumin

1 tsp Old Bay Seasoning

1 tsp fine ground black pepper

2 cups (491 g) ketchup

½ cup (120 ml) maple syrup, dark amber grades are preferred

1 tbsp (14 g) your favorite dry rub, or the latest hyped-up dry rub on the competition circuit

In a medium saucepan over medium heat, combine the brown sugar, vinegar and Worcestershire sauce. Bring to a gentle boil. As soon as the sauce base begins to boil, remove it from the heat. Add the garlic powder, chili powder, onion powder, ground cumin, Old Bay and black pepper. Mix very well, cover and let it sit for 15 minutes.

Stir in the ketchup and maple syrup. Return to the stove and simmer, uncovered, over low heat for 30 minutes. DO NOT let the sauce boil.

Using a spice grinder, process the dry rub into a fine powder. Remove the sauce from the heat and add the rub. Let it cool. Transfer to a quart-sized (liter-sized) glass mason jar and store in the refrigerator for up to 1 month.

KANSAS CITY GLAZE

WILBUR'S REVENGE

This Kansas City–style sauce is sweet and smoky with a little bite. Feel free to increase or decrease the amount of cayenne to your taste preference.

YIELD: MAKES 4 CUPS (946 ML) • COOK TIME: 20 MINUTES

2 cups (491 g) ketchup

½ cup (120 ml) clover honey

½ cup (120 ml) agave

½ cup (120 ml) water

⅓ cup (79 ml) apple cider vinegar

⅓ cup (73 g) brown sugar

2 tbsp (31 g) yellow mustard

1 tbsp (7 g) onion powder

1 tbsp (10 g) garlic powder

½ tsp cayenne

Combine all the ingredients in a saucepan over low heat. Stir occasionally. Simmer for 20 minutes. The sauce should be thin but not watery. Allow to cool. Store in an airtight container and refrigerate. The sauce can be used immediately but is best if you allow it to cure for 24 hours.

QUICK CARAMEL SAUCE

LUCKY Q

This is a rich, sweet caramel sauce that can quickly be made at the last minute. It's great on just about anything you want to put it on, especially desserts!

YIELD: 2 CUPS (475 ML) • COOK TIME: 5–10 MINUTES

1 cup (220 g) brown sugar

½ cup (115 g) salted butter

½ cup (120 ml) cream or half-and-half, optional for creamier sauce

Chopped roasted pecans, optional

Place all the ingredients in a small, disposable loaf pan. Place the pan on your grill at medium-low heat, stirring frequently, until the mixture boils and the sugar dissolves. In less than 10 minutes, the sauce will thicken.

Remove from the heat and serve warm over your favorite dessert or cool to use later.

KAYLIN'S AWARD-WINNING STEAK RUB

KAYLIN GRONEMAN, RECKLESS AND BRAVE BBQ

When you're looking for the perfect rub to use on any cut of beef, look to Kansas City for inspiration. This award-winning rub, created by a young competition cook from Kansas City, will inspire your meals to stimulate your taste buds!

YIELD: ABOUT ¾ CUP (87 G) • COOK TIME: NONE

2 tbsp (16 g) ancho chile powder

2 tbsp (11 g) finely ground coffee

5 tsp (23 g) dark brown sugar

1 tbsp (7 g) hot paprika

1½ tsp (1 g) dried oregano

1½ tsp (4 g) freshly ground black pepper

½ tsp freshly ground pink/white pepper

1½ tsp (3 g) ground coriander

1½ tsp (3 g) mustard powder

1 tsp chipotle powder

1 tsp ground ginger

1 tbsp (18 g) kosher salt

Combine all the ingredients in a bowl and mix well. Store in an airtight container.

SMOKIN' HOGGZ ALL-PURPOSE DRY RUB

SMOKIN' HOGGZ

Everyone needs a good dry rub in their barbecue bag of tricks. A good dry rub has to be well balanced with the sweetness, the heat and a touch of the savory. This rub does just that.

YIELD: ABOUT 2 CUPS (230 G) • COOK TIME: NONE

½ cup (96 g) granulated sugar

½ cup (110 g) brown sugar

¼ cup (36 g) ancho chile powder

¼ cup (72 g) kosher salt

2 tbsp (15 g) paprika

1 tbsp (6 g) ground black pepper

2 tsp (6 g) garlic powder

2 tsp (5 g) onion powder

1 tsp white pepper

½ tsp allspice

Mix all the ingredients together and store in an airtight container.

MYRON MIXON'S VINEGAR SAUCE

JACK'S OLD SOUTH BBQ

This type of sauce is popular in the Carolinas, and it's one of the oldest sauces invented in the South. You can use this as a basting sauce or just mix it with cooked meat when you are ready to eat.

YIELD: 3 CUPS (710 ML) • COOK TIME: 6–8 MINUTES

2 cups (473 ml) apple cider vinegar

1 cup (245 g) ketchup

½ cup (120 ml) hot sauce

2 tbsp (30 g) salt

2 tbsp (12 g) coarsely ground black pepper

1 tbsp (3 g) red pepper flakes

½ cup (96 g) sugar

In a stockpot over medium heat, combine the vinegar, ketchup and hot sauce. Stir together for about 5 to 7 minutes (you don't want to lose the acidity). Pour in all the remaining ingredients and stir to dissolve. Do not boil.

When the spices are thoroughly dissolved, take the pot off the heat and funnel the sauce into a bottle. The sauce will keep, refrigerated, for up to a year.

SWEET &AND& SPICY CHILI SAUCE

SWEET SWINE O' MINE BBQ TEAM

Sweet and a little spicy, this versatile chili condiment can be used with any meat or vegetable dish, or as a dipping sauce. Made-in-minutes, it's a great substitute anytime a recipe calls for plain, bottled chili sauce.

YIELD: ABOUT 2 CUPS (473 ML) • COOK TIME: NONE

2 cups (473 ml) Frank's RedHot Sweet Chili Sauce

2 tbsp (28 g) minced ginger

2 whole chopped scallions or 1 diced shallot

½ cup (24 g) chopped cilantro

1 tbsp (15 ml) toasted sesame oil

1 tsp toasted sesame seeds

1 tbsp (15 ml) ponzu

2 tbsp (30 ml) Sriracha

1 tsp minced garlic

Black pepper, to taste

Combine all the ingredients in a bowl. Store in an airtight container in the refrigerator.

SWEET SWINE O' MINE ALL-PURPOSE BRINE

MARK LAMBERT, SWEET SWINE O' MINE BBQ TEAM

Brining adds moisture and flavor to a cut of meat. You can also impart great flavors into your meats if you heat, cool and strain this brine, and then inject the liquid mixture into large cuts of meat, such as pork butts or pork loin.

YIELD: ABOUT 1 GALLON (3.8 L) • COOK TIME: 15 MINUTES

1 gal (3.8 L) distilled water

1 cup (241 g) salt

2 cups (383 g) cane sugar

4 cloves garlic, chopped

1 onion, chopped

1 large bunch fresh thyme

2 ribs celery, chopped

1 large bunch rosemary

2 bay leaves

½ cup (120 ml) Worcestershire sauce

½ cup (120 ml) soy sauce

Mix all the ingredients in a large food-grade container that has a lid. When you brine a cut of meat, make sure the meat is fully submerged below the liquid. Always brine the meat in the refrigerator. Place the lid on the container to help eliminate food contamination. You can brine small items, such as chicken wings, pork chops or pork tenderloin in about an hour. Larger cuts, such as a whole turkey or a pork butt will likely take 6 to 12 hours. Alternatively, you can use brining liquid to inject large cuts of meat, such as pork butt, pork loin or whole chickens.

To make the brine injection, mix all of the ingredients in a large pan. Place a lid on the pan, and bring the water to a boil, about 15 minutes. Carefully strain the hot liquid, to remove the dry ingredients. Removing the dry ingredients helps prevent the injector from getting clogged. Inject the meat just before you cook it.

ALL-HERB PESTO

THE BASIC BBQ TEAM

Here is a fresh, tasty pesto that you can make with herbs from your garden. It's delicious spread on a sandwich, or as a dip for vegetables. Store the pesto in an airtight container, and it will keep in the refrigerator for up to one week. Use this recipe for all your pesto needs, as pesto can also be frozen.

YIELD: 1 CUP (180 G) • COOK TIME: NONE

¼ cup (55 g) light brown sugar

½ cup (120 ml) extra-virgin olive oil

¼ cup (72 g) kosher salt

2 tbsp (12 g) coarse ground black pepper

1 whole bulb garlic, diced (do not pulverize)

¼ cup (7 g) finely chopped fresh rosemary leaves

¼ cup (10 g) finely chopped fresh thyme leaves

2 tbsp (7 g) finely chopped fresh sage leaves

One by one, prepare the ingredients and then place in a hard bowl. Avoid plastic bowls. When all the ingredients are in the bowl, mix thoroughly using a fork. Cover and place in the fridge for up to 1 week.

BASIC TOOLS AND TECHNIQUES

The book you are holding contains over 200 recipes from competition chefs and national cooking champions. This section provides an overview of the basic techniques these cooks use to produce their winning results. Designed for the beginner cooking enthusiast, these backyard basics will help take your skills to the next level! In this section, you'll find insights about charcoal, smoking, ways to configure your grill and where to purchase the same products the champs use. Read on to learn about the methods and tools you'll need to barbecue like a pro!

GUIDE FOR COOKING TEMPERATURES

Low heat: 250 to 275°F (121 to 135°C)

Medium heat: 300 to 400°F (149 to 204°C)

High heat: 500 to 600°F (260 to 316°C)

ESSENTIAL EQUIPMENT

Aluminum foil

Butane lighter

Food-grade thermometer

Full roll of paper towels

Grill brush

Heat-resistant or leather work gloves

Long-handled basting brush

Metal tongs

Metal spatula

Charcoal chimney

CHARCOAL

The fuel of choice for most backyard cooking enthusiasts is charcoal. Sure, it takes a little longer to cook on a charcoal grill than on a gas grill, but the flavor of the finished product speaks for itself. Charcoal comes in two basic varieties: lump charcoal and charcoal briquettes. Lump charcoal is essentially large, mismatched hunks of burned wood. It usually burns at a slightly hotter temperature than charcoal briquettes. By comparison, charcoal briquettes are composed of burned wood that is mixed with fillers and chemical binding agents that help form their square shape. A variety of manufacturers provide natural briquettes, which typically use an alternate binding agent such as cornstarch. Because of the uniform shape, charcoal briquettes usually provide a more even and consistent burn than lump charcoal. When firing up your charcoal, never use lighter fluid. The preferred starting method is a charcoal chimney.

CHARCOAL CHIMNEY

A charcoal chimney is a round, metal cylinder with a slotted bottom that you use to light charcoal. You can light the charcoal by burning some crumpled-up newspaper or a paper towel doused with olive oil beneath the base of the charcoal chimney.

CHARCOAL BASKETS

A charcoal basket is a third-party product that contours to the curved edge of your grill and retains hot charcoal in a confined area. Charcoal baskets enable you to more easily configure your grill for the indirect and two-zone cooking methods.

SMOKE WOODS

A wonderful way to enhance the flavor of food is to cook using smoke wood. Pairing smoke wood with different proteins is actually quite simple. If you're just learning to cook with smoke wood, a simple thing to keep in mind is that fruit woods pair well with pork and poultry, while nut woods offer a fine complement to red meats. Above all else, as you're learning, let your taste buds guide you. Don't use too much smoke wood, as it can build up a bitter taste in the food you are preparing.

Most home improvement stores carry a small selection of smoke woods next to the grills. Sometimes, you can also find smoke woods at fireplace specialty stores. Smoke wood is usually available in the form of chunks or chips. Chunks are roughly fist-sized (or half fist-sized) pieces of wood and are typically large and robust enough that you can place them directly on the hot charcoal. Chips are much smaller. They tend to burn quickly, and many cooks let them soak in water for about an hour before placing them onto hot charcoal. Chips are also a good choice if you want to smoke food using a foil packet.

HOW TO MAKE A FOIL PACKET

Cut a square of heavy-duty aluminum foil that is roughly 10 to 12 inches (25 to 30.5 cm) on each side.

Place a handful of wood chips in the middle of the square.

Fold the edges of all four sides of the square in towards the center.

Use a knife or fork to make 6 to 8 holes in the foil packet.

Place the packet onto the hot charcoal.

Put the cooking grate on the grill and you're ready to cook.

DIRECT, INDIRECT AND TWO-ZONE COOKING

Throughout the book, you'll notice that recipes often require that you set up your grill for direct, indirect or two-zone cooking. Each of these methods has its benefits for working with certain ingredients and different types of meal or dessert preparation. Getting comfortable with these methods will enable you to barbecue a variety of dishes and desserts.

Direct Cooking

Direct cooking is a method of preparing food where hot charcoal is directly beneath the food you are cooking. Generally speaking, this is a fast cooking method and is what most people see when they're at a family cookout or tailgating at a football game: think of grilling hot dogs or chicken wings and you're on the right track.

SETUP FOR DIRECT COOKING:

Light a full charcoal chimney.

When you see the edges of the briquettes at the top of the chimney begin to turn gray, the charcoal is ready to use. (It usually takes about 20 minutes.)

Carefully dump the hot charcoal into the grill.

Using metal tongs, form the charcoal into an even cooking layer across the bottom of the grill.

Quickly coat the cooking grate with olive oil.

Put the cooking grate on the grill, and let it heat up for 3 to 5 minutes.

Place the food on the grill and follow the instructions in the recipe.

Indirect Cooking

For the indirect cooking method, the hot charcoal is not directly beneath the food you are cooking. Instead, the heat source is offset from the food you are preparing. This slower cooking method, which might not be readily familiar to newer backyard cooks, usually produces more tender results than direct cooking.

SETUP FOR INDIRECT COOKING:

Light a full charcoal chimney.

When you see the edges of the briquettes at the top of the chimney begin to turn gray, the charcoal is ready to use. (It usually takes about 20 minutes.)

Carefully dump the hot charcoal into the grill.

Using metal tongs, form the charcoal into a pile on one side of the grill.

Quickly coat the cooking grate with olive oil.

Put the cooking grate on the grill, and let it heat up for 3 to 5 minutes.

Place the food on the grill so it is not directly over the hot charcoal, and follow the instructions in the recipe.

Two-Zone Cooking

Don't let the fancy name scare you; two-zone cooking is exactly what you think it is—a method of food preparation that uses both the direct and indirect cooking methods. Most experienced backyard cooks tend to prefer the versatility of this cooking method. The grill setup for two-zone cooking is the same as indirect cooking. The differentiating factor is that you take advantage of the benefits that both cooking methods provide. Essentially, you're creating two cooking zones. Use the hot zone for direct cooking and searing meats. This allows you to seal juices inside the meat and form a flavorful surface char. The cool zone is where you perform indirect cooking. This slower, gentler cooking process helps create a tender and moist finished product.

WATER PAN

Some cooks like to use a water pan to help create moisture inside the grill during the cooking process. You can use a disposable aluminum pan, a rigid metal pan, or try forming aluminum foil into a bowl. A water pan can either be placed beneath the cooking grate, next to the charcoal or directly on the cooking grate—wherever you have sufficient space for it.

LETTING MEAT REST

After you finish cooking the meat, you should let it rest for at least 10 minutes. During the cooking process, the protein strands that make up the meat become rigid. Letting the meat rest allows the protein strands to relax and helps redistribute the meat's natural juices throughout the finished product.

CLEANING AND MAINTAINING YOUR GRILL

Keeping your grill clean and well maintained can be simple and straightforward. For starters, when your grill is not in use, it should be stored with a cover to help protect it from rain and the elements. At the beginning of each spring, tighten the screws, nuts and bolts that fasten the grill together. You should also visually inspect the product for signs of rust and decay. You can clean the exterior of your grill using a damp rag. Every three or four cooks, you should also wipe down the interior of the grill to help prevent grease from collecting. This helps prevent flare-ups, or worse, a grease fire. Some cooks like to use a disposable aluminum pan to collect food drippings, particularly when they're using either the indirect or two-zone cooking method. You can add water to the drip pan so it doubles as a water pan.

RESOURCES

ATLANTA BBQ STORE

Providing all things BBQ to the competition and backyard enthusiast

https://www.atlantabbqstore.com

BBQ SUPERSTORE

Great selection of products and accessories

https://www.thebbqsuperstore.com

BIG POPPA SMOKERS

The best online selection of BBQ rubs, seasonings, sauces, marinades, BBQ tools, meats, BBQ grills and smokers for sale

https://www.bigpoppasmokers.com

FRUITA WOOD

Premium-quality BBQ smoking wood chunks

https://fruitawood.com

HAWGEYES

Online outlet for all your championship barbecue cooking needs

http://www.hawgeyesbbq.com

HUMPHREY'S SMOKERS

Custom and cabinet-style smokers

https://humphreysbbq.myshopify.com

KANSAS CITY BBQ STORE

The world's biggest inventory of BBQ sauces, seasonings, smokers and supplies

https://www.thekansascitybbqstore.com

MOJOBRICKS

Clean, easy and convenient compressed wood chunks

https://mojobricks.com/

SMOKIN' HOGGZ

Award-winning sauce by a national champion pitmaster

http://www.smokinhoggzbbq.com/shop

VAUGHN WOOD

Kiln-dried smoke woods

http://www.vaughnwoodproducts.com

ABOUT THE BBQ TEAMS

407 BBQ

Bryan McLarty has been competing in BBQ and steak competitions for 12 years, and has been in the catering business for 18 years. Since opening his doors to the public in October of 2016, he has expanded twice, and is in the process of building a full-scale, brick-and-mortar restaurant. Though the restaurant and catering keep his plate full, he still manages to compete on the professional circuit!

A MAZIE Q

Jayna Todisco began attending barbecue competitions in 2002, and as her enthusiasm grew, she served as a KCBS judge for five years. Inspired by memories of cooking with her grandmother, Jayna decided to take the plunge into the crazy world of competition barbecue in 2012. Supported by her husband, Pete Coulon, and two sons, Jake and Jaron, Jayna has won eighteen grand championships, including the World Food Championship Fire & Ice Women's BBQ Championship, five reserve grand championships and earned eleven perfect scores of 180 in Northeast Barbecue Society grilling contests. A Mazie Q cooks on Humphrey's Smokers, 270 Smokers and Weber Smokey Mountain cookers. Jayna's sons have also won Kids Q contests cooking on a Mini Big Green Egg at Brookline, New Hampshire, and Ridgefield, Connecticut.

BABEÉ BLUE'S BBQ

Babeé Blue's BBQ was established in 2010. Team members Damon Blue and Rachel Blue are members of numerous barbecue associations and have come away from many cookoffs with awards. They cook using a Pitmaker Vault smoker, and Blue 22½-inch (57-cm) Weber Kettle.

BARK BROTHERS BBQ

Bark Brothers BBQ from Columbus, Ohio, have been competing on the KCBS circuit since 2012. They cook on Humphrey's Smokers and Weber Grills. The team won the Madison Ribberfest in Madison, Indiana, in 2015, their 1st KCBS Grand Champion win. In 2016 they decided to compete in the dessert category. Lori-Ann's Chocolate Salted Caramel Cheesecake earned a 180 perfect score at CCS Festival, Indianapolis, Indiana, and again at Madison Ribberfest in Madison, Indiana.

THE BASIC BBQ TEAM

Patrick Paquette, Wendy Paquette and Ellie Huyser are a professional competition BBQ team out of Hyannis, Massachusetts, that also do festival vending and catering. In 2015 they won two grand championships and a reserve grand championship. Their delicious hickory-smoked turkey recipe brings a "Cape Cod" twist to your Thanksgiving table.

BBQ GURU

Over the years, Bob Trudnak, or "BBQ Bob," grew to love all cooking and has tirelessly worked to perfect the craft of making delicious food. As a result, he has amassed over 200 awards, plus numerous trophies and titles, cash and prizes at national and international competitions.

A Jack Daniel's World Championship Reserve Grand Champion, "BBQ Bob" helped create an entire line of high-tech cooker accessories made by BBQ Guru, headquartered in Warminster, Pennsylvania. These devices include the top-selling PartyQ, DigiQ and CyberQ, all of which the majority of America's award-winning BBQ competition teams use. Trudnak runs a catering business with his wife, Tammy, juggles a competition schedule and still found time to create a line of award-winning sauces and rubs. He says there's nothing better than creating a food, handing it to someone and seeing that smile when they bite into it. That's what makes him go.

BBQ LONGHORN RANCH HANDS

Team Captain and Chief Cook, Hannes Handle, joined by his wife, Heike, form the basis of BBQ Longhorn Ranch Hands. Joined by their dedicated team members Eddie Stern, Kristin Otto, Mario Hammerer and Sabrina Visneider, the BBQ Longhorn Ranch Hands have won three grand championships and three reserve grand championships. In only their second year on the competition circuit, they were ranked #27 in Team of the Year America, and #4 in Team of the Year Europe. Hannes and Heike own the BBQ Longhorn Smokehouse and run the Steak and Fisch Steakhouse, both located in Dornbirn, Austria.

BEHIND BBQ

Kim Perry is the pitmaster for Behind BBQ. Based out of Spencerport, New York, Behind BBQ has been competing in KCBS and amateur competitions since July 2010, starting with local Western New York competitions and then expanding into New York's Southern Tier, the Adirondacks, Canada and Pennsylvania. In 2014, Kim Perry won the Travel Channel's American Grilled episode, filmed in Latrobe, Pennsylvania. Then, in 2016, Kim and her team went on to win World Champion Dessert and Third Cook's Choice at the Jack Daniel's World Championship Invitational in Lynchburg, Tennessee.

BIG BOB GIBSON BAR-B-Q

Widely recognized as one of the oldest and best barbecue restaurants in the country, Big Bob Gibson Bar-B-Q was founded in Decatur, Alabama, back in 1925. Big Bob Gibson was a railroad worker who honed his backyard BBQ skills in a hand-dug pit. This pitmaster's world-renowned cooking techniques and his Original White BBQ Sauce have stood the test of time.

Five generations and 90 years later, the Big Bob Gibson Cooking Team has racked up fifteen world BBQ championships in competition meat categories, including: pork shoulder, ribs, chicken and brisket. They have won a record four Memphis in May World Grand Championships (2000, 2003, 2011 and 2014), and won the American Royal International Invitational Cook-Off. Their reserve grand championship honors include the Jack Daniel's World Barbecue Championship and the World Series of Barbecue, the American Royal Open. Big Bob Gibson Bar-B-Q also displayed their culinary talents abroad by capturing the grand championship at the International Jamaican Barbeque Cook-Off. In 2012, they won the title of "King of the Smokers" at a national barbecue invitational.

The Big Bob Gibson Crew has appeared on *Live with Regis and Kelly*, *Today*, *The Martha Stewart Show*, *ESPN College Football Live* and *ESPN Game Day*, as well as numerous Food Network programs. In addition to television appearances, Big Bob Gibson Bar-B-Q has been featured in *Southern Living*, *People*, *Food and Wine*, *Food Network Magazine*, *The New York Times*, *Men's Health*, *The Wall Street Journal* and *Maxim* magazine.

Ken Hess, who manages the day-to-day operations at Big Bob Gibson's restaurants, is a pitmaster from North Alabama and four-time winner of the World Championship of Pork. Hess also appeared on the Food Network's *Chopped Grill Masters* and competed in the seafood category at the 2017 World Food Championships in Alabama after qualifying at the Music City Cookoff.

BIG POPPA SMOKERS BBQ TEAM

The Big Poppa Smokers BBQ Team, founded in 2009, was the grand champion of the 2012 American Royal Invitational, and was featured on the second season of TLC's BBQ Pitmasters.

BIG UGLY'S BBQ (BUBBQ) TEAM

Big Ugly's BBQ (BUBBQ) was founded in 2007 by Chris Hall and his children. They competed in one contest in their inaugural season, getting a third-place call in brisket at the Maryland State BBQ Championships. The following year, 2008, saw them win two grand championships and a reserve grand championship. BUBBQ took a rather long hiatus while Chris became a member of 3 Eyz BBQ from 2009 thru 2013, winning the KCBS Team of the Year in 2012. Kitty Sambucco also joined 3 Eyz in 2012 and was an instant success, dominating the alternate categories. In 2014, Chris and Kitty decided to compete separate of 3 Eyz. They resurrected BUBBQ and experienced immediate success with two grand championships and four reserve grand championships.

BUBBQ's arsenal of cookers includes a Humphrey's Qube'd Battle Box, a Backwoods Competitor, a Weber Smokey Mountain Smoker, a Gateway Drum Smoker and BPS Drum Smoker. They travel with their gear in an Extreme BBQ Trailer, affectionately called the "War Wagon."

In 2015, BUBBQ won six reserve grand championships. In 2016 they won a grand championship and several top-ten finishes. When Chris is not competing, you can find him teaching his winning rib recipe at competition rib classes in Maryland.

BLAZIN' BUTTS BBQ

Blazin' Buttz BBQ is a competition cooking team from Long Island, New York, made up of two coworkers who initially came together to cook a local barbecue competition in 2007. Pitmasters Bob Schwarz and Frank Sacco, along with team leader Laura Schwarz, now compete around the country. In the past few years, they have won seven BBQ grand championships, eight grilling grand championships and competed at the Jack Daniel's Invitational in 2013, 2015 and 2017.

BOO BOO QUED BBQ TEAM

When mid-May rolls around, you will find Mic and Kim Stanfield taking time away from their busy Northeast competition schedule to head to Memphis, where they walked up to the stage for their award for Mic's Mustard Sauce.

BOOTYQUE BBQ TEAM

Bootyque was created in 2012 by Patrick and Kathy Banks, and this professional barbecue team competes on the KCBS, IBCA, FBA and ABA circuits. Patrick Banks is the Director of Disaster Response for Operation BBQ Relief. He and his wife Kathy live in Fairhope on the Alabama Gulf Coast. They became involved with Operation BBQ Relief in the spring of 2012. Prior to his involvement with OBR, Patrick worked disaster relief in Tuscaloosa, Alabama, after the horrific tornado on April 27, 2011. Patrick spent two weeks in Tuscaloosa directing the distribution of 50,000 meals and over 100,000 pounds (45,360 kg) of food across north Alabama.

ELYSE BROWN

Seven-year-old Elyse Brown was the 2016 Kid's Que Grand Champion at the Gold Ribbon BBQ Festival in Green Bay, Wisconsin. Cooking on a Weber Smokey Joe, she presented the judges with a mouthwatering burger that was juicy and spicy. There's a good chance you and your guests will like her ground beef hamburger recipe just as much as the judges did!

BUSH KITCHEN BBQ

For the past seven years, Saffron Hodgson has judged, competed in and won countless cooking competitions, from barbecue and chili contests to dessert and seafood cook-offs across America and Canada, as well as in Australia, her native country. In addition to these activities, she is the digital content manager for the Allrecipes' Australia and New Zealand sites. Currently she's devoting all her free time to her signature webpage, BushCooking.com, which focuses on outdoor cooking tips, techniques and recipes.

CAN U SMELL MY PITS

In 2012, Michael Pelletier and his Can U Smell My Pits team broke into the barbecue competition world with a bang, winning NEBS Rookie Team of the Year. Beginning in 2013, they won grand championships for four consecutive years, each of which resulted in a trip to the Jack Daniel's Invitational World Championship. These days, Mike spends less time on the competition circuit and more time with his five grandchildren, but it won't be long before barbecue contestants will be smelling his pits again!

CHECKERED FLAG 500 BBQ

The Checkered Flag 500 BBQ team, based out of Fawn Grove, Pennsylvania, consists of Mark Gibbs, his wife Sharon and their silver labrador, Sterling. They have been competing on the KCBS circuit for five years, mostly in the mid-Atlantic region, but they travel south and west on occasion. The team was the Mid-Atlantic BBQ Association Rookie Team of the Year in 2012, and they have won numerous grand championships and top ten overall finishes since then. Checkered Flag 500 BBQ proudly cooks on a Deep South Smokers' GC-28.

COUNTY LINE SMOKERS

County Line Smokers is a competition BBQ team in the Kansas City, Missouri, area. Stan Hays co-founded Operation BBQ Relief in response to the May 2011 tornado that struck Joplin, Missouri. At the urging of his wife, Amy, Stan contacted Jeff Stith and gathered up a group of volunteers. They traveled to Joplin to cook barbecue for those in need, and from that single call, Operation BBQ Relief started. Stan and Amy have two children, Nathan and Anna. When they are not on the road catering, competing or fundraising for OBR, Stan is working on his recipes from *Chopped Grill Masters* tournament season two, where he finished as runner-up.

Ten-year-old Anna Hays started cooking when she was only six years old. Anna already has two grand championships under her belt, earned in 2012 and 2015, and she contributed her noteworthy Apple Pork Chop recipe (page 16) to this book!

Twelve-year-old Nathan Hays competes in BBQ with County Line Smokers, but in Steak Cookoff Association (SCA) competitions he goes by CLS Grillers. Nathan is the youngest SCA steak champion in the history of the Steak Cookoff Association and has been competing since the age of five. Nathan won two Kid's Q grand championships and four reserve grand championships, including Reserve Grand Champion at the American Royal Kid's Q in 2012. He has already achieved a perfect 180 score and has beat adults in an SCA Adult Steak Championship. Make sure you check out his Perfect Score Burger (page 134) recipe!

JOHN DELPHA, IQUE BBQ

John Delpha is a member of the world champion IQUE BBQ team. He joined the IQUE team in 2006, and his chef's choice dish helped his team win the Jack Daniel's World Championship in 2009. He is also the partner and chef of Somerville, Massachusetts, Rosebud American Kitchen and Bar, and the author of *Grilled Pizza the Right Way*.

DISCO PIGS

Mike, Karen and Sam Espey first started competing in BBQ contests when they lived in the Kansas City area, back in 2009. At their first contest, they competed under the name Smokin' BBQ Boys. In 2012 they decided to change their team name, and then nine-year-old son, Sam, suggested Disco Pigs. The first contest with their new name in Bonner Springs, Kansas, also saw them win their first grand championship!

DIVA Q, AKA DANIELLE BENNETT

Danielle Bennett's excitement for BBQ knows absolutely no boundaries, as is apparent when her team name is called to the stage at award ceremonies. Diva Q is the 2011 Jack Daniel's Pork Champion. She certainly knows her pork, as she is also the 2013 World Bacon Champion from the Roc City BBQ Festival in Rochester, New York.

The proud owner of forty smokers and grills, Diva Q has won fifteen grand championships on the Kansas City BBQ Society circuit and more than 300 other awards, including the 2013 Jack Daniel's I Know Jack . . . About Grilling event.

Danielle has appeared on the Food Network, Travel Channel, TLC, A&E, *BBQ Pitmasters, Chopped Grill Masters, American Grilled, Today* and *The Marilyn Denis Show*. She also published the cookbook *Diva Q's Barbecue: 195 Recipes for Cooking with Family, Friends & Fire*.

DIZZY PIG BBQ TEAM

Under the direction of pitmaster and Dizzy Pig owner Chris Capell, the Dizzy Pig Barbecue Team made its competitive debut in August 2002. Since then, they have cooked in over 100 competitions, with over half of those being top ten overall finishes, including fifteen grand championships.

These grand championship wins earned Chris Capell and his team invites to the American Royal and the Jack Daniel's World Championships, where the Dizzy Team was honored to cook among the best teams in the country for six straight years, from 2004–2009.

One element that has directly resulted in their overall success is the exclusive use of Dizzy Pig rubs: the very rubs they sell at their headquarters in Manassas, Virginia, and at chosen retailers across the country. Capell's headquarters have been described by customers as the BBQ "pro shop." His barbecue store has become a thriving business that offers some of the best outdoor cooking equipment, sauces, cooking classes and championship seasonings on the market. When the Dizzy Pig's are not grinding and bottling their seasonings, they're cooking it up in the test kitchen, at home, at demos and in Dizzcovery classes at their headquarters.

FAMOUS DAVE ANDERSON, FAMOUS DAVE'S BBQ

Dave Anderson has dedicated his life to making the best barbecue in America. Famous Dave is a BBQ encyclopedia, a man who has spent years pursuing BBQ perfection, and he's won some of the biggest BBQ awards in the nation. In 2017 he was one of three inducted to the Barbecue Hall of Fame at The American Royal World Series of Barbecue at the Kansas Speedway.

Dave Anderson has appeared on all major networks, including appearances on *Live! with Regis and Kathie Lee*, *Oprah*, CNBC's *The Big Idea with Donny Deutsch*, *Crook & Chase*, the Discovery Channel, the Food Network, National Public Radio and over 200 radio shows. As a highly sought-after keynote speaker, Dave shares his heartfelt optimism using his life's story to communicate valuable insight and life lessons in dealing with today's fast changing and challenging world. Dave is an enthusiastic advocate of the American dream; he stresses that no matter how tough things may seem today, if you never give up your dream and work hard, tomorrow's rewards will always come.

Dave Anderson, best known as the founder of the Famous Dave's restaurant chain, is the former Assistant Secretary of Indian Affairs in the Department of the Interior, and is a Choctaw and Ojibwe Indian. Dave lives in Minnesota, travels the country speaking and is the author of several award-winning books.

FEEDING FRIENDZ

Based in Deerfield, New Hampshire, and no longer competing, Tim and Wendy Boucher still love to gather with large crowds and cook for their "Friendz." Over a ten-year period, they won several grand championships and have been fortunate enough to be invited to "The Jack" twice (2010 and 2011). In 2013 they made it to the finals of the Sam's Club National Barbecue Tour, finishing with a second-place brisket and thirteenth overall.

FERGOLICIOUS BBQ TEAM

Fergolicious BBQ is a KCBS competition BBQ team from Gardner, Kansas, that was featured on season five of *BBQ Pitmasters* on Destination America. Richard Fergola's journey into the world of BBQ began in the kitchen, learning how to prepare family favorites with his mom and grandmother. Today, he still carries on the family secrets and has found a way to stay true to his roots. His love of Italian food opened the door and led him to his current obsession with smoke and fire. Richard's passion, preparation, organization, determination and planning made him a successful wrestler and coach, and now he applies those same attributes to the competition cooking arena. His commitment and desire to be the greatest at everything he does helped make Fergolicious BBQ what it is today.

FINN'S FINEST BBQ

Established in 2010, Finn's Finest BBQ is a family-run competitive BBQ team and catering company located in Middletown, Delaware. From the start, their focus has been to integrate their award-winning, competitive BBQ flavors into their backyard barbecue recipes. Past performances have earned Finn's Finest invitations to the most prestigious BBQ contests in the world, including the Jack Daniel's World Championship and the Sam's Club National BBQ Tour.

FIRE DOWN BELOW

Ed Roach has always loved BBQ, especially pork ribs. Many years ago on Father's Day, his wife, Ginny, bought him an inexpensive offset smoker. They were able to produce some decent BBQ on it, but the smoker needed constant attention. They upgraded to a Weber Smokey Mountain Smoker (WSM) and started enjoying BBQ much more often. Shortly after getting the WSM, the BBQ bug hit hard and Ed eventually convinced Ginny to enter a competition with him. Initially she was apprehensive and told him this was going to be a one-shot deal. At the contest, Ginny even went so far as to tell a neighboring team that this was their first and last competition. During the awards ceremony at their first contest, they got a fifth place call in brisket. Ginny was jumping up and down with such excitement that both of them have been hooked ever since!

Since 2013, Fire Down Below has competed in over twenty contests and have made several upgrades to their smokers and trailers. Ed and Ginny have had category calls at the majority of their competitions. The highlight of their short time on the circuit was a first-place call in pork, with a perfect score at the 2014 Jack Daniel's World Championship Invitational.

FREDDY RAY'S BBQ

In 2010, Freddy Ray's BBQ started as a catering company and quickly found its way onto the competition BBQ circuit. After changing from backyard cooking to professional circuit, they quickly learned to write down all recipes, even while testing new rubs and sauces. It was during a competition that they discovered both of their BBQ sauces were a big hit. Since 2016, with numerous awards and a gold medal finish at a national BBQ sauce competition, their all-natural, small-batch, award-winning sauces and rubs can be purchased all over America and abroad.

GUADALUPE BBQ COMPANY

Ty Machado is a fourteen-year-old pitmaster from Seguin, Texas, who has been competing in the Texas BBQ scene for the last three years. His father, Joey Machado, competed for over sixteen years and has turned over the reins to Ty. Ty has cooked over twenty non-sanctioned events and earned several grand championships and reserve grand championships, sometimes while cooking against teams who have been competing longer than Ty has even been on this earth!

Schooled in the Texas IBCA (International Barbeque Cookers Association) style, and with the support of his family, Ty has hit the IBCA Central Texas circuit running for the 2016–17 season. He earned his first Sanctioned IBCA Grand Championship with a first-place brisket, third-place chicken and fifth-place ribs in Sergeant, Texas, in September of 2016. Since Ty is only fourteen, the IBCA rules will not allow him to be a head cook on paper but everyone who has cooked against him knows he has earned his spot.

Ty most recently was a contestant on Food Network's *Kids BBQ Championship*, where he appeared on four of the six episodes. He is the real deal and cooks with the best of them every other weekend. Ty enjoys mentoring other kids on cooking and loves to volunteer where he can for great causes and folks in need.

HERE PIGGY PIGGY BBQ

Here Piggy Piggy BBQ consists of the husband and wife team of Mike and Chris Peters. They don't just compete, though. For those of you familiar with KCBS, you will recognize Mike and Chris as the faces of the KCBS Great American BBQ Tour. They have been traveling around America promoting all that is good with barbecue for the last four years.

Here Piggy Piggy BBQ won Smoking on the Water in Lakeport, California, in 2011, which then got their bung pulled at the lucky draw for the Jack Daniel's Invitational eight days later. They also scored a perfect-perfect in the chicken category at their home event in Springfield, Missouri, using a Southern Pride MLR-150 for competition cooking.

IQUE BBQ

IQUE is one of the first teams in New England to see major BBQ success. Their 2010 win at the Jack Daniel's World Championships in Lynchburg, Tennessee, positioned them as the first New England team to become world champions. They also took first place out of 510 teams in the brisket category at the American Royal in 2007.

KG COOKERS

KG Cookers' pitmaster, Carlo Casanova, founded KG Cookers BBQ competition team and catering company in 2011. Carlo has always loved to cook, and his passion for perfecting his barbecue has grown over the years. KG Cookers BBQ spent five years working hard on the Texas BBQ competition circuit. In one season, they were awarded seven grand championships and two reserve grand championships. In addition to barbecue, KG Cookers produces an award-winning brisket and rib rub, along with their famous Cherry Habanero Pepper Jellies.

LAKESIDE SMOKERS BBQ TEAM

Mike and Kris Boisvert won an astounding seventeen grand championships in a short five-year period before moving on from competition barbecue. When Superstorm Sandy hit the Northeast, Mike was one of the first to jump in to volunteer with Operation BBQ Relief. While he's no longer competing, Mike still loves to cook for a crowd!

LIL' LOOT BBQ

Sterling James "Jimmy" Smith, a nine-year-old from Scottsdale, Arizona, has entered several Kids Q competitions. He has three first-place wins and two second-place wins. He also loves to play soccer and video games when he's not cooking. His favorite food to grill is burgers, so be sure to check out his Epic Sauce Bacon Cheeseburger recipe (page 131)!

LO'-N-SLO' BBQ TEAM

The Lo'-N-Slo' BBQ Team consists of Tom and Michele Perelka and their German Shepherd, River, from New Providence, Pennsylvania. Their first official contest was in 2006 and they have earned more than fifteen grand championships, fourteen reserve grand championships and more than 275 top-ten category calls. Earning an invitation to the Jack Daniel's World Invitational, they finished second place in the Cook's Choice category. They returned to Lynchburg in 2010 and earned a first-place Cook's Choice with a perfect 180 score. Their team has been named the Pennsylvania State BBQ Champions in 2011, 2012, 2013 and 2014, as well as the Mid-Atlantic BBQ Association's Pennsylvania State Cup Champions in 2011.

LOCAL SMOKE BBQ TEAM

Local Smoke BBQ was created in 2007 when Steve and Loren Raab, with Eric Keating, decided to spin off from their former team, Lost Nation Smoke Company. After years of working as apprentices they decided that they were ready for the major league. Local Smoke BBQ has represented New Jersey at contests all over the country, including: Missouri, Tennessee, Arkansas, Georgia, Nevada and in almost every state from Virginia to Vermont. They have collected over 100 awards, including four New Jersey State Championship titles. Competition highlights include first place in ribs against 488 teams at the American Royal BBQ contest in Kansas City, and first place in brisket at the National BBQ Festival in Douglas, Georgia.

LONESTAR SMOKE RANGERS

The Lonestar Smoke Rangers came up with the team name from a former team member who passed away a few years ago. His name was Boyd Preckwinckle and he was a retired Texas Ranger. They took the Texas Ranger badge as their logo and fashioned the name. The Lonestar Smoke Rangers team consists of Tony Balay; his wife, Kim; their four kids, Doug, Matt, Carly and Wyatt; Tony's mom, Rosa and his dad, Tony, Sr; his Shiggin' brother-in-law Keith and sister Becky. Cooking on a Memphis Elite Pellet Smoker and a Stumps Stumpster XL, Lonestar Smoke Rangers has won thirteen grand championships and five reserve grand championships. They have competed in the Jack Daniel's Invitational World Championship for the past three years, qualified for the American Royal Invitational the last four years and the World Food Championship the last four years.

LOOT N' BOOTY BBQ

Pitmaster Sterling Smith leads this family BBQ team from Scottsdale, Arizona. While competing nationally on the professional barbecue circuit, Loot N' Booty BBQ has earned seventeen grand championships, twelve reserve grand championships and 250 top-ten calls. Sterling is also available for catering work and teaches barbecue cooking classes.

LUCKY Q

Lucky Q started competing in KCBS-sanctioned events in 2010, partaking in five that year. Justin, their head cook, made a smoker out of a 55-gallon (208-L) air compressor tank, and he and his wife, Kate, soon hit the road to compete. Once they received their first ribbon, they were hooked! They have over 100 contests under their belt in their short career. In 2011 they received their first grand championship in Owatonna, Minnesota, which in turn qualified them to compete at the Jack Daniel's Invitational. In between their first grand championship and "The Jack," they were joined by their first child, Gavin. Lucky Q has fifteen grand championships, many reserve grand championships and numerous category wins and perfect scores of 180. The sauce recipe on page 111 is from Artie Inouye.

BRYAN MCLARTY

Bryan has been competing in BBQ and steak competition for twelve years, and has been in the BBQ and steak catering business for eighteen years. Since opening his doors to the public in October of 2016, he has expanded twice and is in the process of building a full-scale, brick-and-mortar restaurant. While the restaurant and catering keep Bryan's plate full, he still manages to compete on the professional trail.

MYRON MIXON, JACK'S OLD SOUTH BBQ

Hailing from Unadilla, Georgia, Myron Mixon is the winning-est man in barbecue. This four-time world barbecue champion was recently inducted into the prestigious Barbecue Hall of Fame and is widely recognized as the most successful and charismatic man in barbecue. He's been dubbed "The King," "The Best Hog Cooker in the World," "The Man in Black" and more nicknames than he can shake a stick at. He's a downright fierce competitor and learned everything he knows about cooking great barbecue from his dad, Jack Mixon. Barbecue has always been and continues to be a family affair for him. His brother Tracy, sons Michael and David and other close family members and friends are part of his Jack's Old South competition BBQ team.

Myron competed in his first competition in Augusta, Georgia, in 1996, where he took first place in Whole Hog, first place in pork ribs and third in pork shoulder. Since then, he's won more barbecue competitions than anyone else in the world. He's won over 180 grand championships and still counting, resulting in over 1,700 total trophies, 30 state championships, eight Team of the Year awards and eleven national championships and counting. Myron's team has taken three first-place Whole Hogs at the Jack Daniel's World Championship Invitational Competition; has been the grand champion at the World Championship in Memphis four times—2001, 2004, 2007 and 2016—and has also taken first place in the Whole Hog category at the World Championship in 2001, 2003, 2004, 2007 and 2016. His team is the only team to win grand championships in Memphis in May, Kansas City BBQ Society and Florida BBQ Association in the same year.

Myron is the star of Destination America's *BBQ Pitmasters* series, which is starting to film its fifth season, and is starting on a new series, *BBQ Rules*. He loves to share his recipes and barbecue know-how, and he is the author of the *New York Times*–bestselling cookbook *Smokin' with Myron Mixon: Recipes Made Simple, from the Winningest Man in Barbecue* (Random House, May 2011), *Everyday Barbecue* (Random House, May 2013) and *Myron Mixon's BBQ Rules* (Abrams, April 2016). He has also made numerous television appearances on shows including *The Tonight Show with Jay Leno*, *The Late Late Show with Craig Ferguson*, *Conan*, ABC's *Good Morning America* and NBC's *Today*. He's been featured on several television networks, including the Food Network, the Discovery Channel, the History Channel, the Travel Channel, the Versus Network and QVC.

When he's not competing or filming, Myron runs a barbecue school out of his cooking pavilion in Unadilla, Georgia, where he welcomes barbecue aficionados of all levels to come and learn from the master. You'll also find him in Waterford, Connecticut, putting his smokers to the test. Myron's relentless pursuit of the best smoker he can design means working closely with the product, sales and manufacturing teams at Seconn Fabrication and results in smokers that use cutting-edge technology to give you the best smoking experience on the market.

MOO COW

Founded in 2007, Moo Cow is a championship BBQ team based out of the Kansas City area. They've won three grand championships, and were the 2010 World Champions in dessert at the Jack Daniel's World Championships. They also cater, teach BBQ cooking classes and offer welding and metal fabrication services for your BBQ-related needs.

NATURAL BORN GRILLERS

John D. Wheeler is the 2008 Memphis in May Grand Champion in Whole Hog and first-place ribs in 2010, and then again in 2013. The co-owner of the Memphis Barbecue Company and winner of 65 grand championships, he contributed a spectacular beef tenderloin recipe (page 56) that's perfect when you're having company for dinner.

NAUGHTY NURSES BBQ

Greg and Kristi Powers are both nurses (Greg is the naughty one). They have been competing for eight years, earning two grand championship wins and two reserve grand championship wins. They also do some catering on the side. For something sweet and delightful, make sure you check out their Peanut Butter Sheet Cake recipe (page 302).

OLD VIRGINIA SMOKE

Competing since 2013, Old Virginia Smoke (OVS) won the Mid-Atlantic BBQ Association Rookie Team of the Year award. Since then, OVS has won four grand championships and two reserve grand championships, including the 2015 National BBQ Cup and the 2015 National Pork Champion at the Safeway BBQ Battle in Washington, D.C.

PHIL THE GRILL BBQ

Phil Johnson, better known as "Phil the Grill," has been seen on a variety of television cooking shows. Phil the Grill (PTG) created his own rubs and spices that enabled him to develop unique flavors. On the competition circuit, Phil the Grill has proven himself to be a championship pitmaster at contests featuring some of the nation's finest cooks. He is the proprietor of a food truck called Sammitch, and serves his mouthwatering BBQ throughout the Phoenix, Arizona, metro area. His signature seasonings include Rub Me All Over and Blue Magic.

PORK BARREL BBQ

The Pork Barrel team is comprised of Heath Hall, Brett Thompson, Rex Hall, Barbara Hall, Nisha Hall, "Mango" Mike Anderson and Bill Blackburn. Over their first 57 KCBS contests, they have won three grand championships, three reserve grand championships, four first-place chicken awards, one first-place rib award, two first-place pork awards and three first-place brisket awards. In total they've received fourteen top-five overall finishes and 26 top-ten overall finishes. They've also received 38 top-five category (chicken, ribs, pork and brisket) finishes and 76 top-ten category finishes.

PRAIRIE SMOKE & SPICE BBQ

A hobby that started in 2000 and transformed into a full-time career, resulting in the most successful competition track record in the country, BBQ is something for which Rob Reinhardt lives, breathes and displays endless passion. Rob and his wife, Jacy, run Prairie Smoke & Spice BBQ, a business and competition barbecue team that started in 2007. Rob's obsession with cooking perfect barbecue has resulted in more grand championships than any other Canadian team. Victories include the Canadian National BBQ Championships, and a two-time World Championship category win at the Jack Daniel's World Championship Invitational in Lynchburg, Tennessee.

With over 180 competition awards won, Rob has blazed a trail across the country. Rob also runs Canada's largest BBQ school, with over 1,800 students trained in the art of Low 'n' Slow cooking so far, and classes running across Canada every spring. He makes appearances at home shows and has had regular appearances on Global, CTV and City's *Breakfast Television Vancouver*.

In addition to success in the competition world, Prairie Smoke & Spice operates as a successful catering and concession company. They worked at the biggest festivals across western Canada and kept their crew running at ribfests for twelve weeks during summer. Prairie Smoke & Spice caters to parties from 50 to 5,000 across Saskatchewan, though their reputation has also brought them into special parties in three additional provinces.

Rob organizes Pile 'o Bones BBQ, Saskatchewan's largest BBQ festival, and was a board member of the Canadian Barbecue Society as well as the Pacific Northwest BBQ Society. He's also a certified barbecue judge.

RECKLESS AND BRAVE BBQ

Reckless and Brave BBQ is a team of two sisters: 14-year-old Lauren Groneman and 16-year-old Kaylin Groneman. Kaylin, who has been cooking since she was four years old, started competing at age five. She has competed in many Kids' Qs, but her most memorable event occurred when she competed at the Junior World Championship in Lake Placid, New York. Here, at the age of eleven, she won against teams of twelve- to fifteen-year-olds. Kaylin and her sister Lauren decided to start their own BBQ team and go up against the people that have taught them over the years. Reckless and Brave BBQ's first competition was in Osage City, Kansas, and they got a 14th-place pork call against some of the best teams around. Kaylin says, "The BBQ community has molded my life in unimaginable ways. I have developed a family I wouldn't ever want to lose. I have many 'aunts and uncles' that I know I can always go to, and I have to thank BBQ for that."

Lauren has also been cooking since a very young age. Growing up in the BBQ world, she's been introduced to some of the most important people of her life. Her BBQ family has not only been there for her but has taught her many things that have helped mold her into who she is today and the person she will be in the future.

Two of Lauren's favorite Kids' Q cooking experiences occurred at Smokin' on Big Creek and at the American Royal. At the 2013 Smokin' on Big Creek, the young contestant struggled a bit, and freaked herself out. She won the event and received a 180 pin—the first 180 pin ever awarded in a kids' competition! Lauren also won the American Royal Kids' Q (younger division) in 2012 with her Mexican Burger.

While Lauren enjoys the feeling of winning, it's the pure happiness she gets while cooking that she loves the most. Today, being able to team up with her sister Kaylin and compete against teams that have molded their knowledge of cooking is a truly amazing experience. Cooking is something Lauren doesn't think she'll ever want to give up!

RI COOK TEAM

Bryan Roppolo from Shreveport, Louisiana, owns Roppolo's Insulation, LLC. Joined by his wife Shawna, daughter Emma Jo and his father-in-law, the RI Cook Team has been competing in steak cook-offs since 2014. Bryan became involved with Operation BBQ Relief in 2015 after meeting Stan Hays at a steak cook-off in Kansas. He instantly knew he wanted to be a part of the organization and has never looked back!

RIBS WITHIN BBQ TEAM

Doug Keiles is a driven competitor and pitmaster who loves BBQ almost as much as he loves his family (and the Mets). Doug has led Ribs Within to grand championship and reserve grand championship victories in BBQ and grilling. He creates a unique mélange of flavors reminiscent of Caribbean and Asian tones, with a zesty Cajun kick. When not actually cooking, Doug spends a lot of time working on new rubs, which you can buy through his website. He is always on a quest for new flavors!

ABIGAIL RICHARDSON

This young lady won first place in the six- to eight-year-old age division of the Kids Que competition at Pork and Brew in Rio Rancho, New Mexico. She used a Weber Kettle grill and Kingsford charcoal for her competition win. Great job, Abby, your kabob recipe (page 204) sounds delicious!

S&S PIT CREW

The S&S Pit Crew of San Marcos, Texas, cooks in the International Barbecue Cookers Association, Lone Star Barbecue Society and Kansas City Barbecue Society events. Established in 2005, they have won two state title grand championships in Texas and several grand and reserve championships.

THE SHED BBQ TEAM

The Shed BBQ Team has won so many awards that the trophy case at their BBQ and Blues Joint in Ocean Springs, Mississippi, is overflowing! Winning more than twenty awards for their sauces at the National BBQ Association Convention, as well as the Grand World Championship in the Whole Hog Division at the Memphis in May World Championship, are just a few of the accolades that belong to The Shed's BBQ competition team.

SLAUGHTERHOUSE FIVE BBQ TEAM

Jeff and Joy Stehney of the Slaughterhouse Five BBQ Team have won more than thirty grand and reserve grand championships at some of the most prestigious BBQ contests in the country. Among the victories are two at the American Royal BBQ, one at the Invitational and one at the Open. They've also won reserve grand championships at both the Royal Open and Invitational, as well as at the Jack Daniel's World BBQ Championship. In 1993, Slaughterhouse Five was named Team of the Year by the Kansas City Barbeque Society, and in 2017, Jeff Stehney was inducted into the Barbecue Hall of Fame.

Though their success in competition BBQ is "legendary"—according to the folks at the American Royal, who awarded them its Legends of the American Royal honor in 2010—Jeff and Joy are best known for their famous BBQ restaurants in Kansas City.

SMOKE ON WHEELS BBQ TEAM

Andy Groneman has been part of the barbecue world for over 23 years. A second-generation pitmaster, Andy started his BBQ journey with the HoDeDo's BBQ team to spend time with his father. By 1996, Andy was cooking more than the HoDeDo's could schedule, so Smoke on Wheels was born and his trek in competition BBQ has taken him from coast to coast, across the borders into Canada and Mexico and as far away as Australia. The Smoke on Wheels team consists of Andy, his wife Kim and their daughters Kaylin and Lauren (see Reckless and Brave BBQ, page 343).

Andy and Kim Groneman have hundreds of awards at all levels for grilling, smoking and outdoor cooking. In addition to over 25 grand championships, and two perfect scores in Kansas City BBQ Society events, some other notable accolades include: two U.S. National Brisket Championship titles at the Chest to Chest Invitational; World Champion Pork at the Jack Daniel's World Invitational; World Champion Pork at the American Royal Invitational; Reserve Grand Champion at the American Royal Open; New York State Empire Cup Champion (seven events throughout New York State) and Chef's Choice Champion at the Jack Daniel's World Invitational.

Andy Groneman's award-winning recipes have been driven to the shelves of over 150 specialty retail storefronts in the United States and Canada, thanks to the production of his line of marinades and injections.

SMOKIN' ACES

Chuck and Nancy Helwig are the Smokin' Aces team from Chicopee, Massachusetts. They won 2nd-place chicken and an overall 9th place at The American Royal Invitational in 2015. Smokin' Aces teaches beginning cooks a versatile grilling method in their Crispy Potato Pouches recipe (page 217).

SMOKIN' HOGGZ

Smokin' Hoggz BBQ Competition team, led by pitmaster Bill Gillespie, started in 2008. After a few years of competing, tweaking recipes and testing them on friends and family, it all came together. The Smokin' Hoggz team, including Shaune Gillespie, Alan Burke and Shakes, won the 2011 Jack Daniel's World Championships, the 2014 American Royal Invitational and 26 grand championships. Bill sells his rubs and sauces across the country, and shared his love of cooking in three cookbooks: *Secrets to Smoking on the Weber Smokey Mountain Cooker and Other Smokers*, *The Smoking Bacon & Hog Cookbook* and *Secrets to Great Charcoal Grilling on the Weber*.

SON SEEKERS BBQ

Son Seekers BBQ team is an award-winning competition team that competes in events sanctioned by the Kansas City Barbeque Society (KCBS). The team members are Johnny Ray and his best friend, Jim Bob. They tell everyone that they are "brothers from different mothers" and have been competing together since 2006.

STICKS-N-CHICKS BBQ TEAM

The Sticks-n-Chicks BBQ team is comprised of Will and Kristie Cleaver, their children, Zack, Kaylee, Kennedy and Madelyn, and Jon Orr. Located in Kansas City, they compete throughout the Midwest, cooking in twelve to fifteen competitions a year, with an occasional drop-in from the Disco Pigs. The Sticks-n-Chicks BBQ team competes using a Yoder 640, a Yoder 1500, Ugly Drum Cookers and an FEC100.

STICKS-N-CHICKS KIDS-Q

The Sticks-n-Chicks Kids-Q team is comprised of Will and Kristie Cleaver's children, Zack, Kaylee, Kennedy and Madelyn. They compete throughout the Midwest, cooking twelve to fifteen competitions a year. Their team consists of the Cleaver family and Uncle Jon, with the occasional drop-in from the Disco Pigs.

SWAMP BOYS BBQ

Based in Winter Haven, Florida, Swamp Boys BBQ is a professional barbecue cook team and championship BBQ sauce purveyor. They began competing on the professional circuit in 2004, and finished 2006 and 2007 as a top-five team in the Florida BBQ Association (FBA). Swamp Boys BBQ earned Team of the Year in 2008 and 2009, and have been in the top five since then. They were ranked the #1 team in the country for 67 straight weeks (including all of 2009) by the National BBQ Rankings and were ranked #1 nationally again in 2013.

Led by pitmaster Rob "Rub" Bagby, Swamp Boys have won 52 grand championships, 44 reserve grand championships and won the World Championship in pork shoulder. They also competed in Season 4 of the TV show BBQ Pitmasters. On two occasions, Rub was hired to train and help open the first American-Style Barbecue restaurant that operated in Brazil. He was spokesman for Kingsford Charcoal at the Daytona Firecracker 400 and on *The Steve Harvey Show*. He has also taught professional BBQ classes to hundreds of people from all over the United States and Canada.

SWEET BREATHE BBQ TEAM

Hailing from Burlington, Vermont, the Sweet Breathe BBQ Team is led by pit boss Eric Gray. Joined by Tony Brown, Chris and Jason Mazur, Bethany Scott and Tawnya Gray, the team entered its first competition at Harpoon Brewery in 2009, and they have been smoking ever since. In 2010 Sweet Breathe BBQ won Rookie Team of the Year honors for the New England BBQ Society.

SWEET SMOKE Q

Jim Elser, pitmaster of Sweet Smoke Q, is one of the hottest names on the championship BBQ circuit. This small farm–town guy with an engineering degree is now being recognized around the world due to his recent BBQ competition success. He has made several television appearances, including being highlighted as a competitor against the four pitmasters on season two of *BBQ Pit Wars* on Destination America. His accomplishments have drawn attention to his line of specialty consumer products, as well as his BBQ classes where he shares pitmaster secrets with cooks of all levels. Jim is the 2014 BBQ World Food Champion, 2014 and 2016 Florida BBQ Association Team of the Year and champion of the television show *Smoked* that aired on Destination America. In just the past three and a half years he has also won other impressive titles, including 24 grand championships, 22 reserve grand championships and multiple top-five finishes overall.

SWEET SWINE O' MINE BBQ TEAM

Established in 1996, Sweet Swine O' Mine was named the Grand Champions at the Memphis In May World Champion BBQ Cooking Contest in 2013 and 2009. Additionally, they were named World Champions in Shoulder at Memphis in May four times: 2005, 2008, 2009 and 2013. They also placed second in 2007 and third in 2010.

At the 2016 National Barbecue Association's Conference in Jacksonville, Florida, Mark Lambert of Sweet Swine O' Mine was well received when he hosted The BBQ Competition Matrix—Inside the Minds of the BBQ Competition Cooks and Judges. Mark also served on the Meet the Masters session panel, which offered a chance for each member to share stories and experiences.

THREE MEN AND A BABYBACK BBQ TEAM

Dana Reed has been competing in grilling and BBQ contests since 2009. In 2016 he left Three Men and a Babyback when he, his wife and their two boys ventured out, creating The Reed Boyz BBQ team. In the short time they have been competing, they've won the New York Bull Burger Contest and consistently get top-ten calls in categories. Their travels in culinary competitions have brought them to The American Royal twice and the World Food Championships.

UNCLE KENNY'S BBQ

Uncle Kenny's BBQ was started by two college friends from Missouri, the BBQ capital of the world. Uncle Kenny's BBQ is a family-run business that prides itself on cooking some of the best barbecue around. Mike Smith and Kenny Nadeau first met in Missouri where they learned to appreciate the intricacies and flavors of smoking and curing meats. Eventually they both moved to Florida and enjoyed barbecuing for family and friends in the Florida sun. After loads of encouragement and prompting from family and friends, they started Uncle Kenny's BBQ and started catering private events and festivals. In 2005 they decided to start testing their skills against the best in the area by participating in BBQ competitions sanctioned under the Florida Barbeque Association (FBA) and Kansas City Barbeque Society (KCBS).

Kenny Nadeau is the Florida State Lead for Operation BBQ Relief. In a short period of time, Kenny got Florida signed up to volunteer. He spent significant time on deployments in 2016 and was instrumental in the procurement of food and supplies. Kenny's tenacious drive to be all things BBQ is infectious. His desire to spread his love of BBQ to the world is evident in everything he does and OBR is just part of that. Kenny's get-it-done, can-do attitude is his calling card!

WILBUR'S REVENGE

David Marks is a franchisee of Famous Dave's BBQ and backed into competitive BBQ as a marketing strategy. Following in the footsteps of his BBQ mentor, Famous Dave Anderson, he fell in love with the BBQ family and adopted the BBQ lifestyle. Beginning in 2010, Wilbur's Revenge Competition BBQ Team has competitively cooked up and down the East Coast. The team saw early success, winning the New Jersey State BBQ Championship Iron Chef Contest in 2010 and 2011. In 2012, David made it to the Sam's Club National Championship in Bentonville, Arkansas, where he won the Tyson's Best Wings on The Planet contest. More importantly, David met Stan Hays, Co-Founder of Operation BBQ Relief, for the first time. Soon thereafter, Hurricane Sandy came down the East Coast and David participated in his first OBR deployment, serving 100,000 meals in New Jersey. From there, David's involvement with OBR has been strong and fast, as he has served on the organization's board of directors for four years and has held the Chief Operating Officer position.

YABBA DABBA QUE!

Pitmaster Eric Mitchell is the author of the bestselling books *Smoke It Like a Pro on the Big Green Egg & Other Ceramic Cookers* and *More BBQ and Grilling for The Big Green Egg & Other Kamado-Style Cookers*. He is a member of the award-winning competitive BBQ team Yabba Dabba Que!, which has competed in both the Jack Daniel's World Championship Invitational Barbecue competition and the American Royal Invitational.

Pitmaster Eric Mitchell and his wife, Cindi, have been competing on the KCBS circuit since 2006 and perform food demonstrations on their Big Green Eggs across the Northeast, demonstrating the versatility of the Egg with everything they cook.

YES, DEAR BBQ

Yes, Dear BBQ hails from Savannah, Georgia, and started competing in professional BBQ contests in 2012. Cooking on a Deep South GC36 at contests and a GMG Jim Bowie at home, they've honed their barbecue craft and have gone on to win multiple grand championships, top-ten calls and first-place finishes in chicken, ribs, pork and brisket.

ABOUT THE AUTHORS

STAN HAYS, co-founder and CEO of Operation BBQ Relief and barbecue competitor, has participated in more than 35 sanctioned barbecue contests with two grand champion awards, four reserve champions and several top-ten finishes. He was runner-up in the 2015 season of *Chopped Grill Master* on the Food Network.

In May 2011, Stan, Will Cleaver and Jeff Stith established OBR after a tornado swept through Joplin, Missouri. At that deployment, the team served 120,000 meals with the original intention of serving 5,000 meals. Before coming home from the first eleven-day deployment, they sat down and developed plans for a 501(c)(3) nonprofit. Stan's passion for barbecue and helping those in distress developed into Operation BBQ Relief, which now has served more than 1.78 million meals in 25 states. During the past seven years, Stan and his team have responded to 51 disasters with the help of more than 6,700 volunteers nationwide.

Stan works so hard to "create normalcy" for the victims of natural disasters through the comfort of a hot barbecue meal. He was recognized as a 2017 Top 10 CNN Hero for his work with Operation BBQ Relief. While he has received congratulations and awards for his leadership, he says that the most rewarding gratitude is from the people he has served hot barbecue sandwiches to during the past seven years.

TIM O'KEEFE has a lifetime membership in the Kansas City Barbeque Society (KCBS). A certified barbecue judge, he has judged over 40 contests sanctioned by the KCBS, and has been part of the Can U Smell My Pits competition team since 2015. Tim has contributed articles for *National Barbecue News*, and co-wrote three cookbooks with Bill Gillespie.

INDEX